MAṆḌANA MIŚRA'S DISTINCTION OF THE ACTIVITY

BHĀVANĀVIVEKA

MAṆḌANA MIŚRA'S DISTINCTION OF THE ACTIVITY

BHĀVANĀVIVEKA

(WITH INTRODUCTION, ENGLISH TRANSLATION WITH NOTES, AND SANSKRIT TEXT)

by

V.P. Bhatta

Assistant Editor,

Sanskrit Dictionary,

Deccan College, Pune.

EASTERN BOOK LINKERS

DELHI : : (India)

Published by :
EASTERN BOOK LINKERS
5825, New Chandrawal, Jawahar Nagar,
Delhi-110007

First Edition : 1994

ISBN : 81-85133-81-6

Typesetting by :
Amar Printing Press
8/25, Vijay Nagar, Delhi-9
Phone : 7252362

CONTENTS

PREFACE

Jaimini's ritualism *(Pūrvamīmāṁsā)*, along with grammar *(Vyākaraṇa)* and logic *(Nyāya)*, has made the most significant contribution to the development of the philosophy of language in India. Pūrvamīmāṁsā was primarily concerned with the investigation of the nature of Dharma and therefore, with the analysis of the Vedic and non-Vedic statements.

However, the advent of Prābhākara and Bhaṭṭa schools gave a new thrust to the linguistic activities of the ritualists and scholars like Prabhākara Miśra, Kumārila Bhaṭṭa, Maṇḍana Miśra and Khaṇḍadeva composed several works on the analysis of sentence and its meaning. The ritualists dealt with the words and the comprehension of the syntactico-semantical relations, i.e. the sentence-meaning, in general, and they dealt with the nature of optative and other injunctive statements and the comprehension of the syntactico-semantical relations involved in such statements in particular. However, the question is 'what do optative and other finite forms of verbs such as 'he cooks' *(pacati)* ,'he should offer' *(yajeta)* etc. express ? Do they express only an action such as 'cooking' or 'offering' or do they express an activity that accomplishes/produces an effect such as 'becoming soft' or 'heaven' in addition to, i.e. as distinct from, such actions as well ? Also, suppose the finite forms of verbs do express the activity, in addition to the verbal actions, then how do the same verbal actions function, i.e. do they function as the means of the accomplishment of the effects or do they function as the effects/grammatical objects by themselves ? Further, the question is 'suppose the finite verbs do express both the activity and the action, then what element in the finite verb, i.e. the base or the ending, expresses the accomplishing/productive activity and what element expresses the action ?

These and other questions, which are relevant even today, for the Philosophers of language and also for the linguists, have dominated the minds of the ritualists and also the grammarians since the ancient times in India. The Prābhākaras, who followed the early school of Bādari, have maintained that the finite forms of verbs express only an action such as cooking or offering. However, the Bhāṭṭas, who followed the later school of Jaimini, have developed the concept of the 'word-efficient-force' (*śābdībhāvanā*) to explain the motivation for the listener to undertake an action after listening to an injunction (Vedic or non-Vedic); and the 'end-efficient-force' (*ārthī bhāvanā*) to explain the accomplishment of an effect such as becoming soft or heaven.

On the other hand, Maṇḍana Miśra has modified the Bhāṭṭa concept of the word-efficient-force into the theory of the knowledge that the Vedic rites are beneficial means to the accomplishment of the desired effect (*iṣṭasādhanatājñāna*), and also modified the Bhāṭṭa concept of the end-efficient-force into the effect-productive/accomplishing activity (*bhāvanā*). According to him, the accomplishing activity needs to be assumed, since the effects such as becoming soft or heaven need an accomplishing activity to accomplish them. Also, according to him, the accomplishing activity needs to be distinguished from the actions expressed by the verbal roots, since the same actions function merely as the means of the accomplishment of the effects/grammatical objects by themselves. Further, Maṇḍana has held that in the static or intransitive usages 'he is/becomes' (*asti/bhavati*), where there is no separate effect to be accomplished, the actions, expressed by the verbal roots, themselves function as the effects/objects to be accomplished through the activity. Thus, the concept of the accomplishing activity (*bhāvanā*) constitutes the heart of the Mīmāṁsā analysis of sentence and its meaning.

Bhāvanāviveka, or 'The distinction of the activity' is the most important book on the topic of the effect-accomplishing (producing) activity in the Bhāṭṭa system of Mīmāṁsā. It is divided into two parts, viz. Pūrvapakṣa and Siddhānta. Maṇḍana gives a detailed account of the arguments of the Niyogavādins against the necessity of accepting the accompllishing activity in the Pūrvapakṣa; whereas he gives the account of his own refutations of the Pūrvapakṣin's argument, and then establishes the accomplishing activity as the distinct meaning of the verbal ending in the Siddhānta.

Maṇḍana, and his followers hold that the accomplishing activity is the chief qualificand (nucleous) of all the syntactico – semantical relations in the analysis of the sentence-meaning, i.e. verbal cognition. To facilitate the understanding of such an epistemological and linguistic aspect of the activity, I have provided a brief account of the analysis of sentence and its meaning according to the ritualists in the General Introduction. Further, to substantiate the theory of the distinction of the activity, I have translated Bhāvanāviveka of Maṇḍana Miśra into English with notes. I hope the translation with notes along with the introduction would provide adequate help to the readers in the understanding of Maṇḍana's theory of the distinction of the activity.

I would like to express my deep gratitude and regards to my teachers : Dr. N.S. Ramanujatatacharya, Vice-Chancellor, K.S. Vidyapeetha, Tirupati, Vidwan Shri Ramabhadracharya and Vidwan Shri Archaka Venkannacharya, both retired Professors, Mahārājā Sanskrit College, Mysore, who have taught me Nyāya and Mīmāṁsā and initiated me into research.

Also, I would like to express my gratitude to my friends and collegues: Late Dr. Shivkumar Sharma, Reader, CASS, University of Poona, for his constant encouragement and moral support which played such a crucial role in the preparation of this work; Dr. H.C. Patyal, Assistant Editor, Sanskrit Dictionary, Deccan College, Pune and Mr. Ashok M. Hedge, in charge English Dept., N.S.B.,Pune, for their suggestions and corrections which were of great help to me.

Finally, I would like to thank sincerely Mr. Shamlal Malhotra and his brothers of Eastern Book Linkers for bringing out this volume very nicely.

Deccan College,
Pune. India., June 1992.

V. P. Bhatta

GENERAL INTRODUCTION

GENERAL INTRODUCTION

Contribution of Pūrvamīmāṁsā to linguistics

Three systems of Indian Philosophy, namely, Pūrvamīmāṁsā, Vyākaraṇa and Nyāya deal with the philosophy of language. Pūrvamīmāṁsā was the first system to undertake the analysis of sentence and its meaning systematically on a scientific basis. Its analysis of Vedic and non-Vedic statements and their meanings is a testimony to the scientific approach it has adopted in the analysis of word and meaning. It has greatly contributed to the development of linguistics, especially semantics, in ancient India by proposing various theories of verbal cognition such as the theory of the reference to the meanings related syntactico-semantically to each other (*anvitābhidhānavāda*), and the theory of the comprehension of the syntactico-semantical relations between the individual word-meanings (*abhihitānvayavāda*).

The Pūrvamīmāṁsā system has established that all the *kārakas* are directly or indirectly related to the accomplishing or productive activity[1] (*bhāvanā*) expressed by the conjugational endings in finite verbs. It has also established that the verbal root-meanings such as 'cooking' or 'offering' etc. are to be considered as the *kārakas*, and therefore, are related directly to the activity as either the objects or instruments.

The nature of Dharma and its relevance to the analysis of word and meaning

The followers of the earlier school of Bādari and also those of the later school of Jaimini have differed between themselves as to the nature of Dharma; and therefore, as

---

1 It will be explained in the course of this introduction that, according to Maṇḍana Miśra, an activity, which is to be distinguished from verbal actions, and which is conducive to the accomplishment of (or efficient in producing) effect, is the meaning expressed by the conjugational endings in finite verbs.

to the nature of the subject-matter of the Mīmāṁsā system. While Bādari and other earlier Mīmāṁsakas have held that the sense conveyed by the Vedas (*dharmaśabdaścātra vedārthamātraparaḥ*) constitutes Dharma; and therefore, the discussion of the sense conveyed by the Vedas constitutes the subject-matter of the Mīmāṁsā system, Jaimini and other later Mīmāṁsakas have held that the actions such as offerings (Vedic rites) constitute Dharma; and therefore, the discussion of the nature of the same actions (Dharma) constitutes the subject-matter of the Mīmāṁsā system.

However, despite their difference in the perception of the nature of Dharma and the subject matter of the Mīmāṁsā system, both the followers of Bādari and Jaimini maintain that Dharma alone is the ultimate goal (end) of human beings and the Vedic injunctions enjoin such a Dharma. This has led the ritulists to undertake the analysis of words (statements) and their meanings in general and the Vedic injunctive statements and their meanings in particular.

Words as valid means of knowledge (pramāṇa)

Pūrvamīmāṁsā recognizes that, besides perception (*pratyakṣa*) inference (*anumāna*), and absence (*abhāva*), words (*śabda*) (both Vedic and non-Vedic) are the valid means of knowledge (*pramāṇa*). It accepts that words are eternal, and therefore, the relationship between the words and the things meant by them is also eternal. According to the Pūrvamīmāṁsā, words have an inherent capacity to signify the things which are connected with the duty (actions), which is always 'to be accomplished' (*sādhya*) and therefore, is never 'already accomplished' (*siddha*).

Śabara, the great commentator on the Jaimini's *sūtras*, holds that the knowledge of things about which nothing is known before, is conveyed by significant words (*śāstraṁ śabdavijñānād asannikṛṣṭe arthe vijñānam*). However, he seems to maintain that the knowledge is derived from the Vedic words alone, although later ritualists, especially Bhāṭṭas, have accepted that both Vedic and non-Vedic words are the valid means of knowledge.

The advent of Prābhākara and Bhāṭṭa schools and its influence over analysis of sentence and its meaning

The advent of Prābhākara and Bhāṭṭa schools in the Pūrvamīmāṁsā system of philosophy was a turning point in the linguistic philosophy of India. It has brought a qualitative change in the analysis of sentence and its meaning in general and in the interpretation of the Vedic statements and their meanings in particular. The two schools have greatly contributed to the Indian theories of analysis of sentence and its meaning by proposing mutually divergent and yet equally rational theories on many important topics of linguistics, such as the nature of words, the concept of sentence, individual word-meaning, sentence-meaning, the syntactico-semantical relations between various word-meanings (referents), and the chief or principle qualificand of syntactico-sementical relations. Following is a brief outline of the Prābhākara and Bhāṭṭa positions regarding words and their meanings.

Prabhākara on words, word-functions and sentence

Prabhākara Miśra, the celebrated author of *Bṛhatī*, was totally opposed to the Jaimini's school of Vedic interpretation; he has followed the Vedic interpretation suggested by the earlier thinkers such as Bādari, Bhartṛmitra etc. According to him, only the Vedic words, which are eternal (*nitya*) and not produced by human beings (*apauruṣeya*), are valid means of knowledge since they are free from human error. He holds that non-Vedic words cannot be accepted as valid in general, since the verbal testimony (authority) of such words is to be obtained through the process of inference. Further, Prabhākara maintains that syllables/words, which are eternal, become manifest by articulatory wind; and hence convey the sense to the listener through the eternal word-signification.

Prabhākara holds that the signification or denotative power of words (*padavṛtti* or *śakti*) is also eternal. According to him, since both words and things meant by words are eternal, the signification must also be accepted as eternal and inherent in words. People obtain knowledge regarding signification only by observing elders' usage and do not establish any new signification as such.

Sentence (*vākya*), according to Prabhākara, is a connected utterance of individual words (*samabhivyāhāra*), and conveys the sense of the accomplishment. For instance, consider the sentence: *yasya parṇamayī juhūr bhavati na sa pāpaṁ ślokaṁ śṛṇoti* ('He, whose laddle is made of parṇa wood, does not hear the evil words'). This sentence, conveys the sense of the accomplishment of the laddle by means of the *parṇa*-wood, despite the absence of the accusative case ending after the word '*juhūr*', (which expresses the laddle) due to the connected utterance of the words '*parṇamayī*' and '*juhūr*' together denoting the subsidiary and the prominent respectively.

According to Prabhākara, sentence cannot be distinguished from the (utterance of) individual words since the same words too, like sentence, have an inherent capacity to signify (denote) semantically competent and syntactically complete idea.

Prabhākara on word - and sentence-meaning

As regards the individual word-meanings, Prabhākara holds a unique theory. According to him, individual words have an inherent capacity or power to denote things 'yet to be accomplished' (*kārya or sāddhya*), or things connected with what are yet to be accomplished (*kāryānvita*). Meanings obtained through the denotative powers of words are never 'what are already accomplished' (*siddha*). Also, according to him, each word is capable of signifying a complete sense as syntactico-semantically connected with a '*kārya*' such as verbal action of offering etc. referred to by an expressed or implied verb. He holds so, because each word is to be recognized as posessing a particular signification in a sense connected with an action. For instance, the word '*svargakāmaḥ*' in '*svargakāmo yajeta*' (he who desires heaven should offer), refers to the person desiring heaven, which is syntactico-semantically connected with the action of offering which in turn is expressed by the verbal root '*yaj*'. Thus, the word '*svargakāmaḥ*' conveys a complete idea of a person, offering an oblation. Prabhākara holds that the words refer to a *kārya* on the ground that reference to an already accomplished entity (*siddha*) does not serve any useful purpose; whereas reference to the entity that is yet to be accomplished (*kārya*) is useful to the accomplishment of the cherished goal of mankind; and hence, must be accepted as word-meaning.

It should be noted here that Prabhākara accepts that the syntactico-semantical relations or connections (*saṁsargas*) between different individual word-meanings too are obtained by the signification or denotative power of words. According to him, each word, when denoting its individual word-meaning, denotes its relation with the action as well. For instance, the word *'gām'* (cow) in *'gām ānaya'* (bring the cow), while denoting the sense of cow as the object of bringing, denotes the syntactico-semantical relation of the objecthood of cow with the action of bringing denoted by the verb *'ānaya'*, i.e. the conditioning as well. Thus, for Prabhākara, the syntactico-semantical relations (*saṁsargas*) between word-meanings too are obtained by words; and therefore, function as the referent-qualifiers (*prakāras*) with respect to actions. Now, as regards the sentence-meaning : Prabhākara maintains a unique theory known as reference to the meanings related to each other (*anvitābhidhāna*) with respect to sentence-meaning. As noted earlier, according to him, each word, in a sentence, refers to its individual word-meaning, as syntactico-semantically related to the action which is to be accomplished. And thus, the listener, when comprehending the individual word meanings, comprehends the syntactico-semantical relations of the same with the action as well. For instance, consider once again the sentence *'gām ānaya'* (bring the cow). Here, the total sentence-meaning comprehended is, according to Prabhākara, that the action of bringing, which conditions, i.e. delimits the objecthood of the cow, must be undertaken by the second person.

Now, such a sentence meaning is obtained by the denotation of the cow as related to the action of bringing or the denotation of the action of bringing as related to the cow, the object. Thus, according to Prabhākara, the comprehension of the total sentence-meaning is based on the reference to (denotation of) the cow, the object, as related to the action of bringing etc. by the words.

Kumārila on words and sentence

Kumārila Bhaṭṭa, the celebrated author of the *Ślokavārttika* etc., who has re-established Jaimini's theory of ritual interpretation by refuting the views of the earlier scholars like Bādari, Bhartṛmitra and others, has regarded the knowledge derived from both Vedic and non-Vedic words as valid. According to him, all words, whether Vedic or non-Vedic, are the valid means of knowledge, since the same, when uttered by pious trustworthy elders, are perceived to be conveying valid sense. Bhaṭṭa, therefore, opposes Prabhākara's view that only Vedic words, which express something yet to be accomplished (*kārya*), are valid.

Now, as regard the sentence: Bhaṭṭa holds that sentence is not merely a collection of words, but rather, is a meaningful unit of words distinct from individual words. According to him, sentence consists of both nouns and verbs (*liṅādipadaghaṭitatvam*). For instance, consider the sentence '*svargakāmo yajeta*' (he who desires heaven should offer). This sentence is a meaningful unit of words and consists of the nouns and verbs such as '*svargakāmaḥ*' and '*yajeta*'.

Kumārila on word - and sentence-meaning

Kumārila Bhaṭṭa firmly opposes Prabhākara's view that each word has an inherent (eternal) capacity to denote something (action) yet to be accomplished (*kārya*) or something connected with what is yet to be accomplished (*kāryānvita*). According to him, each word denotes only its individual word-meaning through the signification (denotative power) established by the usage of elders and then such an individual word-meaning is to be comprehended as syntactico-semantically connected with another individual word-meaning. For instance, consider the words '*gām*' (cow) and '*ānaya*' (bring) in '*gām ānaya*' (bring the cow). Here, the word '*gām*' refers to the individual cow, as delimited by the cowness; whereas the verb '*ānaya*' refers to the activity (*bhāvanā*), as conducive to the bringing. And, the listener comprehends at first only the individual word-meanings as such; i.e. the 'cow' and 'the activity' individually without comprehending any syntactico-semantical relation between such word-meanings. This stage is considered as the cognition in parts (*sakhaṇḍabodha*) since the same does not involve the comprehension of any syntactico-semantical relations between the word-meanings. Thus, the words, according to Bhaṭṭa, refer to the individual word-meanings as such; and not to word-meanings as mutually connected with each other by any syntactico-semantical relation.

Kumārila holds, further, that the sentence-meaning is the comprehension of the different syntactico-semantical relations between various individual word-meanings which are denoted by individual words (*abhihitānvaya bodha*). Kumārila holds so on the ground that the individual words cannot be established to refer to the syntactico-semantical relations. According to him, the words denote only the individual word-meanings, which are then comprehended as related to each other by syntactico-semantical relations obtained through the relational seam or power of syntactico-semantical relations (*saṁsargamaryādā*). For instance, consider, once again, the sentence '*gām ānaya*' (bring the cow). Here, the words '*gām*' (cow) and '*ānaya*' (bring) refer to their individual word-meanings, namely, the cow (the object of bringing) and the activity leading to bringing; and then the same cow (the object) and the activity leading to the bringing are comprehended as related together by the relation of conditioning (describing) and producing respectively since the action of bringing conditions (describes) the objecthood of the cow and the activity produces the action of bringing. Thus, the sentence-meaning, for Bhaṭṭa, is the comprehension of syntactico-semantical relations between various word-meanings denoted by individual words.

It should be noted here that Kumārila, like logicians, conceives a separate power of syntactico-semantical relations (*saṁsargamaryādā*) to obtain the syntactico-semantical relations. He conceives so because the individual words such as '*gām*' and '*ānaya*' etc. are established to have denotations only in the sense of individual word-meanings such as the objecthood of the cow, and the activity conducive to the bringing and not in the sense of any syntactico-semantical relations such as conditioning; whereas the sentence-meaning is the comprehension of the syntactico-semantical relations between various individual word-meanings and not simply the comprehension of unrelated individual word-meanings. Since the syntactico-semantical relations, which are comprehended in the sentence-meaning, cannot be obtained through the words, the same must be obtained through the power of syntactico-semantical relations.

Kumārila Bhaṭṭa proposes a unique theory regarding the chief qualificand or nucleus of syntactico-semantical relations (*mukhyaviśeṣya*) between different individual word meanings (*padārtha*) as well. According to him, the activity expressed by the verbal endings or *ghañantas* is the chief qualificand (nucleus) of all the relations and all other individual word-meanings are directly or indirectly related to such an activity. For instance, consider the statement *'jyotiṣṭomena yajeta svargakāmaḥ'* (He who desires heaven should make offering by *Jyotiṣṭoma*). Here, the verb *'yajeta'* has two morphs: the verbal root *'yaj(i)'* and the verbal ending*(e)'ta'*; and while the root *yaj*(i) refers to the action of offering, the ending, '(e)*ta*' refers to the accomplishing activity conducive to such an offering. And, the word *'jyotiṣṭomena'* refers to the instrumentality of Jyotiṣṭoma, and the word *'svargakāmaḥ'* refers to the objecthood of the heaven. And all these individual word-meanings are related to the accomplishing activity directly or indirectly. Thus, the verbal cognition such as "one who desires heaven should undertake the activity, conducive to the offering, which has heaven as its object to be accomplished and Jyotiṣṭoma as its instrument of accomplishment", which has the same activity as the chief qualificand of all the syntactico-semantical relations, is produced in such a case.

Theory of bhāvanā - a historical background

Undoubtedly, the single most important contribution of the Mīmāṁsā system of philosophy to the study of linguistics in India, is the theory of the accomplishing (productive) activity (*bhāvanā*). The accomplishing activity is the heart of the Mīmāṁsā-theory of sentence-meaning since all the *kārakas*, including the root-meanings such as actions (actions too are *kārakas* according to Mīmāṁsakas), are related to the activity as qualifiers (modifiers). The accomplishing activity functions as the qualificand (nucleus) of all the relations and hence constitues the primary sense of all the sentences.

The term *'bhāvanā'* is a primary derivative (*kṛdanta*) from the causative base *'bhāva'* of the root *bhū* (to be or to become); and hence, means literally something that causes to be or to become. However, Maṇḍana has developed his theory of the accomplishing (productive) activity (*bhāvanā*) on the ground that every effect or result (*phala*) requires some accomplishing activity to accomplish it; and therefore, all finite expressions (verbs) including optatives must be held to express an accomplishing activity that accomplishes an effect by means of root-meanings (actions). Thus, Maṇḍana's concept of the accomplishing (productive) activity (*bhāvanā*) can be defined as an operation or effort of the producing agent that is conducive to the accomplishment of the effect to be produced (*bhavituḥ bhavanānukūlaḥ bhāvayituḥ vyāpāraviśeṣaḥ*).

Maṇḍana's concept of *Bhāvanā* as the accomplishing (productive) activity had such a dominating influence over the scholars that in later times scholars of both *Mīmāṁsā* and other systems of Indian Philosophy have come to regard *'bhāvanā'* as standing for only the accomplishing (productive) activity; and therefore, *'bhāvanā'* becomes almost a synonym of *'ārthībhāvanā'* or an activity that accomplishes (produces) an effect (end-efficient-force). However, it should be noted that originally for Bhāṭṭas, *bhāvanā* meant to signify either an activity (force) that is efficient in accomplishing an effect (*ārthībhāvanā*) or an activity (force) that verbally impels the people to undertake some action (*śābdībhāvanā*). Thus, the Bhāṭṭas divided *bhāvanā* into two types; the end (effect) – accomplishing activity (*ārthī-bhāvanā*) and an activity (force) that verbally impels the people to undertake some action (*śāddībhāvanā*).

Maṇḍana, however, modified the theory of the end (effect)-accomplishing activity (*ārthībhāvanā*) to suit into his concept of accomplishing (productive) activity (*bhāvanā*) and the verbal impellent activity (*śābdībhāvanā*) to suit into his concept of knowledge that the actions imposed are beneficial means to the desired results (*iṣṭasādhanatājñāna*). Since the theory of the accomplishing activity is a modification of the *ārthī-bhāvanā* of the Bhāṭṭas, a brief account of the historic background that had led to the establishment of the accomplishing activity is in order.

Niyoga as the sentence-meaning (vākyārtha)

Bādari, the earliest known exponent of Mīmāṁsā, had held that the Vedic injunction (*vidhi*) means the optative suffix '*(e) ta*' etc. in the finite forms such as '*yajeta*' (one should offer) (and not the optative form such as *yajeta*) etc. According to him, such injunctions impose (enjoin) only the compulsory duty (*niyoga*) of performing the Vedic rites which are of three types: obligatory (*nitya*), conditional (*naimittika*) and optional (*kāmya*). However, such performances cannot be considered to be the cause of any effect (result). While no Vedic statement expressing any result exists in the case of the performance of the first two types of rites, the phrase '*svargakāmaḥ*' (he who desires heaven) found in the statement '*svargakāmo yajeta jyotiṣṭomena*' (he who desires heaven should offer by *Jyotiṣṭoma*) does not indicate any direct causal relationship between the Jyotiṣṭoma rite and the heaven in the case of the third type of the rite. Thus, Bādari has held that the Vedic injunction has only the enjoining (imposing) of the performance of the compulsory duty (*niyoga*) of Vedic rites as its sense. This theory of Bādari is known as *niyogavākyārthavāda* since the same recognizes the imposition of the compulsory duty (*niyoga*) of the Vedic rites, which have no causal relationship with the effects, heaven etc., as the sense of the injunctive suffix.

Now, the question arises as to how to account for the inducement of the people to undertake the performance of the Vedic rites since the same are not conducive to any result. Bādari answers the question by stating that the Vedic injunction (*vidhi*) is an impellent (*codanā*). According to him, the Vedic injunction is to be regarded as an impellent (*codanā or pravartaka*) since the same impeles the people by conveying the sense of the performance of the compulsory duty like the command or order of the elders that impels or induces the listeners to obey. Thus, Bādari and other earlier Mīmāṁsakas have held that the Vedic injunction (*vidhi*) is an impellent (*codanā*) and the imposing of the performance of the compulsory duty (*niyoga*) is the sense conveyed by such injunction.

Apūrvakārya as the sentence-meaning (vākyārtha)

However, Prabhākara Miśra and other later followers of Bādari have modified the *niyogavākyārthavāda* of Bādari by proposing *apūrvakārya vākyārthavāda*. According to them, the Vedic injunction *(vidhi) such as* the suffix *'(e)ta' in 'yajeta'* (one should offer) etc. cannot be accepted to refer to the enjoining (imposing) of mere performance of the compulsory duty of Vedic rites (*niyoga*); for, the performance of the compulsory duty of Vedic rites or offering (*yāga* or *homa*) do not constitute Dharma as they are momentary. What constitutes Dharma is only the things to be accomplished (*kārya*) such as the transcendental effect (*apūrva*) and never something already accomplished (*siddha*). And therefore, the Vedic injunctive suffix such as (e)*'ta'*in *'yajeta'* (one should offer) etc., should be accepted as referring to the same transcendental effect (*apūrvakārya*). This modified theory of Prabhākara is known as *'apūrvakāryavākyārthavāda'* since it recognizes the things to be accomplished, i.e. the transcendental effect (*apūrvakārya*) etc., as the sense conveyed by the sentence with injunctive suffix. According to Prabhākara, offering (*yāga*) etc. are subordinate to the transcendental effect (*apūrva*), since the same is accomplished by offerings; and therefore, injunctions refer to the duty means they refer to the transcendental effect caused by the compulsory undertaking of the duty. Prabhākara maintains further that the undertaking of the compulsory duty of Vedic rites invariably leads to the effect 'heaven' etc. although no cause and effect relationship between *apūrva* and heaven can be visualised.

According to Prabhākara, the *apūrvakārya*, which is Dharma, is the most important sense (i.e. chief qualificand) in a sentence. And all the other words excepting injunctive suffix in a sentence, therefore, refer to only the things subordinate to such an *apūrvakārya*. Even the phrase *'svargakāmaḥ'* (he who desires heaven) in *'svargakāmo yajeta'* (he who desires heaven should offer) refers to only the person who undertakes the duty; and therefore, who is subordinate to the *apūrvakārya* and not to any result (like heaven).

Also, it should be noted that Prabhākara and other followers of Bādari have argued that the knowledge of *apūrvakārya* as the item to be accomplished is sufficient to induce the people to undertake the performance of the actions like the Vedic rites (i.e. offerings) etc.; and therefore, the Vedic injunctions need not indicate the actions like Vedic rites as being conducive to the result of heaven etc; rather, the same injunctions can indicate the transcendental effect (*apūrvakārya*) which does not produce any result (the result of 'heaven' is merely an accident).

According to them, injunction (*vidhi*) is an impellent (*codanā*) means the same impels (induces)the people to undertake the Vedic rites by merely indicating the sense of Dharma, namely, the *apūrvakārya;* and therefore, it is not necessary that the Vedic injunctions refer to the Vedic rites as the means of accomplishing some result such as heaven. Thus, Prābhākaras have established their theory that Vedic injunctions refer to the duty such as the transcendental effect (*apūrvakārya*) which is to be accomplished, but which does not, in turn, produce any result.

'Bhāvanā' as the sentence-meaning (vākyārtha)

Kumārila Bhaṭṭa and his followers have brought significant change in the analysis of Vedic statements. They have reestablished Jaimini's school of thought by refuting the theories of Bādari and that of his followers. They have held that injunction (*vidhi*) meant the complete injunctive statement such as *'jyotiṣṭomena svargakāmo yajeta'* (he who desires heaven should offer by means of Jyotiṣṭoma) etc. and not simply the optative suffix'(e) ta' etc. in the finite forms such as *'yajeta'* etc. According to them, simple optative suffix'(e) ta'' etc., without functioning as the part of a statement, cannot indicate any sense of duty. Thus, they have held that injunction is a complete injunctive statement consisting of *vidhiliṅ*'(e)*ta'* etc.

Also, Bhāṭṭas have held that the injunction is the section of the Veda which teaches an unknown sense, i.e. duty or action (*ajñātārthajñāapko vedabhāgaḥ*). For instance, the statement *agnihotraṁ juhuyāt svargakāmaḥ,* 'He who desires heaven should undertake the making of Agnihotra oblations' which teaches Agnihotra, is an injunction. Here the statement enjoins the undertaking of the making of Agnihotra oblations which is not known by any other means.

However, when the main action (duty) is already understood, the same injunction enjoins merely the quality of the action which is unknown. For instance, *dadhnā juhoti* 'He makes the Agnihotra oblations with curd,' is an injunction of quality. Here, since the primary action of Agnihotra is already understood by some other means, the injunction enjoins merely the quality, i.e. the curd to be used in the Agnihotra. Also, when neither the action nor the quality is understood, the injunction enjoins the sense of both the action of offering and the quality. For instance, *somena yajeta* 'One should make the oblations with Soma is an injunction of both since neither the action nor the quality are previously understood by any means.

Now, as regards the sense conveyed by injunction: Bhāṭṭas have established the theory of *bhāvanāvākyārtha*. They oppose Bādari's theory of *'niyogavākyārtha'* and also Prābhākara's theory of *apūrvavākyārtha* on the ground that mere reference to the undertaking of compulsory duty (offering) (*niyoga*) or to the transcendental effect to be accomplished (*apūrvakārya*) does not serve any useful purpose, since the same are not conducive to any desired result such as heaven etc. And unless, the injunctions impose some actions conducive to the desired result, the inducement towards the undertaking of the action cannot be explained. The knowledge that the action imposed is beneficial (*iṣṭasādhanatā jñāna*) is essential to the undertaking of actions. Thus, the injunctions must be accepted as imposing some actions conducive to some desired result for facilitating the inducement of men.

Bhāṭṭas explain their theory of the imposition of the actions which are conducive to the desired result such as heaven and also their theory of the inducement of the persons to undertake such actions by proposing *bhāvanā* as the sense conveyed by the injunctive statements (*bhāvanāvākyārthavāda*). According to them, *bhāvanā* is to be analysed as having two different aspects : namely, (i) the aspect of impellent force (*codanā* or *pravartanā*) inducing the persons to undertake actions and also (ii) the aspect of an inherent energy, effort or activity (*prayatna*) conducive to the desired effect (*phala*). The first aspect of *bhāvanā* is visualized as the word-impellent force (*śābdī bhāvanā*), which impels or induces (*pravartaka*) people desirous of the result, heaven, etc to undertake an action (*puruṣapravṛtyanukūla-bhāvaka-vyāpāra*). That is to say, the Vedic injunctions refer to a certain force which impels the people to undertake the actions. The second aspect of *bhāvanā* is visualized by the Bhāṭṭas as an end-efficient-force (*ārthībhāvanā*) which is pure energy, effort or activity (*anyotpādanānukūlavyāpāra*). Thus, *bhāvanā* can be generally defined as an impellent force or inducement (*pravartaka*) impelling people to undertake the action and also as an effort or activity (*prayatna*) conducive to the desired effect.

Kumārila's concept of 'śābdībhāvanā'

According to Kumārila, words, both Vedic and non-Vedic, must be recognized as having a particular inducement (*preraṇā* or *pravartanā*) which can impel the people to undertake the actions. For, in Vedic and non-Vedic injunctions, the words are found to induce the people to undertake the actions. For instance, consider the word *'yajeta'* (one should offer) in *'svargakāmo yajeta'* (he who desires heaven should offer). Here the word *'yajeta'* impels the people to undertake the action of offering. Further, according to Kumārila, such an inducement (*preraṇā*) must be identified with 'word-impellent force' (*śābdī bhāvanā*). This is so because, in such cases, no external agency that can impel the people to undertake the action of offering, can be recognized to be present. It is the sheer power or force of words that impels the people to undertake the actions. Thus, the words have an inducement (*preraṇā*) means the words have an impellent force (*śābdībhāvanā*) that impels the people. Now, the inducement (*preraṇā*), which is identified with the word-impellent force (*śābdī bhāvanā*), must be admitted to be the sense referred to by the injunctions such as *'yajeta'*. This is so because, nothing that is not referred to or denoted by the words, can be admitted to be the sentence-meaning. Thus, in the injunction *'jyotiṣṭomena svargakāmo yajeta'* (he who desires heaven should make offerings by means of *Jyotiṣṭoma*), the inducement (*pravartanā* or *preraṇā*), which is visualized as word-impellent-force (*śabdī bhāvanā*), is the meaning referred to by the word *'yajeta'*.

Kumārila's concept of ārthībhāvanā

Also, according to Kumārila, men possess an inherent energy/effort (*prayatna*) which can be visulized as an efficient-force in producing the desired effect. He holds that when men undertake to perform certain actions, such as offerings, which are the means to the accomplishment of the desired effect (heaven etc.), they must be accepted to possess certain inherent energy or effort since, without the productive energy or effort, no result can be accepted as being accomplished. Further, he holds that such an effort must be recognized as an 'end-efficient/accomplishing force (*ārthībhāvanā*), since the same is efficient towards the accomplishment of the effect such as heaven. Thus, for instance, the person desirous of heaven, who is imposed to undertake the action of offerings, possesses the effort conducive to the production of heaven which must be recognized as the end-efficient/productive force (*ārthībhāvanā*). Now, such a force is held to be the meaning expressed by the injunctive words such as '*yajeta*', in the case of the injunctions '*jyotiṣṭomena yajeta svargakāmaḥ*' (he who desires heaven should make offerings by means of Jyotiṣṭoma) etc.

Maṇḍana's modification of śābdībhāvanā into iṣṭasādhantājñāna and ārthībhāvanā into bhāvanā

Ācārya Maṇḍana Miśra has brought a qualitative change into the analysis of sentence-meaning by modifying the Bhāṭṭas' concept of 'inducement' (*preraṇā*) or 'word impellent-force' (*śābdībhāvanā*) into the theory of 'the knowledge that the actions imposed are the beneficial means to the desired results (*iṣṭasādhanatājñāna)* and the concept of 'effort' (*prayatna*) or 'end-efficient (productive) force' (*ārthībhāvanā*) into the theory of the productive (accomplishing) activity (*bhāvanā*). He has established that the injunctions (*vidhi*) have a reference to the 'inducement' or 'word-impellent force', which impels the people, desirous of the result 'heaven' to undertake the actions, means the injunctive words convey the knowledge that the actions imposed are the beneficial means to the desired result (*iṣṭasādhana*). For instance, consider the injunctive statement *jyotiṣṭomena svargakāmo yajeta* 'he who desires heaven should make offerings by means of Jyotiṣṇoma' . Here, the injunctive word *'yajeta'* has a reference to an inducement or word-impellent force, that impels the listener to be undertaken the offerings, means that the same word conveys the knowledge that the action of offering imposed to undertake is the beneficial means to the desired result of heaven. Thus, the injunctive words must be recognized as conveying only the knowledge that the actions imposed are the beneficial means to the desired result (*iṣṭasādhanatājñāna*).

Maṇḍana has also established that 'men are known by Vedic and other statements to possess a particular inherent energy/effort (*prayatna*) or an 'end – efficient-force' (*ārthībhāvanā*), which is conducive to the production of desired result', means men are known to possess a productive or accomplishing activity (*bhāvanā*) expressed by the injunctive and other conjugational endings in the finite expressions. According to him, conjugational endings such as (e)'*ta*', '*ti*' etc., in finite expressions such as *'yajeta'* (one should make offerings), *'pacati'* (he cooks)etc., must be accepted as expressing the activity (*bhāvanā*) of men etc. which is conducive to the production of the desired effect, since no effect can be accomplished without a productive activity. Thus, energy or effort (*prayatna*) or 'end – efficient-force' (*ārthībhāvanā*) must be viewed as the accomplishing or productive activity (*bhāvanā*), since the same is conducive to the production of the desired effect. Maṇḍana has further established that the productive activity must be accepted as the meaning expressed by all the conjugational endings, since no other expressions can be found to express it; and no meaning can be cognized without being expressed by an expression. It should be noted here that influence of Maṇḍana's interpretation of *bhāvanā* as the accomplishing (productive) activity was so dominant that in later times, the term *bhāvanā* came to be recognized as standing for only the concept of the accomplishing (productive) activity. *Bhāvanā* was regarded, no longer, to represent the concept of word – impellent – force. And thus, Kumārila's original concept of *bhāvanā*, as representing both the aspects; namely, the word - impellent-force' and the 'end-efficient-force' was totally overshadowed. Thus, later writers such as Laugākṣi Bhāskara etc. defined the *bhāvanā* as the operation of the producing agent that is conducive to the accomplishment of the effect to be produced (*bhavituḥ bhavanānukūlaḥ bhāvayituḥ vyāpāraviśeṣaḥ)*. This definition of *bhāvanā* clearly identifies *bhāvanā* with only the accomplishing activity.

Also it should be noted that while the knowledge that the actions imposed are the beneficial means to the desired effect (*iṣṭasādhanatājñāna*) (the modification of 'word-impellent-force' *śābdībhāvanā*) was established as the sense conveyed by only the injunctive words such as '*yajeta*' etc., the accomplishing activity (*bhāvanā*) (the modification of 'end-efficient-force' *ārthībhāvanā*) was established as the sense conveyed by conjugational endings of all the finite expressions such as '*yajeta*', '*pacati*' etc.

Author : Maṇḍana Miśra, the author of the Bhāvanāviveka, was an acknowledged scholar of many disciplines such as Mīmāṁsā, Advaita and grammar. He has written number of books on all the three disciplines. He is believed to be a disciple of Kumārila Bhaṭṭa, the great Mīmāṁsaka, who has founded the Bhāṭṭa School of Philosophy. According to Ānandagiri's *Śaṅkaradigvijaya*, he married the sister of his own teacher, namely, Kumārilla Bhaṭṭa. He was a staunch follower of Bhāṭṭa school of Mīmāṁsā and therefore, supported Bhāṭṭa doctrine in all of his works devoted to the system of Mīmāṁsā.

However, the identity of Maṇḍana Miśra poses a problem. *Śaṅkaradigvijaya* of Vidyāraṇya identifies Maṇḍana with both Suresvarāchārya, the author of the *Naiṣkarmyasiddhi*, and Vārttikas on the *Bṛhadāraṇyakopaniṣadbhāṣya* and *Taittarīyopaniṣadbhāṣya* of Śaṅkarācārya, and also with Viśvarūpācārya, the author of the *Blākrīdā*, a commentary on the *Yājñavalkyasmṛti*. However, the view-points expressed by Maṇḍana in his *Brahmasiddhi*, one of the greatest of pre-Śankara Advaita works, differ completely from that expressed in the *Naiṣkarmyasiddhi* etc. On this ground, Prof. Kuppusvami Sastri has convincingly argued in his introduction to the *Brahmasiddhi* that Maṇḍana was a pre-Śaṅkara Advaitin, and therefore, cannot be identified with Sureśvarācārya or with Viśvarūpācārya. Also it should be noted that the pattern, viz. *kārikas* followed by prose explanatory passages, found in the *Brahmasiddhi* is similar to the pattern, viz. *kārikas* followed by prose-explantory passages found in his *Bhāvanāviveka* and in other known works by him; whereas the pattern of the *Naiṣkarmyasiddhi* etc. with only prose passages is quite distinct from that of the *Brahmasiddhi* etc. Thus, it should be admitted that Maṇḍana is to be identified with the author of the Brahmasiddhi and not with the author of the *Naiṣkarmyasiddhi* etc.

As far as Maṇḍana Miśra's date is concerned, it can be fixed around 680-720 A.D. The *Brahmasiddhi* does not manifest post-Śaṅkara Advaita tendencies such as the establishment of *anirvacanīyatva* of Brahman etc. (it actually holds that Brahman is to be obtained, i.e. understood, through the Vedas); consequently, Maṇḍana can be admitted to have lived prior to Ādiśaṅkara, who flourished around 788-820 A.D. Also, since Maṇḍana has studied under Kumārila Bhaṭṭa and explained many of his doctrines in his works, he cannot be placed earlier than 680 whrein Kumārila flourished. Thus, Maṇḍana's date can be fixed between 680 and 720 A.D.

Works of Maṇḍana

Maṇḍana Mishra is known to have composed six works in all. They are : The *Brahmasiddhi, Sphoṭasiddhi, Mīmāṁsānukramaṇī, Vibhramaviveka, Vidhiviveka* and *Bhāvanāviveka*. Out of the six works, the first work, the *Brahmasiddhi*, deals with the Advaita system of Philosophy; the second work deals with theword essence or *sphoṭa* theory of Bhartṛhari and the remaining four are devoted to the establishment of the Bhāṭṭa tenets of Pūrvamīmāṁsā.

BRAHMASIDDHI

The *Brahmasiddhi*, the celebrated work of Maṇḍana on pre-Śaṅkara-Advaita philosophy, is set out to establish Brahman as the only ultimate goal of mankind known by the Vedic and also Upaniṣadic statements. It holds firmly that the Vedas (words) must be accepted as establishing the existence of Brahman, since the same words are not contradicted by the perception etc. in establishing the oneness of Brahman. Further, it establishes that the Vedic injunctions do not refer to the existence of Brahman as it is already known by the *karmāvabodha*, but refer to the same Brahman as the qualificand of *samanvaya*. The *Brahmasiddhi* finally concludes that Brahman needs to be established as the qualified entity by words.

SPHOṬASIDDHI

The *Sphoṭasiddhi* is a work on grammar and it deals with the establishment of *sphoṭa* or word-essence and also the eternality and validity of words. It is a useful monograph for students and scholars interested in the comparative study of Bhartṛhari's *sphoṭavāda* and also Bhāṭṭa's analysis of word and meaning.

MĪMĀṀSĀNUKRAMAṆĪ

The *Mīmāṁsānukramaṇī* is a metrical composition intended to index and enumerate the topics of different *adhikaraṇas* found in the 12 chapters of *Pūrvamīmāṁsā;* and it illustrates the arguments of Mīmāṁsakas by summarising both *pūrva* and *siddhāntapakṣa* of various *adhikaraṇas*.

VIBHRAMAVIVEKA

The Vibhramaviveka establishes the *khyātivāda* of the Bhāṭṭa school by refuting the well-known theory of *akhyātivāda* of the Prābhākara school. It explains briefly, in the beginning, the four theories of error (*bhrama*), viz. *ātmakhyāti*, *asatkhyāti*, *akhyāti* and *anyathākhyāti*, and then argues that the Prābhākara's notion of *akhyāti* (non-perception) fails to explain satisfactorily the erroneous knowledge such as 'this entity is silver' (*idam rajatam*). According to Vibhramaviveka, error (*vibhrama*) must be held to be a distinct entity for explaining the error in erroneous perceptions such as 'this entity is silver' etc. The Vibhramaviveka is thus, a useful monograph for the understanding of the Bhāṭṭa theory of *khyāti*.

VIDHIVIVEKA

The Vidhiviveka establishes 'the knowledge that the actions imposed are the beneficial means to the accomplishment of the desired effect' (*iṣṭasādhanatājñāna*) is the meaning denoted by both Vedic and non-Vedic injunctions (*vidhi*). It holds that the injunctions such as *'yajeta'* (one should offer), *'paceta'* (one should cook) etc. must be held to have a distinct denotation in (reference to) the *iṣṭasādhanatājñāna;* otherwise the inducement to undertake the actions such as offering or cooking cannot be explained. According to the Vidhiviveka, as explained earlier, only 'the knowledge that the actions imposed are the beneficial means to the desired effect' can induce the people to undertake the actions such as the offering since the mere imposition of the performance of the compulsory duty of actions (*niyoga*) without a cause and effect relationship with the effects to be accomplished is not sufficient enough to induce, i.e. to motivate the people to undertake the actions. Thus, the injunctions such as '*yajeta*', '*paceta*' etc. in '*svargakāmo yajeta*' (he who desires heaven should offer, by means of offering), '*taṇḍulaṁ paceta*' (one should cook the rice grains) etc., must be held to denote the *iṣṭasādhanatājñāna* as its meaning.

It should be noted here that Maṇḍana's proposal that *iṣṭasādhanatājñāna* is the meaning expressed by injunctions is a modification of the Bhāṭṭa's concept of inducement (*preraṇā*) or word-impellent-force (*śābdībhāvanā*); and such a concept of *preraṇā* or *śābdībhāvanā* was in direct contrast to the Prābhākara's theory of reference to *apūrvakārya*. The theory of reference to the transcendental effect to be accomplished (*apūrvakārya*) by the injunctive affixes has been refuted on two grounds: Firstly, because such an *apūrvakārya* is not recognized to be Dharma by anyone and secondly, because knowledge of mere *apūrvakārya* is not sufficient to induce men to undertake actions.

BHĀVANĀVIVEKA

The Bhāvanāviveka, the work being translated into English with notes, is the most important treatise in the Bhāṭṭa school of the Pūrvamīmāṁsā system on the topic of the accomplishing or the productive activity (*bhāvanā*). Its main purpose is to establish that while the *iṣṭasādhanatājñāna* is the meaning expressed by the optative suffixes in the injunctive statements, the accomplishing activity (*bhāvanā*), which is a modification of the Bhāṭṭa theory of effort (*prayatna*) or end (result)-efficient-force (*ārthībhāvanā*), is the meaning distinct from the verbal root meanings (actions or effects); and therefore, is the meaning expressed by all the conjugational/verbal endings in all the finite expressions such as '*yajati*' (he offers), '*pacati*' (he cooks) etc. It establishes the theory of the accomplishing activity by refuting the Prābhākara's theory that the imposition of the performance of the compulsory duty of the actions (*niyoga*) which have no causal relationship with the effects, is the meaning conveyed by the optative and other finite verbs; and further, it establishes the theory that the accomplishing/productive activity (*bhāvanā*) is the distinct meaning of the conjugational endings. The Bhāvanāviveka sets aside the theory of the Pūrvapakṣins, mainly the niyogavādins, aided by the grammarians, that the activity (*bhāvanā*) is nothing but the actions such as 'offering', 'cooking' etc. or qualities such as the *vikledana* etc. expressed by the verbal roots (*dhātvarthabhāvanāvāda*).

The Bhāvanāviveka consists of 59 *kārikas*, alongwith their explanatory prose passages by Maṇḍana. It is divided into two parts : viz. the *pūrvapakṣa* and the *siddhānta*. The *Pūrvapakṣa* explains first the theory that *bhāvanā* is nothing but the root meaning, i.e. actions or effects (*dhātvarthabhāvanā*) by refuting the necessity for the acceptance of a distinct accomplishing activity (*bhāvanā*) from the root-meanings; and then establishes the theory of *niyogavākyārtha* of Bādari and his followers as an inevitable consequence. The *Siddhānta*, on the other hand, refutes the *dhātvarthabhāvanāvāda* by explaining the necessity for accepting a distinct accomplishing activity from the root-meanings as the meaning expressed by the conjugational endings on the ground that otherwise the accomplishment of the desired effect such as 'heaven' etc. would be untenable; and then establishes the theory of *bhāvanāvākyārtha* of Maṇḍana as the necessary consequence.

Edition :

For the purpose of the translation of the Bhāvanāviveka, the text edited by Sri V.A. Ramaswami Sastri and Sri K.A.Sivaramakrsna Sastri (Annamalai University, Annamalainagar, 1952), is used.

Methodology :

I have explained Maāḍana's theory of the distinction of the activity in the following pages. Further, to facilitate the understanding of Maṇḍana's theory of the activity, I have included the translation of the Bhāvanāviveka which consists of 59 verses along with their explanatory prose passages, in the present edition. While translating the text of the Bhāvanāviveka, an attempt is made to provide 'literal translation' as far as possible. This has been done without neglecting clarity of the text. Nevertheless, since the text is highly technical in nature, and the literal translation does not become quite intelligible by itself as such, notes become an absolute necessity for the clear understanding of the technicalities and the intricacies of the arguments. Thus, in order to facilitate the understanding of the arguments, I have provided notes for both the verses and the explanatory passages. However, in providing notes, I have made extensive use of the commentary of Viṣamagrannthibhedikā by Narayaṇa, although I had many occasions to refer to the commentary by Umvekabhaṭṭa as well.

EXPOSITION OF MAṆḌANA MIŚRA'S DISTINCTION OF THE ACTIVITY

The concept of the accomplishing activity (bhāvanā)

Maṇḍana's concept of accomplishing (productive) activity (*bhāvanā*) or operation (*vyāpāra*) is a modification of the concept of 'end-efficient-force' (*ārthībhāvanā*) of the Bhāṭṭas. According to Maṇḍana, Kumārila's theory that "there exists an inherent energy (*pravṛtti*) or effort (*yatna*) that is conducive to the production of the effects such as heaven; and therefore, the same (energy or effort) must be viewed as an 'end-efficient-force' (*ārthībhāvanā*)", means that the energy (or the effort) is activity (*bhāvanā*) or operation (*vyāpāra*) which is efficient in producing the effects such as heaven and is distinct from action. Maṇḍana holds that a separate producing or accomplishing activity must be accepted in addition to the action of offering etc. expressed by the verbal roots such as '*yaj*' (to offer) etc.; otherwie the production of the desired effect such as heaven cannot be explained. No effect can be accomplished without an accomplishing factor and nothing except the activity can be conceded as the accomplishing factor. The actions such as 'offering', expressed by the verbal roots such as '*yaj*' (to offer) etc., cannot be identical with the producing or accomplishing activity, since the same actions function as merely the grammatical objects or the instruments (means of accomplishment) with respect to the activity.

Actions are either grammatical objects or instruments

Actions, expressed by verbal roots, are either grammatical objects or instruments (means to the accomplishment) with respect to the activity. Consider, for instance, the following statements : (i) *taṇḍulaṁ pacati*' (he cooks the rice grains), and (ii) '*jyotiṣṭomena svargakāmo yajeta*' (he who desires heaven should offer by means of the Jyotiṣṭoma through the activity). The two instances can be phrased (analysed) usually as follows : (i) *'taṇḍulasya pākaṁ karoti'* (he makes (performs) the action of cooking of rice grains), and (ii) *'jyotiṣṭomena yāgena svargaṁ bhāvayet'* (one should exert in such a way as to accomplish the heaven by means of the Jyotiṣṭoma offerings) respectively. Here, the analysis of the first instance, namely, *'taṇḍulaṁ pacati'* as *'taṇḍulasya pākaṁ karoti'* clearly establishes the fact that the action of cooking, which is the meaning of the verbal root *'pac'* (to cook), is the grammatical object with respect to the activity (i.e. performance), since the word expressing the same (cooking), i.e. *'pākam'*, is found to occur in the accusative (*'am'*) ending. Also, the analysis of the second instance, namely, *'jyotiṣṭomena svargakāmo yajeta'* as *'jyotiṣṭomena yāgena svargaṁ bhāvayet'* clearly establishes the fact that the action of offerings of Jyotiṣṭoma, which is the meaning expressed by the verbal root *'yaj'* (to offer), is the instrument, i.e. means of the accomplishment of heaven. Thus, it becomes established that the action of 'cooking', 'offering' etc., expressed by the verbal roots such as *'pac'* (to cook), *yaj* (to offer) etc., function as either the grammatical object or the instrument (means of accomplishment) with respect to the activity expressed by the conjugational ending.

Basis of the objecthood of verbal root-meanings (actions)

The theory of Maṇḍana that the actions such as cooking, expressed by the verbal roots such as *'pac'* (to cook) etc., function as the grammatical objects with respect to the accomplishing activity is based on the possibility of the analysis of the finite forms of verbs such as *'pacati'* (he cooks) etc. as *'pākaṁ karoti'* (he makes or performs cooking) etc. In such an analysis, the verbal derivative *'pākam'*, expressing the action of cooking, is a noun found to occur in the accusative case ending which signifies the objecthood of its base-meaning. And the explanatory verb *'karoti'* expresses the activity accomplishing such an action.

Most of the Indian languages such as Bengali; Kannada etc. as well as French have usages wherein the root-meanings are construed as the grammatical objects with respect to the accomplishing activity expressed by a separate verb equivalent to *'karoti'*. Consider the following sentences :

Bengali : *'āmi pāk kari'*
(I make / perform cooking);
Kannada : *'avanu aḍigeyannu māḍuttāne'*
(He makes cooking);
French : 'Il fait curire'
(He makes / performs cooking).

In all these instances, the action of cooking, expressed by the verbal nouns such as *'pāk'*, *'aḍigeyannu*, and *'curire'* is construed as the grammatical object with respect to the accomplishing activity expressed by the explantory verbs *'kari'*, *'māḍuttāne'*, and *'fait'* respectively.

These examples clearly illustrate the fact that the root-meanings (actions) can be construed in many of the Indo-European languages as the grammatical objects with respect to the accomplishing activity; and hence Maṇḍana's theory of the productive activity, which is based on the linguistic analysis of finite verbs such as *'pacati'* etc. as *'pākam karoti'* etc., wherein the verbal noun in the accusative expresses the objecthood of the verbal action of cooking etc. with respect to the activity expressed by the explantory verb *karoti*, is the earliest recognition of the fact that the verbal actions function as the objects to be accomplished through the activity.

Activity is the meaning expressed by conjugational endings

The productive or accomplishing activity (*bhāvanā*) is held to be the meaning expressed by the conjugational (verbal) endings by Maṇḍana. According to him, all finite verbs (*tiṅantas*) must be divided into two morphs : viz. (i) verbal root (alongwith the conjugational mark), and (ii) conjugational/verbal ending. Consider, for instance, the finite verb *'pacati'* (he cooks) or *'yajeta'* (one should offer). Here the verb *'pacati'* can be divided into the morphs *'paca'* (i.e. the root *'pac'* along with the class mark or infix 'a') and *'ti'*; whereas the verb *'yajeta'* can be divided into the morphs *'yaja'* (i.e.the root *'yaj'* with the mark *'a'*) and *'ta'*. While the morph, consisting of the verbal root and the conjugational mark, such as *'paca'* (or *'yaja'*), refers to the action of cooking (or the action of offering), the morph *'ti'* (or *ta*) refers to the productive activity. Thus, the sense of the activity, which is conducive to a desired effect, and which has the action functioning as either the grammatical object or the instrument (i.e. means of accomplishment), is referred to by the conjugational ending in a finite form of verb such as *'pacati'* or *'yajeta'*. etc.

Treatment of finite forms of verbs 'tiṅantas'

It may be stated now that Maṇḍana's treatment of finite forms of verbs (*tiṅanta*) comes very close to the modern concept of accomplishment verbs since Maṇḍana regards them as conveying the sense of an activity accomplishing the desired effect. Nevertheless, the main distinction is that while the accomplishment verbs convey the sense of an activity accomplishing certain objects, the finite verbs, for Maṇḍana, convey an accomplishing activity and also an action to be construed as either object or instrument, since the same finite verbs are to be divided into two morphs, viz. verbal roots and conjugational endings.

Grammatical agreement (sāmānādhikaraṇya) is the basis of reference to the accomplishing activity by verbal endings.

Maṇḍana holds that the conjugational endings must be accepted as having a reference to the accomplishing activity due to the grammatical agreement (*sāmānādhikaraṇya*) of the finite verbs (in which they occur) with the verb *'karoti'* (he accomplishes) in question and answers. For instance, consider the question *'kim kaṛoti'* (what does he do) and answer' *pacati'* (he cooks). Here, *'pacati'* has grammatical agreement with the explanatory verb *'karoti'* in person and number. Since the verb *'karoti'* refers to the accomplishing activity in such questions, the finite verbs *'pacati'* etc., agreeing with such explanatory verb *'karoti'*, too must be accepted as referring to the same activity. And between the verbal roots such as *'pac'* and also the conjugational or verbal endings such as *'ti'* found in such verbs as *'pacati'* etc., only the latter, which are common to all the finite verbs, and not the former, which are different in each case, and therefore, are not common to any verb as such, must be accepted as referring to the accomplishing activity. Thus, the grammatical agreement of the finite verbs *'pacati'* etc. with the explanatory verb *'karoti'* is the basis for considering the conjugational endings as referring to the accomplishing activity.

Objection that sāmānādhikaraṇya is not the basis

However, the Pūrvapakṣin (Niyogavādin aided by grammarian) argues that the grammatical agreement (*sāmānādhikaraṇya*) of the finite verbs *'pacati'* etc. with the explanatory verb *'karoti'* cannot be regarded as the basis for the reference to the accomplishing activity by the conjugational endings. According to him, the grammatical agreement functions as the basis for only the establishment of the reference to the individual/particular actions such as 'cooking' by the finite verbs *'pacati'* etc. He argues that the word, which has the grammatical agreement with the word expressing a general notion of an item, can be expressive of only a particular notion of the item. For instance, the word *'śiṁśapā'*, which has the grammatical agreement with the word 'vṛkṣaḥ' expressing the general notion of 'tree (-ness)', in *'vṛkṣaḥ' 'śiṁśapā;* expresses only the particular notion of the tree *'śiṁśapā.'* Thus, the finite verb *'pacati'* etc., which have the grammatical agreement with the verb *'karoti'*, expressing the general notion of actions, must be accepted as expressive of only the particular notion of the action such as cooking etc.

Moreover, between the two morphs, viz. verbal roots such as *'pac'* and also the conjugational endings such as *'ti'* constituting the finite verbs such as *'pacati'* etc., only the former (roots), which are distinct in each case, and not the latter (endings), which are common to all the cases, must be accepted as expressing the particular notion, i.e. the action of cooking etc.

Establishment that sāmānādhikaraṇya is the basis

Siddhāntin (Maṇḍana) establishes that the agreement (*sāmānādhikaraṇya*) between the finite verb such as *'pacati'* etc. and the explanatory verb *'karoti'* is the basis for the reference to the accomplishing activity by the conjugational endings by refuting the Niyogavādin's argument that the verb *'karoti'*, which is used in question, refers to the general notion of actions. He holds that *'karoti'* in instances like *'ghaṭaṁ karoti'* (he makes a pot) must be established to refer to the accomplishing activity since the general notion of actions cannot have any syntactico-semantical relation with the object 'pot'. The general notion of actions expects only a particular item of action, and not any object to be accomplished like pot. And the pot is not a particular item of action such as cooking. Now, since the verb *'karoti'*, in such cases, does not refer to any general notion of actions, but refers to only the accomplishing activity, the same *'karoti'* must be accepted to refer to the same accomplishing activity in the instance of question and answers such as *'kim karoti'* - *'pacati'* etc. as well. Otherwise, suppose *'karoti'* refers to some other meaning, i.e. general notion of actions in such cases, then the accepted convention of reference to the known sense, i.e. the accomplishing activity, would become violated and a new convention would be needed to accommodate the polysemy of *'karoti'*. Now, since the verb *'karoti'* is established to refer to the accomplishing activity, the finite verbs such as *'pacati'*, which are in agreement with *karoti*, must also be admitted to refer to the activity.

Now, between the two morphs, viz. the verbal roots and the conjugational endings, the latter refer to the activity, since the same are common to all verbs. However, in association with different, i.e. particular roots, the conjugational endings could be accepted to refer to the particular type of activity such as the one accomplishing the cooking etc., since the endings refer to those meanings which have syntactico-semantical competency for being related to their base-meanings; or, as an alternative, it could be accepted that the conjugational endings refer to the activity in general; but only as delimited by the accomplishment of particular actions such as cooking. Thus, there would be neither any difficulty in explaining the grammatical agreement between the two verbs *'karoti'* and *'pacati'* due to their reference to mere general notion unlike between the two synonyms *'karaḥ' and 'hastaḥ'* etc.; nor any redundancy in reference to one and the same activity twice.

Bhāvanā is the generality of root-meanings (actions)

Accomplishing activity (*bhāvanā*) is explained as 'doing', i.e. 'performing' (*karoti*), and is distinguished from the root-meanings (actions) such as 'cooking', 'offering' etc. which are perceived as distinct objects in cognitions of statements such as 'he cooks' (*pacati*), 'he offers' (*yajati*), etc. However, the Niyogavādin opposes such a theory of the activity as follows : The accomplishing activity cannot be established to be an entirely distinct entity from the root-meanings (actions); rather, the same must be held to be merely a generality of different root-meanings such as the action of cooking etc., since the same accomplishing activity is continuous in various root-meanings, and hence has the form of root-meanings in general.

According to the Pūrvapakṣin (Niyogavādin), Maṇḍana's theory may be reconstructed as follows : The activity is a generality of root-meanings (actions), since the same is invariably associated with (i.e. continuous in) all the root-meanings. However, unlike the cowness, which is a generality of all the cows due to its occurrence in all the cows, and hence, is identical with, i.e. inseparable from all the cows, the accomplishing activity is a generality of actions due to its accomplishing nature of all the root-meanings. That is to say, the accomplishing activity, despite being a generality, is not identical with the root-meanings (actions), but is a different entity from the root-meanings due to its nature of producing all the root-meanings.

Also, the accomplishing activity in statements such as '*mandam karoti*' (he does slowly) and '*śīghram karoti*' (he does quickly) has the slowness etc. as something to be accomplished through it; and hence manifests its accomplishing nature.

However, the Pūrvapakṣin opposes such a reconstructed theory as follows :

In finite expressions such as '*pacati*' (he cooks) etc., the two items, viz, (i) the generality of the accomplishing activity and (ii) the generality of actions, the means to the accomplishment, are never perceived. Therefore, the finite verbs such as '*pacati*' etc. cannot be accepted to refer to the accomplishing activity and to the action of cooking etc. and hence, the two different items, i.e. the accomplishing activity and the actions could not be accepted. Also, the slowness etc. in '*mandam karoti*' etc. are the secondary generalities (*avāntarasāmānya*) of the root-meanings such as the action of cooking etc., and hence, the theroy that the accomplishing activity has the slowness etc. as something to be accomplished through it is unrealistic. Thus, no distinct accomplishing activity can be established.

Refutation of the view that bhāvanā is the generallity of actions

Maṇḍana refutes the view of the Pūrvapakṣin as follows : The Niyogavādin, who believes that the activity is the generality of the root-meanings (actions), must state as to which morph of finite verb, i.e. the verbal root or the conjugational ending, expresses such a generality. He cannot maintain that the verbal root such as *'pac'* in *'pacati'* etc. expresses the generality, since he has himself stated that the verbal roots express the particular actions such as cooking. Nor can he maintain that the conjugational endings express the generality, since no scholar has ever accepted the theory that the endings refer to the generality of actions. Thus, neither of the two morphs can be stated to express the generality. The accomplishing activity, therefore, must be conceded to be a distinct entity from the root-meanings; and hence must be accepted as expressed by the conjugational endings in finite expressions.

It should be noted that the objection of the Pūrvapakṣin is based on the fact that he cannot conceive a distinct accomplishing activity which is conducive to the root-meanings, actions. According to him, activity is common to all the root-meanings, that means it is the generality of all the root-meanings; whereas according to the Siddhāntin, the activity accomplishes the root-meanings everywhere, and hence can be conceived to be a common quality present in all finite expressions.

Objection that intransitives (akarmaka) cannot refer to the activity

Pūrvapakṣin objects also to the position that the intransitive verbs such as *'dhvanati'* (it rings or sounds) too can refer to some accomplishing activity. According to him, *'karoti'* (he does or performs), due to the agreement with which, the intransitives are held to refer to the activity, cannot itself be explained to refer to the activity in question and answers involving intransitives such as *'kim karoti ghaṇṭā'*? - *dhvanati* (what does the bell do ? - it rings or sounds) etc. In such cases, *'karoti'* refers to simply a state of existence or mere being etc., and hence cannot be established to refer to the accomplishing activity. Also, in such cases, no object that could be accomplished through such an activity can be visualized; and hence the reference to the accomplishing activity would be totally useless. The intransitive verbs such as *'dhvanati'* are not established to refer to any sense of the objects that can be accomplished through the activity. Thus, the intransitives such as *'dhvanati'* etc. cannot be held to refer to the activity accomplishing an object due to their agreement with *'karoti'*. Also, Pūrvapakṣin objects to the position that the *ghañanta* derivatives such as *pākaḥ'* in question and answers involving *'ghañanta'* derivatives such as *'kā kriyā - pākaḥ'* (what is the action - it is the action of cooking) can be held to refer to the activity. According to him, they cannot refer to the activity, since there exists no conjugational ending. Since intransitives and *ghañantas* cannot be established to refer to the activity, (they refer to the actions in general), the verbs *pacati* etc. too cannot be accepted to refer to the activity (they refer to the actions in particular such as cooking).

Refutation of the objection that intransitives cannot refer to the activity

Maṇḍana however, refutes the Pūrvapakṣin's objection as follows : Intransitives can be established to refer to the activity, since *'karoti'*, with which they agree, does refer to the activity in question and answers involving intransitives. For instance, in question and answers such as *'kim karoti ghaṇṭā- dhvanati'*, the happiness etc. are the objects to be accomplished by means of ringing or sounding; and to accomplish such objects, the activity becomes necessary. Such an activity must be admitted in the question to have been referred to by the verb *karoti*; whereas the same in the answer must be admitted to have been referred to by the intransitive *'dhvanati'*. Thus *'karoti'* must be admitted to refer to the activity in the question and answers involving intransitives; and therefore, intransitives too, which agree with *karoti*, must be held to refer to the activity.

Also, according to Maṇḍana, suppose happiness etc. are not intended to be the objects, then the root-meaning 'ringing' (sounding) itself can be construed as the object to be accomplished through the activity. When, there exists a separate object to be accomplished, such as rice, the root-meanings (cooking etc.) function as the means of accomplishment; however, when there exists no separate object to be produced in intransitives, the root-meanings 'actions' themselves function as the objects to be accomplished through the activity. Thus, the action of ringing itself can be construed as the object to be accomplished in *'kiṁ karoti ghaṇṭā ? - dhvanati'* etc.

The construing of the root-meanings such as the 'action of ringing' etc. as the objects to be accomplished is not against the established convention either. For instance, in obligatory rites such as *'agnihotraṁ juhoti'* (he makes offerings of Agnihotra) etc., the offering of Agnihotra, the root-meaning, is construed as the object to be accomplished, since there is no separate object to be accomplished like heaven.

Further, Maṇḍana establishes that in *ghañanta* usages such as *'kā kriyā ? - pākaḥ'* etc. too, the reference to the activity is necessary. For, the object such as rice needs to be accomplished through the activity. However, the difference is that while the activity is indicated, in the case of *ghañantas,* due to the absence of conjugational endings, that can express the activity, the same activity is expressed, in the case of finite forms of verbs such as *'pacati'*, due to the presence of the conjugational endings. Thus, both intransitives and *ghañantas* can convey the activity.

Existential verbs too express the activity

Maṇḍana holds that verbs conveying existence such as *'bhavati'* (he becomes) and *'asti'* (he exists) too express an activity. According to him, all sorts of finite verbs, including existential verbs, can be analysed as expressing an operation/activity conducive to the accomplishment of certain effect (object). For instance, consider the existential verbs *'bhavati'* and *'asti'* in *'ghaṭaḥ bhavati'* (Pot becomes) and *'ghaṭaḥ asti'* (Pot exists). Here, *'ghaṭaḥ bhavati'* can be analysed as *'ghaṭaḥ bhavanaṁ karoti'* (pot operates in such a way that the same accomplishes the state of becoming, i.e. manifestation) and *'ghaṭaḥ asti'* can be analysed as *'ghaṭaḥ sattāṁ karoti'* (pot operates in such a way that the same attains the state of existence). Now, in such an analysis, the agent of becoming or existing (i.e. the pot) accomplishes the state of becoming or attains a certain state of existence means the same agent becomes the object of becoming or existence by acquiring a particular state of existence. Thus, the activity, expressed by the existential verbs, cannot be ruled out to lack any effect to be produced; and hence, the existential verbs too can be explained to express an accomplishing activity.

It should be noted here that Maṇḍana's theory of reference to the activity by existential verbs such as *'asti'* is consistent with his general theory of reference to the activity, accomplishing the effect by finite verbs; and is based on the possibility of the analysis of existential verbs such as *'asti'* as *'sattāṁ karoti'*, etc. This theory gains further credibility from the fact that something exists, can be explained to mean something operates or acts in such a way that the same comes into being (existence); and therefore, a certain effect, namely, a state of existence etc. is accomplished through the operation in the case of existential verbs.

Objection that the activity is not distinct from root-meanings (actions)

The most serious objection of the Pūrvapakṣin against the theory of the activity is that the same activity cannot be distinguished from the root-meanings (actions) such as cooking etc. According to the Pūrvapakṣin, the activity, which is conducive to the effects such as becoming soft of the rice grains etc., cannot be distinguished from the root-meanings such as the action of cooking etc. Also, according to him, in cases like *'yajeta svargakāmaḥ'* (he who desires heaven should offer), it is not possible to perceive any activity distinct from the action of offering of oblations.

Further, the Pūrvapakṣin holds that when the activity is held to be an operation distinct from the root-meanings, the same, being conducive to the accomplishment of root-meanings such as the action of cooking etc., needs to be accomplishing always the root-meanings (actions). Consequently, the root-meanings would become only the objects (i.e. the effects) to be accomplished through the activity; and, therefore, the same would not become the instruments of the accomplishment. Thus, the Siddhāntin's own theory that the root-meanings such as the action of cooking or that of offering are the instruments of the accomplishment, would become contradicted. Since the activity cannot be established as distinct from the root-meanings, the same must be considered to be identical with the root-meanings.

Refutation of the view that the activity is not distinct from root-meanings

Maṇḍana refutes the Pūrvapakṣin's objection that the activity cannot be distinguished from the root-meanings (actions) as follows : Suppose the activity is not distinct from the actions, then the usages such as *'svaṁ yajñaṁ yajate'* (he performs his own sacrifice), and *'aśvamedhena yajeta'* (one should make offerings by means of the Aśvamedha) would become inexplicable. In such instances, the words *'yajñam'* and *'aśvamedhena'*, referring to the root-meanings, i.e. the action of offering and the *Aśvemedha* respectively, have the accusative and instrumental case endings respectively. And such case endings could be justified only if the root-meanings function as the objects or the instruments with respect to the activity; and, to function as either the objects or the instruments, the root-meanings must be distinct from the activity.

Maṇḍana, refutes also the objection of the Pūrvapakṣin that when the activity is accepted to be distinct, the root-meanings would become only the objects and never the instruments with respect to the activity as untenable. According to him, the cognition and illustration of the objecthood of the *kārakas* which are originally instruments are not contradictory. The phenomenon of the cognition and illustration of the objecthood of the *kārakas* which are originally the instruments can be illustrated in the case of the cutting of wood by means of an axe. The operation (of cutting) of the agent, namely, the wood-cutter, never reaches, i.e. produces, the effect such as separation directly; it reaches (produces) the same indirectly through the operation of the instrument such as the axe which produces directly the separation. Thus, the same axe is cognized as the instrument with respect to the production of the effect 'separation' in the statements such as *paraśunā chinatti* 'he cuts with an axe'. However, the same axe (instrument) is cognized as the object with respect to the operation of the agent (wood-cutter), namely, the lifting and also the dropping down of the axe in statements such as *paraśuṁ udyacchati nipātayati.* 'he lifts and drops down the axe'. Similarly, the cognition and the illustration of the objecthood of the root-meanings, which are originally the instruments of accomplishment are not contradictory. The operation/activity of the agent, i.e., 'sacrificer', produces the effect 'heaven' indirectly through the operation of the instrument, namely, the offerings which produces the heaven directly. Thus, the same root-meaning such as the offering of the Viśvajit is cognized as the instrument of accomplishment in *viśvajitā yajeta* 'he offers through the Viśvajit' etc. However, the same root-meaning such as the offering is cognized as the object with respect to the operation/activity of the sacrificer in the statement *svaṁ yāgaṁ yajati* 'he offers his own offerings' etc. Maṇḍana, further, holds, that otherwise all the *kārakas* would become only the objects with respect to the activity, since all the *kārakas* are employed through the activity of the agent. Thus, only those *kārakas,* which are sought most to be accomplished through the activity, are the objects; and those, that function as the means of accomplishment, are the instruments.

Objection that activity cannot be established to be the operation (vyāpāra)

Pūrvapakṣin objects to the theory of the activity by holding that the same cannot be established to be the operation (*vyāpāra*) distinct from the root-meanings; for, a distinct operation cannot be established. Supposing the operation means a certain property to be accomplished (*sādhya*), which in turn, accomplishes the desired effect, then only the root-meanings such as the action of offering etc. would become established as the activity, since the same accomplish the effect 'heaven' etc. Also, suppose the operation is held to be a movement (*spanda*), then the activity could not be explained in the case of non-moving agents such as *asti*', 'he exists' *yajate* 'he offers' etc. Again, suppose the operation is held to be an effort (*prayatna*), then the use of finite verbs such as '*gacchati*', which have inanimates such as the chariot as the agents, in *'ratho gacchati'* (chariot goes) etc., would become inexplicable since the inanimates (chariot etc.) cannot possess such an operation, i.e. the effort which is a property of the animate beings.

Explanation that accomplishing activity is operation

Maṇḍana, however, refutes such an objection by holding that the accomplishing activity (*bhāvanā*) can be explained as the operation (*vyāpāra*). According to him, the activity is the cause of the effects which may be either the actions such as the becoming soft (moistening) of rice grains or the qualities such as the 'contact', 'separation' etc. Also, according to him, the activity, which is explained as an operation, must be analysed to be either the movement (*spanda*) or the effort (*prayatna*) characterised by the loss of inactivity or passivity (*audāsīnyaviccheda*). For, when the movement and the effort are present, the cognition of the activity such as *'ghaṭam karoti'* (he makes a pot) is obtained. That is to say, when a person is engaged in some movement and has an internal effort causing some effect, he ceases to be inactive, i.e. he loses the passivity; and is perceived to be possessing the activity; and thus, the same activity is to be explained as the operation common to both movement and effort.

Maṇḍana strongly criticizes the Pūrvapakṣin's objection that the operation, with which the activity is identified, can neither be explained as the movement nor as the effort, since the statements, which have 'non-moving' or 'inanimate' entities as the agents such as *ghaṭaḥ asti* 'pot exists' and *ratho gacchati* 'chariot moves' etc. would become untenable. According to him, such statements can be explained to be secondary usages (*upacāra*), wherein the operations, i.e. movement or effort, of moving or animate entities (agents) have been imposed on the non-moving or inanimate entities (agents). Maṇḍana explains this phenomenon as follows : The operation, which is a movement or an internal effort, can be considered as belonging to the self, since the same operation is dependent on the self. This is in spite of the fact that the movement may actually be inhering in the non-self; and therefore, may not be found to be present in the self as such. This incident is similar to the incident of considering the action of becoming soft, which is inherent in the rice grains, as the operation of Devadatta etc., since such an operation is dependent on Devadatta.

Objection to the assumption of the activity as the operation of the form of movement

Further, the Pūrvapakṣin objects to the theory that the activity be assumed as the operation (*vyāpāra*) of the form of a movement (*spanda or karma*) to facilitate the expressions of movement such as *'calati'*. '(bird or a person) moves' According to him, such expressions of movement cannot be based on the movement. He argues that only the effects, which are accomplished (*siddha*), are the basis for such expressions of movement. The unaccomplished movement (*asiddhakarma*) cannot be considered to be the basis for the expression, since the same movement is not accepted universally. Also, he argues that occasionally produced effects such as 'contact' and 'separation' cannot be taken as the basis for establishing the existence of a separate movement. According to the Pūrvapakṣin, if the movement is established on the basis of producing the effects, then the same must be established either as eternal or as an occasional cause. If eternal cause, then the same would need to produce the effects always. If occasional cause, then the same would need another cause (movement) to produce itself.

Moreover, the movement, being established through the effects, could be considered to exist only prior to the effects, and not at the time of the effects; and also, the movement, which is destroyed by the production of the effect 'contact', could never be considered as existing at the time of the effect 'contact'.

Now, since the movement cannot be established through the effects, the activity cannot be assumed as the operation of the form of the movement to facilitate the expressions of movement such as *'calati'*.

Avodiance of the incorrect statement 'sthāṇuḥ calati'

According to the Pūrvapakṣin, the expressions of movement such as *'calati'* are based on the effects which are delimited by a particular point of region or location (space) *'deśa'* and not merely on the effects. And the points of region or location (space) are only the points of sky, since only the sky is perceived as the region delimiting the effects 'contact' and 'separation'. Since the points of post etc. are never perceived as the points of region, or location, the incorrect expression of movement such as *'sthāṇuḥ calati'* (post moves) cannot be insisted to be made despite the post possessing the effects such as 'contact' and 'separation' when the bird moves away from the post. Also, he maintains that the sky, although imperceptible, is rendered perceptible by the perceptions, such as *'iha khagaḥ patati'* (here, in the sky, the bird flies) etc; and therefore, the effects such as contact and separation, delimited by the points of sky, can be considered as the basis of the movement. The Pūrvapakṣin, further, holds that no movement *(spanda)* distanct from the effects 'contact' and 'separation' can be established. According to him, the movement cannot be established to be a separate entity. In expressions of movement such as *'calati'* (the bird moves) etc., no distinct movement beyond the effects such as the contact with the upper region and the separation from the region behind can be established. This is so because, the person, though recognizing the movement as distinct from the effects 'contact' and 'separation', cannot gain the knowledge of the movement as 'bird moves' etc. unless and until he perceives the effects such as the contact and separation.

Explanation that the activity is the operation analysable into the movement

Maṇḍana, however, explains that the activity must be held to be the operation analysable into the movement, otherwise the expressions of movement cannot be explained. According to him, expressions of movement such as *calati* '(bird) mvoes' etc. must be considered as based on the movement; and cannot be considered as based on the effects 'contact' and 'separation'. Suppose the same is held to be based on the effects, then the expression could become applicable to the person who has stopped after making a certain movement, but possesses the effects 'contact' etc. Also, then the expressions of movement such as *'calati'* etc. would become necessary with respect to the post, since the same too possesses the effects 'contact' and 'separation' like the bird does. Further, the effects, delimited by the delimiting points of location or space, i.e. sky etc., too cannot be considered to be the basis for the expressions of movement; for, such expressions are not found with respect to the stationary fish despite the same possessing the effects 'contact' and 'separation' delimited by the delimiting points of location or space, i.e. water. Thus, in view of such undesired consequences, only the movement, and not the effects, can be considered to be the basis for the expressions of movement; and once a separate movement is accepted, the activity can be establsihed to be the operation of the form of movement or effort.

Objection that phalotpādikā avasthā cannot be the activity

A disputant of Mīmāṁsakas has held that the activity is not an entity distinct from the actions expressed by the verbal roots; rather, the same is the particular state or condition of the actions that are conducive to the accomplishment of the effects (*phalotpādikā avasthā*). According to him, the verbal roots such as *'pac'* refer to the actions in general as cooking etc.; and the conjugational endings such as *'ti'* refer to the particular state or condition of the actions (cooking etc.) that is conducive to the effect such as the becoming soft of the rice grains. And such a state of actions is called the accomplishing activity (*bhāvanā*), since the same is conducive to the accomplishment of the effect. Also, such an activity is itself to be accomplished, since, nothing that is not accomplished by itself, can ever accomplish any effect.

However, the Pūrvapakṣin opposes such a position on the ground that the knowledge of the beginning and also the end, i.e. the accomplishing state of the actions, which is dependent on the accomplishment of the effects, would become untenable. Although the knowledge of the beginning and the end, i.e. the accomplishing state of the actions, is tenable in the case of the actions that have a perceptible effect such as the husking, the same is not tenable in the case of the offerings etc. that have an imperceptible effect such as heaven. Thus, the motivation of the persons to undertake such actions becomes impossible to explain. Also, when someone undertakes such actions due to *niyoga* etc., he could never stop performing the same, since he cannot consider himself as one who has accomplished his duty even after accomplishing the effect.

Observation that phalotpādikā avasthā can be the activity

Maṇḍana does not make it clear as to what is his position regarding the Mīmāṁsakaikadeśin's theory that the accomplishing state or condition of the actions is the activity. Nevertheless, it can be assumed that since Maṇḍana's own theory that the activity is distinct from the root-meanings (actions) is also based on the fact that the same activity is conducive to the accomplishment of the effects, his theory does not essentially differ from such a theory of the Mīmāṁsakaikadeśins except that it admits such an activity to be a distinct entity from the root-meanings (actions). As regards the Pūrvapakṣin's criticism, it can be argued that the motivation or inclination of persons to undertake the performance of the actions such as 'offerings', which have an imperceptible effect, such as 'heaven', is equally difficult to explain in their own theory as well, since such actions can never be perceived to have the accomplishment of their effects. Thus, the Pūrvapakṣin's criticism could be ignored. Also, the theroy that the accomplishing state of actions is the activity is probably the most radical explanation of the 'end efficient-force' (*ārthībhāvanā*), since it rightly recognizes the accomplishing nature of the actions as the activity and hence Maṇḍana has rightly not criticised it.

Objection that finite verbs cannot express two kriyās

The Pūrvapakṣins hold that the verbal roots such as *'pac'* in *'pacati'* etc. are accepted by both the Pūrvapakṣins and the Bhāvanāvādins as referring to a *'kriyā'*, namely, the action of cooking etc; however, suppose the conjugational endings such as *'ti'* in 'pacati' etc. too are accepted to refer to another *'kriyā'*, namely, the activity, then it would follow that finite verbs refer to two different types of *'kriyās'*. However, finite verbs like *'pacati'* etc. are never perceived to refer to two different *kriyās* by anyone. Thus, the Bhāvanāvādins' theory that the conjugational endings refer to the activity is untenable.

The Pūrvapakṣins hold, further, that the Bhāvanāvādins cannot explain the root-meanings such as the action of cooking etc. as the means of accomplishment (*karaṇa*) with respect to the activity so that the reference to the two different *'kriyās'* can be explained as feasible by finite verbs. According to them,, such an explanation would render the syntactico-semantical relation of the instrumentality of the woods expressed by *'kāṣṭaiḥ'* etc. as untenable in *'kāṣṭhaiḥ pacati'* (he cooks by means of woods) etc. The instrumentality of the woods etc. cannot be construed with the root-meanings (actions) such as cooking etc., since the same are construed themselves as the means (instruments) with respect to the activity; also, the same instrumentality of the woods etc. cannot be construed with the activity expressed by the endings either, since the syntactico-semantical relations of the woods would be interrupted by the instrumentality of the root-meanings towards the activity.

Justification that finite verbs can express both the action and the activity

Maṇḍana justifies the reference to the action and the activity by finite verbs on the ground that such a reference to the action and the activity does not amount to the reference to two different *kriyās*. He explains that the actions such as cooking etc. expressed by the verbal roots 'pac' etc. are construed as only the means of the accomplishment with respect to the activity; and hence are only the instruments and not *'kriyā'*. Thus, out of the actions and the activity, only the latter (activity) is a *kriyā*, whereas the former (actions) are only *karaṇas*.

He also explains that the actions such as cooking etc. function as the instruments only when they are viewed to be already accomplished (*siddha*). However, the same actions function as the objects to be accomplished (*sādhya*) when they are viewed to be associated with the activity; and hence the instrumentality of the woods can be construed directly with the actions such as cooking, since they function as the objects to be accomplished; and thus have a syntactico-semantical expectancy for an instrument for their own accomplishment.

Expressions such as 'viklidyanti' and 'pacanti' cannot be distinguished

Another of the objections of the Pūrvapakṣin is that the finite expressions such as *'viklidyanti'* (rice grains become soft) and *'pacanti'* (they cook rice grains) could not be distinguished as expressing two distinct ideas when both the actions and the activity are held to be the meanings of finite verbs. He argues that in both cases, according to the Bhāvanāvādin, the verbal roots *'viklid'* and *'pac'* would express the action of cooking and the ending *'ti'* would express the accomplishing (productive) activity. The Pūrvapakṣin further, argues that the ditinction between the senses conveyed by the two finite expressions cannot be explained as due to the distinction between the agents of such expressions such as rice grains in the first case, and Devadatta in the second case either. According to him, a satisfactory explanation of the agenthood is untenable. Suppose the agenthood is defined as the employment of the *kārakas,* then the inanimate entities like rice grains would never become the agents since they cannot employ any *kārakas.* On the other hand, suppose the agenthood is defined as the possession of the operation (activity) referred to by the verbal roots as the qualificand, then the same operation (i.e. activity) would cease to be the meaning of the conjugational endings since it is already referred to by the roots.

Also, according to him, it cannot be inferred that there are two distinct operations : viz. (i) one producing the effects such as becoming soft (or heaven), and (ii) the other producing the verbal actions such as cooking (or offering); and while the conjugational endings such as 'ti' express the operations producing the effects, the verbal roots express the operations producing the verbal actions. For, excepting the root-meanings (i.e. the actions such as cooking) and the effects (such as becoming soft), there exists no distinct activity that can produce the effects. The effects are produced immediately after the performance of the actions (root-meanings) such as cooking. In the cases like *sāṅgrahāyaṇeṣṭi,* where a distinct operation is perceived due to the production of the effects interrupted by some other activity, the same activity is the meaning of some other root.

Explanation of distinction between 'viklidyanti' and 'pacanti'

Maṇḍana explains the distinction between the finite expressions *'viklidyanti'* (rice grains become soft) and *'pacanti'* (they cook rice grains) on the basis of the distinction between the agents of such expressions. According to him, the agenthood can be defined as the possession of the operation expressed by the conjugational endings (the agenthood is not to be defined as the possession of the operation expressed by the verbal roots). Consequently, since *'ti'* in the expression *'viklidyanti'* expresses the operation of the rice grains such as becoming soft, and since *'ti'* in the expression *'pacanti'* expresses the operation of Devadatta such as accomplishing of the becoming soft, the agents in the two expressions differ mutually.

It should be noted here that, according to Maṇḍana, the endings such as *'ti'* can be accepted to denote distinct meanings due to the distinction between the preceding bases such as *'viklid'* and *'pac'* in *'viklidyanti'* and *'pacanti'* despite the bases being synongmous, i.e. referring to the same action of cooking. The distinction between the references to different operations by the conjugational endings is similar to the distinction between the references to the distinct pluralities occurring in the parts of wife and also in the wives respectively by the plural endings of *'bhāryāḥ'* (wife) and *'dārāḥ'* (wives) due to the distinction between the preceding bases, i.e. *'bhāryā'* and *'dāra'' respectively.*

Observation :

It can be observed now that the difficulty of non-distinction between the senses of the expressions *'viklidyanti'* and *'pacanti'* is equal for both the Pūrvapakṣin and Maṇḍana, since both hold that the roots are referring to the action of cooking. Also, the solution to the non-distinction between the senses too is equal for both, since they try to explain the distinction due to the distinction between the agents. However, the difference lies in the fact that while the Pūrvapakṣin explains the distinction between the agents due to the possession of the operations expressed by the verbal roots, Maṇḍana explains the same distinction due to the possession of the operations expressed by the verbal endings. Now, the question is which of the two explanations is correct ? Maṇḍana maintains that in the quasi-passive statements such as *'pacyante,* i.e. *viklindyante taṇḍulāḥ svayam eva'* (the rice grains cook, i.e. become soft by themselves) and *'yajate yajamānaḥ'* (yajamāna offers), the finite verbs *'pacyante'* i.e. *'viklidyante'* and *'yajate'* express the mere action of becoming soft and offering (i.e. a resolve to make oblations), since the operation of putting the vessel on fire and the operation of offering is not perceived. On the other hand, in the active *'pacati'* (Devadatta cooks rice grains), and *'yajati'* (he offers), the active verbs *'pacati'*, and *'yajati'* etc. express the sense of the operation of putting the vessel on fire, and the operation of offering etc. which are conducive to the cooking and the making of oblations since the verbs *'pacati'* and *'yajate'* are analysed as *'pākaṁ karoti'* (he performs cooking) and as *yāgam karoti'* (he performs the offering). Thus, Maṇḍana may be justified in his view on the ground that the active verbs *'pacati'* etc. are analysed as referring to the activity.

Objection that the conjugational endings cannot be synonymous with the verb 'karoti'

The Pūrvapakṣin argues as follows : The verb *'karoti'* (he makes or performs) is invariably associated with an object. For instance, it is associated with the object *'ghaṭa'* (pot) in *'ghaṭaṁ karoti'* (he makes a pot). Now, suppose the conjugational endings are held to be synonymous with the verb *'karoti'*, then the same too must always be associated with the objects. However, the incorrect statements such as *'yajeta svargam'* (he should offer the heaven) and *'śayīta svāsthyam'* (he should sleep the comfort), wherein the ending *'ta'* could be associated with the objects *'svargam'* and *'svāsthyam'*, are never made in actuality. On the contrary, only the statements such as *'yajeta svargakāmaḥ'* (he who desires heaven should offer) wherein the ending *'ta'* is not associated with any object, are made, i.e. are grammatically correct. Now, it may be held by the Siddhāntin as follows : The conjugational endings are indeed associated with the objects such as heaven etc. in *'svargakāmo yajeta'* etc; however, they are not perceived to be so (as associated with the objects) due to the fact that the words capable of expressing the object-activity relationship are absent. The case endings such as accusative, instrumental etc., found in the analysis of*'svargakāmo yajeta'* etc., are, on the other hand, expressive of only the *kāraka* relationships with respect to the actions expressed by the verbal roots; and they are not expressive of any *kāraka* relationships with respect to the activity expressed by the conjugational endings. This is established on the ground that the accusative case endings such as *'am'* etc. are not seen used in the sense of the object of the compulsory duty of offering (*niyoga*) expressed by the conjugational endings in the statement *'svargakāmo yajeta'* etc. Thus, the conjugational endings too are associated with the objects such as heaven.

However, the Pūrvapakṣin refutes such a position of the Siddhāntin as follows : The Siddhāntin must concede that the declensional (case) endings express the *kāraka* relationships with respect to the activity expressed by the conjugational endings as well, otherwise the instrumentality of the Viśvajit with respect to the activity expressed by the conjugational ending *'ta'* in *'viśvajitā yajeta'* (one should make offerings by means of the Viśvajit) would become untenable.

Also, suppose it is not accepted that the declensional (case) endings denote the *kāraka* relationships with respect to the activity, then the word *'svarga'* in *'svargakāmo yajeta'* would require the genitive case ending, since only the genitives are used in general for all sorts of relationships. Now, in view of these difficulties, the case endings must be held to refer to the *kāraka* relationships with respect to the activity. Since the absence of the accusative case ending must be held to be due to only the absence of the object to be accomplished and not due to the impossibility of denoting the *kāraka* relationships with the activity, the Siddhāntin's position that the conjugational endings are synonymous with the transitive verb *'karoti'* is not tenable.

Justification that conjugational endings can be synonymous with 'karoti'

Maṇḍana justifies the synonymity of the conjugational endings with the verb *'karoti'* on the ground that the same can be shown to be associated with the objects. In statements such as *'svaṁ yajñaṁ yajate'* (he performs his own offerings), and *'agnim cinute'* (he piles up the fire) etc., the conjugational endings (*te* etc.) are perceived to be associated with the objects, namely, the 'offerings' and the 'fire'. Also, in statements such as *'svargakāmo yajeta'* etc., where no specific object is mentioned, the verbal root-meaning such as the offering may itself be construed as the object to be accomplished through the activity; and hence the conjugational endings can be explained to be associated with the objects such as the root-meanings that are to be accomplished. Now, since the conjugational endings do not deviate from the objects, the same may be considered to be synoymous with the transitive *'karoti'*.

Objection that the causative and primitive expressions cannot be distinguished

The Pūrvapakṣin objects further, that the causative and primitive expressions such as *'ghaṭam bhāvayati'* (he causes the pot to become) and *'ghaṭo bhavati'* (pot becomes) cannot be distinguished in the theory of the Bhāvanāvādin. For, the Bhāvanāvādin must concede that the causative sufix *'aya'* in causatives *'bhāvayati'* etc. and the conjugational ending *'ti'* in primitives *'bhavati'* etc. refer to the accomplishing activity. Thus, both the causative and primitive expressions would become indistinguishable, i.e. would convey only the sense of an accomplishing activity. Also, the Bhāvanāvādin cannot explain the distinction by stating that the causatives express the activity of the causative agent; whereas the primitives express the activity of the primitive agent. For, the causative and the primitive agents cannot be properly defined. Suppose the agent is defined as the one who employs the *kārakas*, then only the animates such as the pot-maker would become the agent in both cases, i.e. in *'ghaṭam bhāvayati'* and *'ghaṭo bhavati'*, and hence both expressions would convey only an identical sense. Also, suppose the agent is defined as the possessor of the activity, expressed by the roots, then no distinct activity can be envisaged as the meaning of the endings. Thus, causative and primitive expressions cannot be distinguished by the Bhāvanāvādin.

Explanation of the distinction between teh causative and primitive expressions

However, Maṇḍana maintains that in the theory of the Bhāvanāvādin, the distinction between the causative and the primitive expressions can be explained due to the distinction between the causative and the primitive agents only. The causative agent is the one who possesses the causative operation (activity) which has the activity of the primitive agent as its object. For instance, the causative *'bhāvayati'* refers to the activity of the pot-maker, the causative agent, which has the operation conducive to the becoming of the pot, the operation of the primitive agent, as its object. On the other hand, the primitive agent is the one who possesses the activity which has the verbal action as its object. For instance, the primitive *'bhavati'* refers to the activity of the pot, the primitive agent, which has the verbal action of becoming, as its object. Now, since the distinction between the causative and the primitive expressions can be explained due to the distinction between the agents, the objection that the acceptance of the reference to the activity by the conjugational endings leads to the non-distinction between the causative and the primitive expressions stands refuted.

It should be noted that Maṇḍana does not confuse causative and primitive expressions. While he accepts that the causatives refer to an activity that causes the activity of the primitive agent to be undertaken, he maintains that the primitives refer to the activity which has verbal action as its object; and hence is a kind of accomplishing activity. So, for him, the causative *'bhāvayati'* refers to the causative activity and the primitive *'bhavati'* refers to the accomplishing activity.

Niyogavādin's conclusion that 'yāgena svargaṁ bhāvayet' cannot be the meaning

The Niyogavādin, assisted by the grammarian's refutation of the existence of a separate activity as the meaning of the conjugational endings, concludes as follows :

The activity, which is distinct from the root-meanings (actions such as offering) and which is conducive to the desired effects such as heaven, cannot be established to be the meaning of the conjugational endings in finite expressions. Consequently, the explanation of the meaning of the sentence *'svargakāmo yajeta'* (he who desires heaven should offer) as *'yāgena bhāvayet svargaṁ'* (one should exert in such a way as to accomplish the effect 'heaven' by means of the offerings through the activity) is mere an assumption of unreality. The actual sense conveyed by such a sentence (*svargakāmo yajeta*) is, therefore, mere performance (undertaking) of the compulsory duty of offering (*niyoga*) by the person who desires the heaven. The effect (heaven) may or may not be accomplished due to the performance of such a compulsory duty of offerings, since no cause and effect relationship between the offerings and the heaven is tenable. The 'sense of the duty' alone impels the person to undertake the performance of the offering, and therefore, no distinct incentive such as an effect is necessary to impel the person.

The Niyogavādin, further, holds that *'svarga'* (heaven) in *'svargakāmo yajeta'* (he who desires heaven should offer) is a qualifier of the person enjoined to undertake the performance of offerings (*niyojyaviśeṣaṇa*). He holds so, although none of the three established purposes of a qualifier, viz. 'exclusion of non-application' (*ayogavyavaccheda*), 'exclusion of application with what is not intended' (*anyayogavyavaccheda*), and 'exclusion of complete non–application' (*atyantāyogavyavaccheda*) is possible to explain.

According to him, *'svarga'* (heaven) in *'svargakāmaḥ'* must be conceded to be the qualifier of the person, otherwise the same *'svarga'* (heaven) would become necessary to be construed as the object of the offering which is untenable due to the absence of the accusative ending.

Refutation of the view that 'svarga' is niyojyaviśeṣaṇa

However, the Siddhāntin opposes the theory of the Niyogavādin that *'svarga'* (heaven) in *'svargakāmaḥ yajeta'* (he who desires heaven should offer) can be construed as the qualifier of the person (*niyojyaviśeṣaṇa*). According to him, when something is construed as the qualifier, the same must be construed as either an effect (*phala*) or the cause (*nimitta*), since the qualifiers are either the effects or the causes. And, in the case of *'svargakāmaḥ yāvajjīvam agnihotraṁ juhoti'* (he who desires heaven offers the Agnihotra during ones entire life), neither of the two options are possible. For, *'svarga'* (heaven) cannot be construed as an effect, since, according to the Niyogavādin, no effect results from the offering. Also, *'svarga'* (heaven) cannot be construed as the cause, since such an option would render either the phrase *'yāvajjīvam'* (during ones entire life) or the phrase *'svargakāmaḥ'* (he who desires heaven) redundant depending upon whether the phrase *'svargakāmaḥ'* is read combindly or separately with the rest of the sentence.

Establishment of the theory that 'svarga' is niyojyaviśeṣaṇa

However, the Niyogavādin holds that *'svarga'* (heaven) in *'svargakāmaḥ'* (he who desires heaven) must be construed as the qualifier of the person (*niyojyaviśeṣaṇa*). According to him, the heaven can be construed as the qualifier by regarding the same as the cause (*nimitta*). He explains that the heaven can be the cause of the offerings inspite of the fact that such a construction would render either the phrase *'yāvajjīvam'* or the phrase *'svargakāmaḥ'* redundant. According to him, just because the phrase *'svargakāmaḥ'* or the phrase *'yāvajjīvam'* would become redundant in *'yāvajjīvaṁ svargakāmaḥ agnihotraṁ juhoti*, the non-meaning such as the heaven being the effect and the activity being the accomplishing factor cannot be accepted. Also, the phrase *'svargakāmaḥ'* would become redudant only in the case of the statements enjoining the obligatiory duties (*nityakarman*) and not everywhere. In statements such as *'svargakāmo jyotiṣṭomena yajeta'* etc., enjoining the optional duties (*kāmyakarman*) like the *Jyotiṣṭoma*, the question of combining the phrase *'svargakāmaḥ'* with the phrase *'yāvajjīvam'* etc. does not arise since such phrases are never used together in such statements at all.

Further, the Niyogavādin states that even the redundancy of the phrase *'svargakāmaḥ'* can be avoided. According to him, the very fact that the phrase *'svargakāmaḥ'* is used again in addition to the phrase *'yāvajjīvam'* suggests that the phrase *'svargakāmaḥ'* is meaningful. And the meaning suggested in such a case is that the person desirous of heaven must perform the Agnihotra as the cause (*nimitta*), and thus the same must be construed as the qualifier of the person.

Finite verbs express merely 'niyoga'

Finally, Niyogavādin cites Bādari to support his theory that finite verbs express merely the performance of the compulsory duty (*niyoga*) such as offerings. According to the Niyogavādin, Bādari has stated that only the subtance (*dravya*) such as rice grains, qualities (*guṇa*) such as tawniness and purification or refinement (*saṁskāra*) such as pounding function as the subsidiary to the action of offering etc., and therefore, the effects such as heaven can never function as the subsidiary to the action of offering. The action of offering is intransitive by its very nature; or if transitive, it has only the deity (*devatā*) as its object. Consequently, the same action can never be regarded as producing the effects such as heaven. Also, suppose, the action does need to produce something, then too, the effect, such as heaven, which functions as the object to be accomplished through the activity, can never be construed syntactico-semantically with the action of offering directly (it can be construed with the action of offering only indirectly through the activity). Therefore, since no effect such as heaven can ever be produced by any action like offering, the assumption of a distinct activity apart from the root-meanings (actions), to facilitate the production of the effects like heaven, is totally unwarranted. Now, since verbs such as *'yajeta'* express merely the undertaking of the performance of a compulsory duty of offerings (*niyoga*) (by the person desiring heaven), the assumption that the conjugational endings in the finite verbs express the accomplishing activity is totally unjustified.

Maṇḍana's explanation of the accomplishing activity.

Maṇḍana, however, rejects the Pūrvapakṣin's argument as fallows : The accomplishing activity (*bhāvanā*), which is distinct from the root-meanings (actions) and which is efficient in producing an effect, is established on the ground that the operation of an agent, which is merely another name for the activity, pervades directly an instrument, and therefore, has the root-meanings (actions) functioning as its instruments. The point that the operation of an agent pervades directly the instrument is best illustrated in the case of the operation of the wood-cutter in *'paraśunā chinatti'* (he cuts with an axe). The operation of the wood-cutter, namely, lifting up and downing the axe, is directly pervasive of only the instrument 'axe'; and by such pervasion it is efficient in producing the effect 'separation'. It should be noted here that the operation of the wood-cutter is directly pervasive of only the instrument 'axe'; and therefore, it does not pervade the effect as such; however, since the operation is meant to produce the effect by means of the instrument, the same is viewed to pervade indirectly the effect as well. Now, since the operation of the agent directly pervades only the instrument 'axe', it requries the separate instrument 'axe' in producing the effect 'separation'. Similarly, in the case of Vedic statements such as *'svargakāmo yajeta'* (he who desires heaven should make offerings) too, the operation of the agent, which is another name for the activity, must be accepted to have a separate instrument in accomplishing the effect such as heaven, since the operation of the agent cannot directly pervade the effect 'heaven' etc. Now, the activity accomplishes the effect of heaven etc. by pervading the instrument, i.e. offering, means the same activity produces the heaven by the instrumentality of the offering. Consequently, the root-meanings, i.e. actions such as offerings, must be held to be merely the instruments of accomplishing the effect 'heaven' etc. The difference between the operation of the wood-cutter and also the operation of the agent in the Vedic statements is that while the former has an accomplished entity such as the axe as its instrument, the latter has only the actions, which are yet to be accomplished, as the instrument. Thus, it is established that the activity requires the actions as its instrument and therefore, the same activity must be distinguished from the actions (expressed by the verbal roots) as the sense conveyed by the conjugational endings.

'Yāgena svargam bhāvayet' as the meaning of 'svargakāmo yajeta'

According to Maṇḍana, the Siddhāntin, the ultimate purpose of establishing the accomplishing activity as the meaning distinct from the root-meanings (actions), is to establish the sentence-meaning (verbal cognition) such as *yāgena svargaṁ bhāvayet* 'one should exert in such a way that he accomplishes the heaven by means of offering through the activity' from the Vedic sentence *svargakāmo yajeta*. 'he who desires heaven should offer'. Also, such a verbal cognition, according to Maṇḍana, should be accepted as obtained through the denotation of words only. For, in such sentences as '*svargakāmo yajeta*', the heaven is perceived to be the effect accomplished through the activity. (This is necessitated by the fact that otherwise the activity, which needs to demonstrate its accomplishing nature, cannot do so without producing an effect). Now, since the effect such as heaven is produced through the activity, and the same activity is the distinct meaning expressed by the conjugational endings, *yāgena svargam bhāvayet* 'one should exert in such a way that he accomplishes the heaven through the activity' is the meaning expressed by the sentence *svargakāmo yajeta* 'he who desires heaven should offer'.

Maṇḍana explains that the phrase '*svargakāmaḥ*' in '*svargakāmo yajeta*' expresses the effect 'heaven' which can be syntactico-semantically related to the activity, despite the same heaven (*svarga*) being construed as the qualifier of the person enjoined to undertake an action. In such a construction, the qualifier, namely the heaven, becomes the primary element (*pradhāna*); whereas the qualificand, namely, the person enjoined to undertake an action, becomes the secondary (*apradhāna*), since only the effect (heaven) is required to be accomplished from the view point of an accomplishing activity. This instance is similar to the instance of the qualifier, namely, *daṇḍin*, the 'staff-bearer' which becomes the primary element in the statement *daṇḍī praiṣān anvāha*, 'the staff-bearer pronounces orders', since the idea of pronouncing orders is already obtained otherwise through some other source; and therefore, only the idea of the 'staff-bearer' needs to be expressed by the statement. In the case of '*svargakāmo yajeta*' too, the idea of the person desiring to accomplish something is already obtained through the accomplishing activity, since the same always implies a person desiring to accomplish something. However, what is needed to be expressed is only the particular item to be accomplished, i.e. the heaven, as only the heaven provides the particular item to be accomplished. Thus, the phrase *'svargakāmaḥ'* in *'svargakāmo yajeta'* expresses only the 'heaven' to be accomplished which is prominent : whereas the same phrase merely repeats the idea of a person desiring to accomplish something which is already obtained and hence is secondary.

Heaven must be considered as the object to be accomplished

It should be noted that, in the Vedic statement *'svargakāmo yajeta'*, the heaven must be considered as the object to be accomplished, since nothing else deserves to be construed as the object. Even the root-meaning, namely, the action of offering cannot be construed as the object to be accomplished; for, the statement cannot enjoin the accomplishment of the action of offering, since the same is not conducive to the achievement of any welfare of persons. Moreover, the root-meaning 'offering' can be construed as only the instrument of accomplishing the heaven with respect to the activity. Now, since it is not possible that the root-meaning 'offering' can be construed as the object of the activity, only the heaven should be construed as the object with respect to the activity; and consequently, the phrase *'svargakāmaḥ'* must be admitted to be expressing the heaven as the prominent, i.e. as the object to be accompolished.

Necessity of expressing the heaven as the object to be accomplished

The Niyogavādin, who holds that the heaven is the qualifier of the person enjoined to undertake the performance of offering (*niyojyaviśeṣaṇa*); and therefore, the phrase *'svargakāmaḥ'* provides the relevant information regarding the eligible person, must also admit that the knowledge regarding the competence or eligibility of the particular person enjoined to undertake the action is obtained through only the implication, i.e. without any word directly denoting such an eligibility. Otherwise, even the incompetent or ineligible persons such as blind etc. could claim their right to perform the action of offering, since no words, that bar incompetent persons to undertake the performance of the offering, are found in the statement *'svargakāmo yajeta'*. Thus, the competence or the eligibility of the person must be admitted to be obtained only through the implication (without the denotations of words). And, therefore, the idea of the qualified person could also be admitted to have been obtained through implication without words. Consequently, the phrase *'svargakāmaḥ'* can be accepted as expressing only the object to be accomplished, i.e. the heaven as the same cannot be implied (implying of the object does not serve any useful purpose). Maṇḍana clarifies, further, that while the implying of the eligibility of the person is necessary, the implying of the effect (object) such as heaven is not necessary. According to him, while the former is required to be implied even without words, as otherwise the incompetent persons could not be prevented from performing the offering, the latter is not required to be implied, since nothing undesirable would become contingent if the same is not implied. Also, he makes it clear that the undertaking of the performance of the offering would not become untenable even without the effect such as heaven being not implied. The Niyogavādin can explain the undertaking of the performance of offering due to the very nature of the enjoining of the compulsory duty of offering (*niyoga*).

Thus, Maṇḍana concludes that since the phrase *'svargakāmaḥ'* in *'svargakāmo yajeta'* must be accepted to have a denotation in the effect or object to be accomplished such as heaven, the meaning comprehended by the sentence *'svargakāmo yajeta'* is, as explained, *yāgena svargam bhāvayet* 'one should exert in such a way that one accomplishes the heaven by means of the offering through the activity'.

Also, thus, Maṇḍana concludes that since the phrases such as *'svargakāmaḥ'* 'he who desires heaven' etc., in *'svargakāmo yajeta'* etc., express an effect (object) to be accomplished such as heaven, an accomplishing activity (*bhāvanā*), which can facilitate the accomplishment of such effects as heaven by means of the root-meanings (action of offering etc.), must be accepted as a distinct meaning of the conjugational endings in finite expressions such as *'yajeta'* etc.

PŪRVAPAKṢA

Statement of subject matter, purpose etc.

Translation : (P.1)

Verse 1

The people, who have their minds confused by the close association, i.e. the subordinate nature, of the root-meanings such as actions, effects etc. to the productive (accomplishing) activity (*bhāvanā*), do not see the real nature of the same productive (accomplishing) activity as distinct from the verbal root-meanings (effects or actions) (*dhātvartha*). Therefore, the real nature of such an activity is analysed here for the benefit of such confused people.

Note : Verse I introduces the topic or subject matter (*viṣaya*), the purpose (*prayojana*), and the person qualified or entitled to undertake the study of the composition (*adhikāri*).

Analysis of the nature of the productive or accomplishing activity (*bhāvanā*) forms the topic (subject matter) of Bhāvanāviveka. However, according to Maṇḍana, scholars are confused as to whether such an activity really exists or not; or if exists, whether the same is distinct from the root-meanings (i.e. quality or effect such as becoming soft or action such as 'cooking' etc.) (*dhāvartha*) or not. Also, they are not certain as to whether such an activity is a meaning denoted by the conjugational ending (such as '*ti*' in '*pacati*' etc.) or is denoted by the verbal roots (such as '*pac*' to cook etc.). The reason for such a confusion is the close association between the activity and also the verbal root-meanings (becoming soft etc.). Thus, the analysis of the real nature of the activity, as a *kriyā*, distinct from the root-meanings, is the subject matter of Bhāvanāviveka. The purpose of the composition of Bhāvanāviveka is to explain the accomplishing activity (*bhāvanā*) as a distinct operation denoted by the conjugational endings, and thereby, to establish the fact that the activity accomplishes the effect such as heaven (*svarga*) etc. by means of the actions expressed by the verbal roots. Also, when the accomplishing activity is explained to be a distinct operation conducive to the accomplishment of the effect 'heaven' etc, the explanation of the verbal cognition (i.e. sentence-meaning) such as (*yāgena svargam bhāvayet*) "one must exert in such a way that he accomplishes the effect 'heaven' by means of the offering through the activity" becomes possible from the statement '*svargakāmo yajeta*'. Finally, as regards the persons qualified or entitled to the study of Bhāvanāviveka: The qualified persons are those who are confused as to whether the activity is distinct from the root-meaning or not and also as to whether the conjugational endings denote the activity or not.

Translation : (P.3)

I.1. The Pūrvapakṣins state that the grammatical agreement between the finite verbs such as '*pacati*' (he cooks)or '*yajati*' (he offers) and the explantory verb '*karoti*' (he makes) cannot be held to establish the reference to the activity by the conjugational endings.

Note : Maṇḍana, the Siddhāntin, likes to establish that "there exists an inherent energy (*pravṛtti*) or effort (*yatna*) that is conducive to the production of the effects such as heaven; and therefore, the same energy or effort must be viewed as an 'end-accomplishing (efficient) - force' (*ārthībhāvanā*)" means the energy or the effect (*pravṛtti* or *yatna*) is an activity (*bhāvanā*) or an operation (*vyāpāra*) which is efficient in producing the effects such as heaven. According to the Siddhāntin, separate accomplishing activity (*bhāvanā*) must be accepted as denoted by the verbal (conjugational) endings such as '*ti*' in finite expressions such as '*pacati*', '*yajati*' etc. in addition to the actions of cooking, offering etc. expressed by the verbal roots '*pac*', '*yaj*' etc. He holds that the assumption of such an activity is necessary on the ground that otherwise the accomplishment of the effect such as heaven cannot be explained. No effect can be accomplished without an accomplishing factor; and nothing except the activity can be considered as the accomplishing factor. The verbal actions such as cooking or offering cannot be identified with the accomplishing activity since they function as either grammatical objects or instruments.

The purpose of establishing such a distinct activity is to facilitate the explanation of the meaning of the Vedic statement *'svargakāmo yajeta'* (he who desires heaven should make the offerings) as *'yāgena svargam bhāvayet'* (one should exert in such a way as to accomplish the heaven by means of offering through the activity).

Maṇḍana holds, further, that the conjugational endings must be accepted to have a reference to the accomplishing activity due to the grammatical agreement (*sāmānādhikaraṇya*) of the finite verbs such as *'pacati'* (he cooks) (in which the conjugational endings occur) with the verb *'karoti'* (he accomplishes) in question and answers. Maṇḍana's theory can be explained as follows :

In question and answers such as *'kim karoti-pacati (yajati)'* 'what does he do'? - 'he cooks (or he offers oblations),' the finite verbs *'pacati'* (*yajati*) etc. are found to have grammatical agreement with the verb *'karoti'*. In such question and answers, the verb *'karoti'* refers to the accomplishing activity. Now, since the finite verbs *'pacati'*, *'yajati'* etc. have grammatical agreement with *'karoti'*, the same finite verbs too must be admitted to have a reference to the accomplishing activity. However, each finite verb consists of two morphs : namely, verbal root such as *'pac'* (or' *yaj'*) and conjugational ending such as *'ti'*. And, between the two morphs, only the latter (conjugational ending) and not the former (verbal root) must be admitted to have a reference to the accomplishing activity since only the latter (conjugational ending) is common to all the finite verbs; whereas the former (root) is different with respect to different verbs. Thus, due to the grammatical agreement, Siddhāntin establishes the conjugational endings as referring to the accomplishing activity. However, the Pūrvapakṣin, namely Niyogavādin, aided by grammarians, opposes such a theory of the activity. According to him, the grammatical agreement of the finite verbs such as *'pacati'* (or *yajati*) etc. with *'karoti'* cannot be held to be the basis for establishing a reference to the same (identical) sense of the accomplishing activity; rather, the same grammatical agreement must be held to be the basis for establishing a reference to the particular notion of actions such as 'cooking', 'offering' etc.

Translation : (P. 3-4)

Verse 2

Since there exists grammatical agreement between the finite verbs such as *'pacati'* (he cooks), *'yajati'* (he offers) etc. and the verb *'karoti'* (he performs or makes) in the question and answers, the finite verbs must be inferred to have the denotations in the sense of particular actions such as 'cooking' or 'offering' which are distinct from the sense of the activity expressed by the verb *'karoti'*. Therefore, it is not possible to have the inference that there is a denotation of the finite verbs such as *'pacati'*, *'yajati'* etc. in the sense of the activity identical with the activity expressed by *'karoti'*. This is established by the fact that the statement such as 'This tree is *śimśapā*' (*vṛkṣaḥ śimśapā*), wherein the word *śimśapā* agrees with the word *'vṛkṣaḥ'*, does not denote the treeness, the general sense of tree expressed by *'vṛkṣaḥ'* (rather it denotes the particular sense of *the śimśapāness*).

Note : The verse (2) states the Pūrvapakṣin's view that grammatical agreement (*sāmānādhikaraṇya*) between the finite verbal forms like *'pacati'* (he cooks), *'yajati'* (he sacrifices) etc. and also the explanatory verb *'karoti'* (he makes or does) in the question and answer series such as *'kim karoti'* (what does he do) - *'pacati'*, (he cooks) (or *yajati'*) (or he sacrifices) should be taken as leading to the inference of the denotations of the finite verbal forms such as *'pacati'*, *'yajati'* etc. in the sense of the particular actions such as 'cooking', 'sacrificing' etc.; and such actions are analysable into different varieties of 'doing' or 'making' (i.e. *karotyartha*). The verse (2) refutes the Siddhāntin's view that such grammatical agreement between the *ākhyātas* such as *'pacati'* etc. and *'karoti'* leads to the inference of the denotation of the verbal forms such as *'pacati'*, (*yajati'*) etc. and also of the finite verb such as *'karoti'* in the identical sense of the activity; and consequently, the conjugational endings, which are common to all the verbal forms such as *'pacati'* etc., like the form *'karoti'*, which is common to all the questions, should be accepted as denoting the activity (*bhāvanā*).

Pūrvapakṣin explains his position by stating the example of *'vṛkṣaḥ śimśapā'* (This tree is *śimśapā*). Here, since the word *śimśapā* is in grammatical agreement with the word *vṛkṣaḥ*, the same expresses the particular idea of *'śimśapā* tree (and not the same idea of merely a tree in general). Similarly, since the finite verbal forms such as *'pacati'*, (*yajati'*) etc. are in agreement with *'karoti'*, the same must express the particular action of 'cooking', 'sacrificing' etc. Also, since the verbal roots, i.e. *'pac'* (to cook), *'yaj'* (to sacrifice) etc., in such forms, are different in each case, the same could be held to express the particular action of cooking etc.

Translation : (P.4-6)

Explanation of verse (2)

Theory of Siddhāntin that verbal forms express the activity : II.1. Siddhāntin holds, in this context, as follows : The agent of becoming, the sense referred to by the verb to 'become' (*bhavati*), is the object of the productive activity, the sense referred to by the verb to 'make' or 'perform' (*karoti*). This fact becomes established by the positive and negative examples that (1) the pot etc., which are the agents of becoming due to their state of being produced, are the objects of the productive activity (i.e. making or performing); and also that (ii) the horn of a rabbit and the sky, which are not the agents of becoming due to their state of non-existing and ever-existing, respectively, are not the objects of the productive activity. Also, it can be stated that the agent of 'making' or 'performing', the sense referred to by the verb *'karoti'*, attains the state of causative (i.e. accomplishing) agent. Consequently, since the accomplishing, i.e. productive, activity is the meaning of the verb *'karoti'* (to make), the causative affix, which is generally enjoined in the sense of the accomplishing (productive) activity of causing to become, resorts to the accomplishing (productive) activity, the sense of the verb *'karoti'* (to make), as its own meaning. Therefore, the accomplishing (productive) activity, (*kriyā*), referred to by the verb *'karoti'* (to make), is the sense conveyed by the word *'bhāvanā'*. Thus, it should be accepted that, since the verbs like *'pacati'* (he cooks) etc. are used in grammatical agreement wth the verb *'karoti'* (he makes), referring to productive activity, the same verbs must be inferred to have the (denotation in the) sense identical with the sense of the verb *'karoti'* (he makes), i.e. the productive activity.

Note : This passage explains Siddhāntin's theory as follows :

Since the verbal forms such as *'pacati'* (or *'yajati',*) etc. have grammatical agreement with *'karoti'*, the conjugational endings such as *'ti'* in *'pacati'* etc. are expresive of the productive activity (*bhāvanā*). Siddhāntin holds that the *'kriyā'* (making), which is expressed by the verb *'karoti'*, is nothing but the productive activity (*bhāvanā*). And such an activity has the agent of becoming as its object (*karma*). This phenomenon has been explained by both positive and negative examples. That is to say that whatever thing functions as the agent of becoming, for instance, the pot (*ghaṭa*), the same becomes the object of making expressed by *'karoti'* (i.e. that *'ghaṭa'* is the agent in *'ghaṭo bhavati'*, and therefore, the same is the object of *'karoti'* in *'ghaṭam karoti'*). And whatever things do not function as the agents of becoming, for instance, the horn of a hare (*śaśaśṛṅga*) and sky (*ākāśa*), the same cannot become the objects of making (i.e. that *śaśaśṛṅga* does not exist and is not the agent of becoming; and therefore, the same is not the object of *'karoti'*; and also that *'ākāśa* is ever-existing and is not the agent of becoming; and therefore, the same is not the object of *'karoti'*).

Consequently, the agent of making, expressed by *'karoti'*, becomes the causative (accomplishing) agent (*prayojaka kartā*) of whatever thing becomes, i.e. is produced. And the making, expressed by *'karoti'*, becomes the causative activity with regard to the production of a thing. Therefore, the same causative activity must be accepted as the productive activity known as *bhāvanā*, since *bhāvanā* is a causative form (*ṇijanta*) and the causative affix (*ṇic*) is used in the sense of the same causative (productive) activity. Thus, it becomes established that the productive activity is the meaning expressed by *'karoti'*. Now, since the finite verbal forms such as *'pacati'* (he cooks), or *'yajati'* (he sacrifices) are found in grammatical agreement with *'karoti'*, the same verbal forms (*'pacati'* etc.) too must be accepted to express the productive activity.

Translation : (p. 7-8)

Refutation of Siddhāntin's theory : II.2. No, this theory is not tenable. Grammatical agreement between the two words (i.e. the use of two words in apposition) is caused by the fact that they have their denotions in two distinct meanings; and therefore, the same (grammatical agreement) does not make us understand, i.e. infer, the identity of denotations of the two distinct words. If that were the case, then the use of the two words simultaneously together would not have been tenable. In the case of *'vṛkkṣaḥ śimśapā'*, wherein the words, *'vṛkṣaḥ'* (tree) and *'śimśapā'* (*śimśapā* tree) are used together in agreement, the treeness (*vṛṣatā*) is never denoted as the meaning by the word *śimśapā*; on the contrary, the same treeness is being understood due to the implication of the meaning denoted by the word *'śimśapā'*. Thus, the grammatical agreement of words is clearly a means to establish the absence of the denotations in the meanings identical to each other.

Note : This portion of the text explains the refutation of Siddhāntin's theory that the conjugational endings such as 'ti' in verbal forms such as *'pacati'*, *'yajati'* etc. denote the productive activity which is identical with the meaning denoted by the verb *'karoti'*. According to the Pūrvapakṣin, the grammatical agreement is not found between the two words which express exactly identical meanings. Therefore, the same grammatical agreement is not enough to suggest the same meanings for the two distinct words. On the contrary, the grammatical agreement suggests that the two words denote particular and genral senses. The two words, which denote exactly the same meanings, cannot be used together in agreement. For instance, the words *'kara'* (hand) and *'hasta'* (hand), which denote exactly the same meaning, i.e. hand, are never used together in grammatical agreement as it would not serve any purpose, i.e. would be redudant.

Pūrvapakṣin refutes, further, the Siddhāntin's position, that the two words, which denote the same meanings, are found used together in the case of *'vṛkṣaḥ śimśapā'* (This tree is a *śimśapā* tree), where both *'vṛkṣaḥ'* and *'śimśapā'* denote only a tree; and such statements are like the statements *'so' yam devadattaḥ'* (This person is the same Devadatta). According to the Pūrvapakṣin, the two words, in such cases, refer to general and particular notions. The word *'vṛkṣaḥ'* denotes the tree in general, whereas the word *'śimśapā'* refers to a particular type of tree, i.e. *śimśapā;* also the word *'saḥ'* refers to the person in general, whereas the word *'devadattaḥ'* refers to Devadatta in particular. In the case of *'vṛkṣaḥ śimśapā'*, the notion of treeness in general is never obtained by the word *śimśapā*. However, the treeness is indirectly understood through the word *śimśupā* because of its necessary occurrence with the word *'vṛkṣaḥ'*. Thus, it becomes established that the grammatical agreement between the two words suggests only the distinct denotations in separate senses for the two words.

Translation : (p.8)

Suggestion of Siddhāntin

II.3. The grammatical agreement (between the verbal forms *'pacati'* etc. and also *'karoti'*), this way, is meant only for the sake of facilitating the inference of the distinct denotations (of the affix *'ti'* of *'pacati'* etc. rather than that of the verbal roots such as *'pac'*, *'yaj'* etc.,) in the particular meanings (of the verb *'karoti,'* i.e. the action of 'cooking' 'offering' etc.)

Translation : (p.8)

Refutation of Siddhāntin's suggestion

II.4. No, if such were the case, then your (Bhāvanāvādins) position could not be tenable. For, (you have accepted that) the activity (making) is the meaning of the conjugational and other affixes (found in *'pacati'* etc.). Also, since the conjugational affix (*'ti'* in *'pacati'* etc.) is only single, the diversity (multiplicity) of the denotated meanings (i.e. particular meanings of the verb *'karoti'* such as cooking, offering etc.) would not be tenable without, the difference between (i.e. multiplicity of) the denoting agents (i.e. words). Therefore, on the contrary, the position that verbal roots such as *'pac'* etc., by being multiple in nature, are denotative of the particular meanings (of the verb *'karoti'*, i.e. the action of cooking etc.) due to their being in grammatical agreement with the verb *'karoti'* is only tenable.

Note : Pūrvapakṣin refutes the suggestion of the

Siddhāntin that suppose the grammatical agreement suggests the difference between the meanings of the two words, then the affix (*ti* etc.), found in *'pacati'* etc. can be accepted to denote the different meanings of the verb *'karoti'* (i.e. 'cooking', 'offering' etc.), since *'pacati'* etc. are in agreement with *'karoti'*. Pūrvapakṣin states that such a position is not tenable because the conjugational affixes *'ti'* etc. are accepted by Siddhāntin (Bhāvanāvādin) to be denoting only the activity. He states also that, since the conjugational affixes *'ti'* etc. are same in all the instances of verbal forms such as *'pacati'* etc., the same cannot be held to have many denotations in different (nuances of) meanings of *'karoti'*. Therefore, only those which are many should be held to denote the many nuances of the meanings of *karoti*; and since verbal roots such as *'pac'* (to cook), *'yaj'* (to sacrifice) etc. are many in number, only the same, found in *'pacati'*, *'yajati'* etc. in grammatical agreement with *'karoti'*, can denote the many nuances of the meanings of *'karoti'*.

'Translation : (p.9)

Pūrvapakṣin's statement that 'bhāvanā' cannot be 'karotyartha'.

Moreover it can be stated as follows :

Verse 3

Since (due to the absence of an object to accomplish and also due to the absence of a word indicating the activity) the verb *'karoti'* is used bothways in the sense of the activity (*bhāva*) and also in the absence of the activity (*abhāva*), the same verb (*karoti*) cannot be held to have a denotation in the sense of the activity. Therefore, only the general notion of action, (as opposed to the activity), which is found occurring invariably in all the root-meanings, becomes very much necessary to be established as the meaning of the verb *'karoti'*.

Note : Pūrvapakṣin refutes Bhāvanāvādin's theory that the activity (*bhāvanā*) is the meaning denoted by the verb *'karoti'*. According to him, no meaning, in the absence of which a word is used, can ever be considered as the word-meaning. And, since the verb *'karoti'* is used in the absence of the activity, (due to the absence of the effect to be accomplished at times in *'dhvanati'* etc. or due to the absence of any word denoting such an activity at times in *ghañanta* usages such as *pākaḥ* etc.), the same activity cannot be considered to be the meaning of the verb *'karoti'*. Also, only the meaning in which a word is always invariably used, can be considered to be the word-meaning; and the meaning, in which the word is occasionally used (i.e. the meaning in the presence and also in the absence of which a word is used), cannot be considered to be the word-meaning. Accordingly, since the verb *'karoti'* is used bothways in the sense of the activity and also in the absence of the activity, the same (activity) cannot be considered to be the meaning of *'karoti'*. On the other hand, the general notion of actions, which is common to all types of actions such as 'cooking', offering (sacrifcing) etc. (and in which the word *'karoti'* is always found used), should be considered to be the meaning of the verb *'karoti'*.

Translation : (P. 10-11)

Explanation of verse (3)

III. 1. For instance, consider the following question and answer : "what does the bell do ? It rings (i.e. it sounds)" (*kim karoti ghaṇṭā - dhvanati*). Here the verb *'karoti'* is used in the absence of the productive activity. And therefore, it cannot be held that the productive activity is the meaning. For, there exists no separate effect (apart from the sounding itself), which is to be produced from the sound. Suppose there does exist some effect (i.e. happiness etc.) (which is to be produced), then too, we shall say that the production of such an effect is not intended. This is so because, in such cases, one wishes to know only the mere verbal root-meaning in general (i.e. the sounding). So, it cannot be supposed that there exists something which is intended to be accomplished, i.e. produced, that did not exist in the past. Thus, how could it be accepted that the verb *'karoti'*, which is being used, in practicality, in the absence of the productive activity, expresses the same sense (of the productive activity). Also, consider the following question and answer : "what is the action ? It is the action such as cooking" (*kā kriyā - pākahḥ).* In this question and answer, the word, ending in *'ghañ' affix, i.e. 'pākaḥ'* (cooking), denotes merely the root-meaning 'action' of cooking (it does not denote productive activity). Here, since there is not any consideration, i.e. cognition, of productive activity from the *'ghañanta'* word *'pākaḥ'* (cooking), the community of locus (i.e. grammatical agreement or equality of status) between the word *'pākaḥ'* and also the verb *'karoti'* cannot be supposed on the ground that the denotation of a particular type of productive activity is a necessity.

III.2. **Suggestion** : The grammatical agreement between the *'ghañanta'* word *'pākaḥ'* and *'karoti'* should be supposed on the ground that a particular type of productive activity is to be assumed as the implied meaning of the *ghañanta* word *'pākaḥ'* as otherwise 'cooking' cannot be produced.

Refutation No, : this suggestion is not tenable. Suppose the grammatical agreement is possible to explain even with an implied activity, i.e. without the denotation of the activity, then, in that case, the grammatical agreement can have an occasion even in the case of the finite verbs such as *'pacati'*, *'yajeta'* etc. on the ground that the productive activity could be assumed as the implied meaning to facilitate the production of the offering etc.

Second suggestion : Since the productive activity is primary, i.e. chief qualificand, the same should be denoted in the case of the finite verbs, (whereas the productive activity is not intended to be primary, the same need not be denoted in the *ghañanta* words).

Refutation : No, this suggestion is also not tenable. Since, in this case (of *ghañanta* usages such as *kā kriyā–?-pākaḥ*) too, the question is about a particular type of activity (i.e. about the activity leading to the cooking), and also, since the root-meaning, i.e. the cooking (expressed by the *ghañanta* word *'pākaḥ'*), is meant to be indicating only the particular type of activity leading to the cooking, the primary nature, i.e. chief qualificandness of the activity, is same in the case of *ghañanta* usages as well.

Note : Pūrvapakṣin explains the first half of the verse by the passage beginning with *'kim karoti ghaṇṭā'* etc. According to him, the verb *'karoti'* is seen to have been used in the language without referring to the activity in both intransitive and *ghañanta* usages. In the statement of question and answer involvidng intransitive verbs such as 'what does the bell do ? - it rings, i.e. it sounds' (*kim karoti ghaṇṭā-dhvanati'*), the verb *'karoti'* is used in agreement with the intransitive verb *'dhvanati'*, and hence does not refer to the activity that can produce some effect. For, in such cases, no effect that can be said to have been produced by ringing or sounding can be envisaged (but merely the root-meaning ringing or sounding, is intended); and therefore, it serves no purpose in accepting that the verb *'karoti'* refers to the activity that can produce something. Also, it is not tenable to accept that an effect such as the happiness is produced from the activity by means of such ringing; for, even supposing that such an effect is indeed produced, then too, the theory does not hold good because the production of such an effect is not intended from the activity by means of the ringing. The perosn, who makes the enquiry as to *'kim karoti ghaṇṭā'*, desires to know merely the action of the bell, i.e. 'ringing' or 'sounding' as such from the answer *'dhvanati'*. He is not interested in knowing the production of any effect from the ringing. Therefore, in such instances, nothing that did not exist prior to the ringing, can be envisaged to have been originated by the ringing. Now, since nothing that did not exist in the past can be produced through the activity, assumption that the verb *'karoti'* has a denotation in such an activity is meaningless. Also, since the verb *'karoti'* is being used without a reference to the sense of the activity in such intransitive usages, the same verb *'karoti'* must be accepted to have been used without a reference to the sense of the activity everywhere.

Also, in the statements of question and answer involving *'ghañanta'* words such as 'what is the action ?, it is cooking' (*kā kriyā ?-pākaḥ*), the *ghañanta* form *'pākaḥ'* expresses merely the root-meaning, i.e. the action of cooking; and it does not express any activity, since it contains no conjugational affix such as *'ti'* that can express the same. Therefore, the same *ghaṇanta* form *'pākaḥ'* cannot be established to have equality of status, i.e. grammatical agreement with *'karoti'* on account of its reference to the particular type of activity; rather, the same form *'pākaḥ'* must be accepted to have the grammatical agreement with *'karoti'* on account of its reference to the root-meaning, i.e. the action of cooking. Thus, the verb *'karoti'* cannot be established to have any denotation in the sense of the activity in either intransitive or *ghañanta* usages; rather, the same gets established to have a denotation in the sense of mere root-meaning, i.e. the action of 'cooking' etc.

Here, Siddhāntin makes a suggestion in defence of his theory of reference to the activity as follows : *Ghañanta* forms such as *'pākaḥ'* can be assumed to have an indication in the sense of the activity on account of the fact that unless the activity is understood, the production of the root meaning 'cooking' etc. cannot be facilitated. And thus, due to the reference to the activity through indication, the same form *'pākaḥ'* can have grammatical agreement with *'karoti'* despite that *'pākaḥ'* does not have a denotation in the sense of the activity. According to the Pūrvapakṣin, however, such a suggestion is not tenable; because, in that case, the grammatical agreement could be imposed between the finite forms of the verbs such as *'pacati'*, (or *'yajati'*) etc. and also *'karoti'* despite that the finite forms do not have any denotation in the sense of the activity, since the same can have an indication in the sense of the activity. Thus, the basic theory that, since finite forms such as *'pacati'* etc. have grammatical agreement with *'karoti'* which expresses the activity, the same must be held to have denotation in the activity becomes defeated.

Again Siddhāntin makes another suggestion in defence of his theory which is as follows : "In the case of finite forms of verbs (*tiṅantas*), the activity is cognized to be the chief qualificand, i.e. nucleus, of all the syntactico- semantical relations. And, therefore, the conjugational endings can be accepted to have denotation in the sense of the activity in finite forms. However, in the case of *ghañanta* forms, the activity is not cognized to be the chief qualificand of relations. And therefore, the *ghañanta* words need not be held to have denotation in the sense of the activity in the *ghañanta* usages".

However, according to the Pūrvapakṣin, this suggestion too is not tenable. For, if the question, in the case of the question and answer, involvidng a finite verb (i.e. *kim karoti* ? - *pacati*), is held as being meant to enquire about the particular type of the activity that is being performed, then the question, in the case of the question and answer, involving a *ghañanta* form (i.e. *kā kriyā* ? – *pākaḥ*), too, can be explained as being meant to enquire about the particular type of the activity that is being performed. Consequently, the answers in both the cases would be about the particular activity leading to the cooking. Thus, the suggestion that, "in the case of finite forms, the activity is cognized as the chief qualificand; and therefore, the conjugational endings express the same; whereas, in the case of *ghañantas*, the activity is not cognized as the chief qualificand, and therefore, the *ghañantas* do not refer to the activity" is not correct. Also, it can be accepted, as a counter-argument, that the *ghañantas* have an indication in the sense of the activity; and therefore, the theory that *ghañantas* are devoid of conjugational endings and so cannot lead us to the cognition of the activity is also unfounded.

Translation (P. 12)

Establishment of the Pūrvapakṣin's theory

III.3. Therefore, since the verb *'karoti'*, which is commonly used in the sense of the root-meanings in general, cannot be explained to have the productive activity as its meaning, the same should be accepted to have only the generality of actions (i.e. the actions in general) as its meaning. So, consequently, the bringing into existence of what has not been already in existence prior to the origination (i.e. productive activity) is not the meaning of the verb *'karoti'*. Thus, the scholars, who understand the function (or the etimological analysis) of words (i.e. grammarians), have established the generality of actions as the meaning of the verb *'karoti'*. Also with regard to establishing the generality of actions, scholars have stated as follows : "The verbal roots are expressive of actions. Now, how is it known that the verbal roots such as *'pac'* (to cook) etc. are expressive of actions (of cooking etc.) ? This is known so, since the verbs such as *'pacati'* etc. have the grammatical agreement with the verb (*'karoti'*) (he makes). The verbs such as *'karoti'* (he makes), *'bhavati'* (he becomes), *'asti'* (he exists) etc. are expressive of the actions in general; whereas, the verbs such as (*pacati*) 'he cooks' etc. are expressive of the particular actions such as cooking".

Note : Pūrvapakṣin (aided by the grammarian) explains his theory, which is explained in the second half of the verse (3) by *'ataḥ'* etc. According to him, since, as explained above, the activity cannot be held to be the meaning of *'karoti'*, only the general notion of the root-meaning, i.e. the action in general, which is common to all sorts of actions such as 'cooking', 'sacrificing' etc., must be accepted to be the meaning of the verb *'karoti'*. And this theory is in accordance with the fact that *'karoti'* is commonly found in agreement with all types of verbs such as *pacati* etc. expressing particular actions such as cooking, sacrificing etc. Thus, it becomes established that, like the general notion of cows, i.e. cowness (*gotva*), common to all types of cows, is the meaning of *'go'*, the general notion of actions (*kriyātva*), common to all types of actions, is the meaning of *'karoti'*; and therefore, the activity, which is nothing but bringing into existence of what has not been existing before production, is not the meaning.

In this connection, the Pūrvapakṣin quotes the well known statement *'kriyāvacanā dhātavaḥ'*, which establishes the grammatical convention that the verbal roots such as *'pac'*, *'yaj'* etc. are expressive of only the actions such as cooking etc. Thus, the Pūrvapakṣin's theory is that since the verb *'karoti'* expresses only the general notion of actions and not the activity as mentioned by the Bhāṭṭas, the finite forms of verbs such as *'pacati'*, *'yajati'* etc., which are found in grammatical agreement with *'karoti'*, must necessarily be accepted to express only the particular type of actions such as 'cooking', 'sacrificing' etc.

Translation : (P. 13)

Siddhāntin's proposition that dhātvarthas imply activity

III.4. Siddhāntin may propose now the following theory : Root-meanings (*dhātvarthas*) are never perceived without the association of the productive activity (i.e. root-meanings are always perceived as being associated with the activity). This is so because, all the root-meanings (whether they are cooking or offering) produce something which did not exist prior to their production. (And since, without the productive activity, nothing can be produced, the same productive activity, which is implied by all the *dhātvarthas,* must be held to be the meaning expressed by *'karoti'*; and thereby the meaning expressed by the conjugational endings)

Refutation of Siddhāntin's proposition that *dhātvarthas* imply activity

No, this theory is not tenable.

Verse 4

Suppose, in all instances of root-meanings (i.e. actions), some thing, that did not exist before, is produced, then let it be accepted that the root-meaning, which produces, is itself the productive activity (i.e. there is no need to accept that there exists a separate productive activity which is implied by all such root-meanings). Also, no productive activity, which is distinct from the root-meanings such as offering and also which is competent to bring heaven etc. into existence, can be accepted in the case of *'yajati'* etc. as no such activity is perceived.

Note : Siddhāntin argues that the root-meanings such as 'cooking', 'offering' etc. which are conveyed by the finite forms of verbs such as *'pacati'*, *'yajati'* etc. must be held to be associated invariably with the sense of the activity. For, all the root-meanings, whether they are animate-actions such as cooking or inanimate actions such as burning of fire, are always found to be producing something (i.e. rice etc.) that did not exist before the production. Therefore, the Pūrvapakṣin's position that the root-meanings are not associated with the sense of the activity is wrong; and so, the very aspect of the productive force, which is implied by the root-meanings, must be held to be the activity expressed by the verb *'karoti'*; and then, due to the grammatical agreement of finite verbs *'pacati'* etc. with *'karoti'*, the same activity must be held to be the meaning expressed by the conjugational endings.

However, the Pūrvapakṣin rejects such a position of Siddhāntin as follows : Suppose the root-meanings are held to be invariably producing something which did not exist in the past, then the very root-meanings such as the action of cooking etc., must be held to be the activity (and the activity need not be a separate entity expressed by the conjugational endings), since the same root-meanings have the nature conductive to the bringing into the existence of the non-existing things. It is not justified, therefore, that the activity is a separate entity. Also, since no other operation, i.e. activity, apart from the action of offering etc., which is leading to the production of heaven, is perceived in the case of *'yajati'* etc., it is totally unjustified that a separate activity be postulated as the meaning of the conjugational endings to facilitate the productin of the effect 'heaven' etc.

Translation : (P. 14)

Explanation of verse (4)

IV.1. Activity (*bhāvanā*) can be stated to be an operation which is competent to bring about ,i.e. accomplish, something that is to be accomplished, i.e. that did not exist before the accomplishment. Now, supposing the root-meaning such as 'cooking' (*dhātvartha*) is itself of the nature of being conducive to the accomplishment, i.e. obtainment, of the self of some, then it must be conceded that the same root-meaning (*dhātvartha*) is the activity. And it cannot be claimed, therefore, that the activity has a body, i.e. form, which is distinct from that of the root meaning (*dhātvartha*).

Note : Pūrvapakṣin explains the first half of the verse 4 with *'bhāvya'* etc. He states that the proposed activity (*bhāvanā*) must be conceded by the Siddhāntin to be an operation which is inherently competent to bring about the effect which did not exist in the past. Now, since the root-meaning (*dhātvartha*) is itself found to have the nature of being an operation competent to bring about some effect,which did not exist in the past, the same root-meaning can be accepted to be the activity as well; and therefore, the activity cannot be claimed to be an operation different from the root-meanings.

Translation : (P. 15)

Explanation of the Purvapakṣins :

IV.2. Verse (4) continued :

We do not perceive certainly any distinct operation

which has particular root-meanings such as offerings as its objects to be accomplished and which is conductive to the effects such as heaven that the word *'bhāvanā'* (productive activity) can resort to, i.e. refer, to as its meaning.

It should be noted that only the root-meanings such as 'offering' (*yāga*) etc., which are enjoined as the means of the production of such effects as the heaven etc., deserve the designation of productive activity (*bhāvanā*), since the same are competent to produce the effects 'heaven' etc. Suppose, now, you Siddhāntin, hold that "since the root-meaning such as 'offering' is of the form of a non-operation (*avyāpāra*), the same cannot be considered to be the productive activity (*bhāvanā*) which is of the form of an operation", then, in that case, you must explain as to what is of the form of such an 'operation' : You may explain that a particular type of property that is of the nature of being accomplished and (at the same time) is of the nature of being congenial, i.e. conducive, to the production of the desired effect is of the form of operation; and only in the case of the same possessing the competence in producing the effect, the same operation is to be called a productive activity. However, in that case, a distinct activity could not be established, since the root-meaning such as offering does not surpass such a state, i.e. incorporates all such characteristics of the operation. You may explain, as a second alternative, that the movement (producing the effect of contact etc.) is the operation. However, in that case too, no distinct activity can be established, since the root-meanings, such as going, being also of the same form as that of the movement, would have the status of the productive activity undisturbed in them. Moreover, when the movement is considered to be the operation, there would arise the undesired contingency of the absence of the state of being the operation with respect to the operations such as 'remaining', 'sleeping' etc. which are expressed by the verbs such as *'āste'* (to remain), *'śete'* (to sleep) etc. that have the non-moving persons as their agents. Also, then, there would arise the undersired contingency of the absence of the state of being the operation with respect to the operations such as 'knowing' and 'offering', which are expressed by the verbs such as *'jānāti'*, *'yajati'* etc. that have the self as their agents.

Note : Pūrvapakṣin states that not only that the activity cannot be cognized to be a distinct entity from the root-meanings, but also that the same activity must be cognized to be merely the root-meanings. This is so because, beyond the root-meanings such as offering (*yāga*), which are conducive to the bringing about the effects such as heaven, no activity that can produce the particular type of root-meanings such as offering, is found to be cognized by any one. Therefore, the word 'activity' (*bhāvanā*) has nothing except the root-meanings (*dhātvartha*) that it can denote.

Now, since only the 'offering' etc. are enjoined as the means of accomplishing the effects such as heaven, the same 'offering' etc. deserve the name 'activity' (*bhāvanā*).

At this stage, Siddhāntin raises another objection to the Pūrvapakṣin's theory : He states that only the operation (*vyāpāra*), that is competent to bring about an effect such as heaven is activity; and, since the root-meanings such as 'offering', 'cooking' etc. are not the operations, the same cannot be considered as the activity despite that the same produce the effect. However, such an objection is refuted by the Pūrvapkṣin by proposing the following three *vikalpas* : namely, that the operation (*vyāpāra*) can neither be i) a peculiar property of the nature of something accomplished which, in turn, is conducive to the desired effect, (*sādhyasvabhāva dharmabheda*) nor be ii) a movement (*parispanda*) nor be iii) conscious effort (*prayatna*). If the first *vikalpa*, namely, that the operation is a property of the nature of some thing accomplished, is accepted, then root-meanings, i.e. the action of offering etc., would attain the status of the operation since the same have the nature of the properties which are accomplished and also since they are conducive to the desired effect such as heaven etc. If the second *vikalpa*, namely, that the operation is a movement is accepted, then too the root-meanings could not be denied the status of an operation since the root-meanings such as going etc. have the nature of being movement. Also, in that case, there would arise an undesired contingency in the form of the non-inclusion of the root-meanings, referred to by the verbs such as *'āste'* (to remain), *śete* (to sleep), *'yajate'* (to offer), *'jānāti'* (to know) etc. in the category of operation. This is so because, all these verbs have non-moving selves (either body or soul) as their agents; and therefore, refer to the actions of 'remaining', 'sleeping,' 'offerring' and 'knowing' which are all non-movements, i.e. which are mere state of existence or mental actions etc.

Translation : (P. 17-18)

Rejection of the theory that *'bhāvanā'* is prayatnavyāpārā

Verse 5

He who holds that the productive activity (*bhāvanā*) is an operation of the form of conscious effect (*Prayatnavyāpāra*) that has animate self as its agent (i.e. productive activity is the operation having the nature of the conscious effort), cannot explain the use of the finite verbs with respect to any other kind of the agent (i.e. the inanimate agent such as the chariot). Also, such a usage as 'the chariot moves' (*ratho gacchati*) cannot be explained away as due to the secondary application; for, there exists a similarity between the cognitions from usages regardless of whether an animate or an inanimate thing is intended to be the agent.

Note : Pūrvapakṣin rejects the third *'vikalpa'*, namely, that the operation, is the conscious effort (*prayatna*) with the verse (5). He states that in the theory that the activity is the operation having the nature of the conscious effort, the *ākhyāta* usages, wherein the verbs have an unconscious (i.e. non-sentient) inanimate thing as the agent, become untenable. For instance, in such usages as *'ratho gacchati'*(a chariot moves) etc., only the inanimate chariot, which cannot possess any conscious effort, is the grammatical agent, and therefore, the conscious effort (i.e. the operation), expressed by the verb *'gacchati'*, could not be syntactico-semantically connected with the agent 'chariot'.

The only possibility, in this theory of conscious effort as the operation, is to explain the usage *'ratho gacchati'* etc. as secondary wherein an inanimate is used as the agent instead of an animate by extension of the agenthood. However, such an explanation is also untenable; for, since the cognition produced from the usage, wherein an animate is the agent, and also the cognition produced from the usage, wherein an inanimate is the agent, are similar, consideration of one usage as primary and the other as secondary is not possible.

Translation : (P. 18-19)

Explanation of the verse (5)

V.1. Any one, who considers that the activity (*bhāvanā*) is the operation (*vyāpāra*), which is to be grasped, i.e. is to be referred to, through the use of the word 'conscious effort' (*prayatna*), must regard that the conscious effort has the nature of being inferred through the loss of passivity or inactivity (lit. indifference) (i.e. through the presence of bodily movement) of the sentient self and also that the effort is realized through the inner self (i.e. mind) of all the (sentient) beings. However, in this theory, he cannot explain the usage of the verbs (*ākhyātas*) with respect to any other kind of agents (i.e. inanimate agents and therefore, non-sentient agents). For instance, he cannot explain the usage of the verbs such as 'shore, i.e. slope, falls' (*kūlam patati*), 'chariot moves' (*ratho gacchaṭi*) and 'fire burns' (*agnir jvalati*) with respect to the inanimate agents, namely, 'shore', 'chariot' and 'fire'.

Suggestion that such usages as '*ratho gacchati*' are to be explained as '*samāropa*'

The usages such as 'O stones listen' (*śṛṇota grāvāṇaḥ*) are made by imposing, i.e. transferring (*samāropa*) the sense of the operation, namely, the effort, referred to by the conjugational affix, to the inanimate agents. Similarly, the usage, such as 'chariot moves', (*ratho gacchati*) can be explained by imposing, i.e. transferring, the sense of the operation, namely the effort, referred to by the conjugational affix, to the inanimate agent.

Refutation : No, this suggestion is not tenable. The cognition produced from the usage with a sentient as agent and also the cognition produced from the usage with a non-sentient as agent have no distinction in any respect. For, instance, the cognitions produced from the usages such as 'chariot moves' (*ratho gacchati*) and 'elephant moves' (*karī gacchati*) do not differ at all.

Note : In the theory that the operation is a conscious effort (*prayatna*), the same (effort) must be understood to be an entity that is internally cognized through mind, and also must be inferred through the movement of the body as only the loss of the passivity or inactivity (indifference) (i.e. the presence of bodily movement) of the sentient self can bring about the conscious effort in the self. And, once such an effort is considered to be the operation, the *ākhyāta* usages such as *'kūlam patati'* (shore falls), *'ratho gacchati'* (chariot moves) and *'agnir jvalati'* (fire burns) would become untenable; for, in all such cases, only the inanimate, i.e. nonsentient things like shore, chariot, fire etc. are used as the grammatical agents; and they cannot be said to posses any conscious effort expressed by the *ākhyātas* such as *'patati', gacchati'* etc.

Also, such *ākhyāta* usages as *'kūlam patati'* etc. cannot be explained by holding that they are secondary usages like *'śṛṇota grāvāṇaḥ' (O stones listen)* wherein the animate, i.e. sentient, agenthood has been imposed on, i.e. transferred to, the inanimate agents such as the stones etc. by secondary attribution. This is so because, the cognition produced from the *ākhyāta* usage wherein an animate is the agent, does not differ in any way from the cognition produced from the *ākhyāta* usage wherein the inanimate is the agent; for instance, the cognitions produced from both *'karī gacchati'* (elephant moves) and *'ratho gacchati'* (chariot moves) do not differ, i.e. they are identical.

Translation : (p19)

Impossibility of accepting the activity as *'prayatnavyāpāra'*

Verse 6

Since the conscious effort, i.e. operation, has the manifestation of the verbal root-meaning (i.e. the action of cooking, offering etc.) as its ultimate goal, the same root-meaning (action) attains the state of being the object with respect to the productive activity which is nothing but a person's conscious effort, i.e. operation. And once the root-meaning is accepted to attain the state of being the object, the same must be accepted to attain the same state every where in general (i.e. with respect to all kinds of duties such as optional and obligatory). Also, it cannot be supposed that the root-meaning functions as a different *kāraka* with respect to the optional duties such as making offerings since the same root-meaning is regarded as the instrument, i.e. means, of accomplshing the heaven; for, there cannot be any different effort, i.e. operation.

Note : Pūrvapakṣin raises another difficulty in the theory that the operation, which is claimed to be the real nature of the activity, has the form of conscious effort. He states that, when the operation is considered to be the conscious effort, producing the root-meaning such as 'cooking', 'offering' etc., the same root-meaning becomes the grammatical object with respect to the activity due to its being produced by the conscious effort, i.e. activity. And, since the root-meaning ('cooking, 'offering' etc.) becomes the object, the Bhāṭṭa's theory that the same root-meaning functions as the means (*karaṇa*) of accomplishing the desired effect such as heaven becomes automatically untenable. The difficulty is explained on the ground that the root-meaning, when functioning as the object of conscious effort, i.e. operation, cannot function as the means of accomplishing the effect with respect to the same conscious effort, i.e. operation, unless the conscious effort is different with respect to the accomplishment of the effect such as heaven and also with respect to the objecthood of the root-meaning such as offering. However, since the conscious effort, i.e. operation, is one and the same with respect to the accomplishment of the effect and also with respect to the objecthood of the root-meaning, distinction between the conscious efforts cannot be envisaged.

Translation (P. 19)

Explanation of the verse (6)

VI.1. The conscious effort of human being has only the manifestation of root-meaning (action) as its end; and therefore, in all cases of duties, i.e. optional, obligatory and incidental, the root-meaning (action) would have the contingency of becoming the grammatical object of such efforts. The root-meaning can never be claimed to be any other *kāraka* such as instrument due to the lack of the availability of any other type of operation (i.e. effort). And this is explained on the ground that even in the case of the optional duties, wherein the root-meaning such as offering is intended to be the instrument, no distinct conscious effort, that can prove the instrumentality of the same root-meaning (offering) in producing a particular effect such as the heaven which, in turn, is to be manifested through the same effort, is found.

Note : The human (conscious) effort must be accepted to have only the accomplishment of the root-meaning such as the action of 'cooking', or that of 'offering' etc. as its ultimate goal. And consequently, the root-meaning would become only the object with respect to the operation, i.e. human effort, in all instances of duties (rites) such as obligatory, optional and incidental.

An action which functions as the grammatical object with respect to some activity, i.e. operation or effort, must be viewed to be the object with respect to the activity in every case. For, no different activity, i.e. operation can be envisaged in the accomplishment of the root-meanings (i.e. obligatory duties, optional duties and incidental duties) and in the accomplishment of the effect such as heaven. Thus, according to the Pūrvapakṣin, the Bhāṭṭa's theory that the root-meaning, which functions as the object of the activity, functions as the means of the accomplishment of the effect such as heaven in optional rites such as Jyotiṣṭoma also would become untenable.

Translation : (P.20)

Suggestion that '*apūrva*' is different effort

VI.2. Yes, there does exist a different effort (i.e.operation), namely, the unseen factor (*apūrva*).

Refutation :

No, this suggestion is also not tenable. The unseen factor (*apūrva*) cannot be regarded as a different effort (i.e. operation), since it is not an operation of the agent. *Apūrva* has been accepted as being an operation of only an instrument such as offering which accomplishes the effect heaven etc. (and therefore, the same cannot be the operation of the agent). Otherwise (suppose even the operation of an instrument can be regarded as that of the agent then) the two distinct operations get mixed up together; and hence, there could occur a contingency of the absence of distinction between the two *kārakas* (i.e. agent and also instrument) due to the non-distinction between their operations. So much deliberation is enough of this matter.

Note : Now, Siddhāntin suggests that the unseen factor (*apūrva*), which is accepted by ritualists as a token, which leads to the accomplishment of the effect such as heaven, can be accepted to be a different effort; and on account of such a different effort, the root-meaning such as offering can be visualized as the means of accomplishing the effect 'heaven' etc. in optional duties. However, this suggestion is rejected by the Pūrvapakṣin on the ground that the *apūrva* is not the operation of the agent, but it is the operation of only an instrument such as the 'offering'. And, since only the operation of the agent can be considered to be the effort, the *apūrva* cannot be considered to be the effort; and therefore, the root-meaning also cannot be regarded as the instrument on the basis of the *apūrva*. Also, on the other hand, suppose the operation of the instrument is considered to be the operation of the agent as well, then there would occur a mix up of the two distinct operations, namely, that of the instrument *kāraka* and also that of the agent *kāraka*; and hence, the distinction between the two *kārakas*, namely, the agent and also the instrument would become untenable. The distinction between the *kārakas* is only due to the distinction between their operations.

Translation :

Theory of a *Mimāṁsakaikadeśīya* that *dhātvartha* is itself the activity with respect to the accomplishment of effect

Verse 7

The Mīmāṁsakaikadeśīya, who advocates that the distinction of the activity from the root-meaning, (i.e. the action such as offering) is based on the fact that the same root-meaning (action such as offering etc.) is efficient in the manifestation of the effect, i.e. heaven, cannot justify as to why the desired performance, i.e. the undertaking of the action (with fixed beginning and completion), is necessary in the case of the offerings, which have only unseen effects such as heaven.

Note : Verse 7 explains the position of a *Mīmāṁsakaikadeśīya* and then refutes it. According to the *Mīmāṁsakaikadeśīya*, the activity is not a totally distinct entity from the root-meaning, i.e. the action of 'offering' etc. He accepts, rather, that the activity is a particular state of root-meaning itself. However, he holds that the state of being an activity is dependent on the fact that the root-meaning such as 'cooking', 'offering' is conducive to the accomplishment of the effect such as 'rice', 'heaven'. That is to say that when the root-meaning such as cooking or offering functions as the means of accomplishing the effect such as rice or heaven, the same attains, the state of being an activity, and otherwise the same remains merely the action such as as cooking or offering etc.

However, this position is refuted by the Pūrvapakṣin. He states that if the root-meanings like the action of cooking and ofering attain the state of being the activity due to their efficacy in accomplishing the effect, then the regular undertaking of such actions could become incompatible since the same actions, at times, have only an unseen effect, i.e. heaven as, their goal.

Translation : (P.21-23)

Explanation of verse 7 (*Mīmāṁsaikaikadeśīya's* theory)

VII.1. For instance, the verbal root conveys (i.e. refers to) (the root-meaning) action in its general form (leaving out its special form of accomplishing the effect such as heaven). However, the same verbal (root-meaning) action is comprehended as being the productive activity due to the association of the verbal roots with conjugational endings. This phenomenon can be explained as follows : The conjugational endings such as *'ti'* in *'yajati'* etc. are used in the sense of the collection of instantaneous actions by which the desired end such as heaven is accomplished. And, therefore, the individual conjugational endings such as *'ti'*, occurring after the individual verbal stems, such as *'yaja'*, refer to a collection of instantaneous actions delimited by (the production of) individual effects such as heaven. Also such individual actions (as offering), which have such individual effects (as heaven), as their final goal, are considered to be the objects (*karma*) to be manifested through the effort (productive activity). For, the actions, which are not themselves being manifested, cannot be considered to be the competent means to produce the effects such as heaven. Thus, the meaning of the conjugational endings is the particular state or condition of the actions which lead to the production of the effects. That is why it has been stated in the Bhāṣya that one should exert in such a way that something (i.e. effect) comes into being, i.e. is produced.

It can be stated, therefore, that the productive activity and also the action (which are held to be the meanings of conjugational endings and verbal roots respectively) are different due to only their difference in states or conditions (i.e. the root-meaning is called action when it is manifested through the effort and the same is called the productive activity when it produces the effect).

Also, (in support of this theory of identity of actions with productive activity), Nirukta states as follows :

"But where both are denoted by becoming, the speaker expresses the becoming arising from a former state to a later state by the verbs such as 'he goes' ('*vrajati*'), 'he cooks' (*pacati*) etc. The embodiment of the whole process from the beginning to the end which has assumed the character of being (i.e. action) is denoted by verbal nouns such as 'going', 'cooking' etc."

Translation : (P.24-25)

Rejection of the theory of *Mīmāṁsakaikadeśīya* :

VII.2. Now you must state, in this context, as to how are the begining and also the end of the collection of actions which are instantaneous and also which meet the end at every moment (i.e. which perish at every moment) tenable ?. You may state that such beginning and also the end of the actions should be assumed due to the fact that they are required for the accomplishment of the effects. And in this theory, the beginning and also the end could very well be assumed in the case of actions which have been established to produce perceptible effects. This is so because, the collective series of instantaneous actions could very well be perceived as lasting upto the accomplishments of the final goal or effect in both past and future times.

However, in this theory, how can any person be claimed to be inclined (i.e. motivated) towards the objects (i.e. actions), which have not been perceived to produce any effect in this world (i.e. which have unseen heaven etc. as their effect), and also which (actions), therefore, are not established to have the distinction between the conditions (i.e. productive activity and action), which last upto the accomplishment of the final goal (i.e. fruit). For, the person, if not fully aware of the particular actions as having been established to have some fruits, cannot be claimed to be motivated to undertake the action despite being prompted (or instigated) by injunctions etc. Also, even supposing that motivation to undertake an action is somehow possible to explain, the person, since no particular fruit could be visualized in the future, would only be considering himself as being one of unaccomplished object of scriptural injunction (i.e. as being one of unaccomplished actions conducive to final goal commanded by the *śāstras*); and therefore, would not be able to retire from (i.e. to give up) the action undertaken.

It may be argued that the person retires from the action undertaken once he understands the accrual (i.e. accomplishment) of the fruit from the scriptures even if he does not understand the same from any other sources (i.e. even if he does not perceive the accomplishment of the fruit).

However, this argument is not tenalbe either. The fruit accrues only to the person who has performed the objects of scriptural injunctions (i.e. who has performed the actions upto the accomplishment of the goal); and only when the goal or fruit accrues to the person the same person can be considered as one who has accomplished the purpose of scriptural injunction. Thus, there occurs a mutual dependence of events. So enough of this fruitless deliberation.

Note : The verbal roots express the actions such as 'cooking', 'offering' etc., in general without including their particular nature of accomplishing effects. However, when the same roots are used with the conjugational endings etc., the action, expressed by them, becomes understood as the activity leading to the accomplishment of the effect. According to the *Mīmāṁsakaikadeśīya*, the conjugational endings and other affixes are used in the sense of the collections of actions, which are generated at every moment, and which lead to the accomplishment of the desired effect; and therefore, the same collections of actions become the meanings of conjugational endings. Now, these collections of actions, which lead to the accomplishment of the effects, must be viewed in turn as the things accomplished since no entity that is not accomplished, can be claimed to accomplish some effects.

Mīmāṁsakaikadeśin insists that the activity, expressed by the conjugational endings, is nothing but the very state or condition of the collection of actions which lead to the accomplishment of the effect. He explains his position by stating that the Bhāṣya that 'one should exert in such a way that something comes into existence,' maintains the accomplishing nature of the action as the productive activity. Thus, the distinction between the activity and also the action is only due to the difference between states or conditions of actions i.e. due to the efficacy and also the lack of it of the action. Thus, he establishes the theory that one and the only action is known as both activity and action depending upon its efficacy to produce or lack of it.

Also, *the Mīmāṁsakaikadeśin* cites the Nirukta passage to support his theory that only the efficacious state of the action is the activity. According to him, the Nirukta passage that "But where both are denoted by becoming, the speaker expresses the becoming arising from a former state to a later state by the verbs such as 'he goes' (*vrajati*'), 'he cooks (*pacati*). etc. The embodiment of the whole process from the beginning to the end which has assumed the character of being i.e. action, is denoted by verbal nouns such as 'going', 'cooking' etc." clearly establishes that the collection of actions, which produces the effect, attains the state of the activity.

However, the Pūrvapakṣin refutes the theory of *the Mīmāṁsakaikadeśiya* as follows : The actions are momentary; and therefore, they cannot be held to attain the state of the activity. According to him, since the actions never occur in two successive moments continuously, the same cannot be explained to have the beginning and also the end. He, further, refutes the claim that "the actions, which are efficacious, could be explained to be continuous up until the accomplishment of their effects; and therefore, the same can be explained to have the beginning and also the end." According to the Pūrvapakṣin, despite the possibility of explaining the actions as having the beginning and also the end in the event of producing the perceptible effects, in this world, the same actions cannot be explained to have the beginning and also the end in the event of producing the imperceptible effects such as heaven enjoined by the *śāstras*. This is so because, such actions are not determined to last up until the accomplishment of such an imperceptible effect. And once the continuation of the actions till the accomplishment of the effect is doubtful, human inclination to undertake such actions would become impossible despite the presence of the injunction for undertaking such actions as the compulsory duty. Also, the injunction enjoining the actions can be accepted as having the capacity to make the qualified people to undertake the actions provided that such actions are well-known to lead to the accomplishment of the effects. Thus, the inclination of humans towards the undertaking of such actions would become impossible to explain in the case of actions of imperceptible effects.

Again, it cannot be held that the humans undertake the actions even without knowing the efficacy of the actions; and therefore,the beginning and also the end of the actions can be explained with respect to even those actions which do not have perceptible effects. For, then, the humans could never stop performing the same actions (such as 'offering) due to the fact that until the effects of their actions are actually produced, the humans cannot consider themsleves as ones who have attained the goal (i.e. purpose) of the *śāstras*. Also it cannot be supposed that by merely inferring the certain accomplishment of the effect, at a later date, one could stop performing the actions despite the actual accomplishment of the effect at present. For, such a supposition would lead to the mutual (reciprocal) dependence as the accomplishment of the effect requires the completion of the duty enjoined by the scripture and the completion of the duty enjoined by the scriptures requires the accomplishment of the effect. Thus, the Pūrvapakṣin concludes that the position that the activity is a mere state of the collection of the actions which are efficacious, i.e. which lead to the accomplshment of the effect, is untenable.

Translation (P.26)

Verbal root and conjugational (verbal) ending cannot refer to two separate 'actions'

Let us follow the present context.

Verse 8

Two separate actions (*kriyā*) (one in the form of verbal action such as cooking and the other in the form of productive activity) are not perceived as the denoted-meanings of the verbal roots (such as '*pac*') and also as that of the conjugational endings (such as '*ti*') respectively. Supposing that were the case (i.e. supposing the verbal roots and also the verbal endings denote the two separate actions), then the relation, i.e. the connected utterances, of the two, viz.. the verbal roots and also the verbal endings could not be possible, since both of them denote only the 'actions' (*kriyā*) to be accomplished.

Note : Verse 8 refutes the position that the productive activity is a distinct sense conveyed by the verbal (conjugational) endings. The verbal roots such as '*pac*' (to cook) necessarily denote an action such as cooking. And suppose, the conjugational endings (*ti* etc.) too are accepted to denote another action in the form of the productive activity, then there would be effectively two distinct actions (*kriyās*), namely, the root-meaning such as 'cooking' and also the conjuational ending-meaning such as the productive activity. However, two separate actions (*kriyās*) are never perceived by any one as denoted meanings in *ākhyāta* usages such as '*pacati*' (he cooks). Therefore, such a theory contradicts the convention that *ākhyātas* are never used in the sense of two separate actions.

Also, when both the verbal roots and the following conjugational endings in *ākhyātas* are held to denote the two separate actions, the connected utterance of the verbal roots such as '*pac*' and also the conjugational endings such as '*ti*' in '*pacati*' etc. would become difficult to justify; for, since the two actions, denoted by the verbal roots and the conjugational endings respectively, are to be accomplished by something else, they become identical in their nature; and therefore, cannot have any syntactico-semantical expectancy for each other, in being uttered together.

Translation : (P.26-28)

Explanation of the verse (8)

VIII.1. (In the analysis of the etymology of words, only

those are to be considered as nouns (*nāman*) which refer to the accomplished form of their referents in their usage. Also, therefore, the nouns have no syntactico-semantical expectancy for other *kārakas*, since their referents are already accomplished at the time of their (nouns) usage. On the other hand, in the analysis of the etymology of words, only those are to be considered as the verbs (*ākhyāta*) which do not refer to the accomplished form of their referents in their usage. Therefore, they are cognized to have syntactico-semantical expectancy for other *Kārakas*, i.e. object etc., since the accomplishment of the effect is to be cognized only through them). In the context of the rule *'yeṣām tūtpattau"*, the verbal roots, which are used with the conjugational endings (in the finite form of predicative usages such as '*pacati*') have been established to denote their meanings which are yet to be accomplished (*sādhya*) and also which have the nature of action (*kriyātma).* However, supposing, the conjugational ending, by itself, can be accepted to denote a separate action, then it would follow that one would cognize two separate actions (i.e. one in the form of verbal action and the other in the form of the productive activity) from one and the same finite form (predicate). And such an instance of cognizing two separate actions would be similar to the instance of cognizing two separate actions in the case ofthe usage of two separate predicates such as *'odanam pacati'* (he cooks rice) and '*ghaṭam karoti*' (he makes a pot). (Here in the case of '*odanam pacati*', the verbal action preceived is the action of cooking; and in the case of '*ghaṭam karoti*', the verbal action perceived is the productive activity of making the pot).However, in general, predicates are not found to generate the cognitions of two separate actions. Thus, it is not possible to establish that the conjugational ending has a (denotation in the sense of a) separate action (i.e. productive activity) which is distinct from the verbal action, expressed by the verbal root.

Also, an entity, which is to be accomplished, cannot have any syntactico-semantical expectancy for another entity, which is also to be accomplished; for, both the entities being equal in their nature of being yet to be accomplished, cannot be perceived to have any mutual expectation for each other. Consequently, the two items, i.e. the verbal root and also the conjugational ending, which denote the two actions, cannot have the connected utterance in the form of a finite verb.

Suggestion that the root-meaning can be construed as *'karaṇa'* (P.27)

VIII.2. Since the meaning of the verbal root, i.e. the verbal action (such as *'udbhid'* offering in the case of *'udbhidā yajeta'*), can be construed as the instrument (*karaṇa*) and not as the thing to be accomplished, (*sādhya*), the same has no difficulty in construction (i.e. has no untenability of relationship with the other action such as productive activity expressed by the conjugational ending).

Refutation (P.27-28) No, this suggestion is not tenable. For, this suggestion is contradictory to the explanation provided in the rule *'yeṣām tūtpattau'* that the verbal root-meaning is something yet to be accomplished (*'sādhya'*). Also, it cannot be supposed now, therefore, that the rule *'yeṣām tūtpattau'* (expressing the *ākhyātārtha* as *sādhya*) is intended to state only the productive activity as something yet to be accomplished (*sādhya*) and hence no difficulty could be envisaged in the verbal cognition of the action as the instrument which is already accomplished (*siddha*). For, such a rule is meant to explain only the required syntactico-semantical relationship between the meaning of a nominal base, which is already accomplished (*siddha*), and also the verbal action, which is yet to be accomplished (*'sādhya*). And, the required syntactico-semantical relationship would be tenable provided that the sense expressed by a nominal base (i.e. rice etc.) has a relation with the verbal action, i.e. cooking etc., expressed by the verbal root (i.e. provided that the sense expressed by the nominal, viz. rise etc., which is *siddha*, is construed with the verbal action, viz. cooking etc. which is *sādhya*); and consequently, the nominal meaning can be perceived as of perceptible purpose.

Note : The rule *'yeṣāmtūtpattau'* has established that nouns such as *'odana'* (rice) or *'ghaṭa'* (pot) refer to the entities such as 'rice' or 'pot' which are already accomplished (*siddha*) as their meanings; whereas the finite forms of predicates, such as *'pacati'* (he cooks) or *'karoti'* (he makes), which end in conjugational endings such as *'ti'* etc., refer to the entities such as 'cooking (or making) which are yet to be accomplished (*sādhya*), as their meanings. And in such a theory, the meanings of the verbal roots such as '*pac*', are held to be entities which are yet to be accomplished. However, suppose, the verbal endings such as '*ti*' are also held to be denoting separate 'action' (*kriyā*), in the form of productive activity, then there would be references to two distinct actions (in the form verbal action such as 'cooking' and also in the form of 'productive activity') like in the case of two distinct statements '*odanam pacati*' (he cooks rice) and '*ghaṭam karoti*' (he makes a pot). However, no one cognizes two distinct 'actions' from the use of a single finite form of verbal predicate like '*pacati*'. Therefore, it cannot be established that the productive activity, which is to be denoted by the conjugational endings, exists apart from verbal action.

An entity, which is yet to be accomplished, expects only a means which is accomplished and hence can accomplish it, and it does not expect another entity, which too is to be accomplished, as such an entity cannot lead to the accomplishment of any thing else but itself by being itself unaccomplished. Thus, the two actions, which have same nature as far as "being yet to be accomplished" is concerned, cannot be claimed to have syntactico-semantical expectancy for each other. And, since the two actions do not mutually expect each other, the words, which denote such two actions, namely, the verbal root such as '*pac*' and also the conjugational endings such as '*ti*', cannot be claimed to have any relation whatsoever; and therefore, cannot be uttered connectedly in '*pacati*' etc.

Also, it cannot be supposed that the verbal action such as cooking can be construed as the means with respect to another action, i.e. the productive activity, referred to by the conjugational endings; and the two 'actions' (*kriyās*) can be explained to have syntactico-semantical expectancy for each other. For, the rules, which begin with '*yeṣām tūtpattau*', have established that the nouns denote entities, which have already been accomplished, as their meanings; whereas the verbal predicates denote the entities, which are yet to be accomplished, as their meanings. And also the rules have established that such noun-meanings are construed with the verbal predicate-meanings. However, suppose the verbal roots such as *'pac'* in *'pacati'* etc. are held to denote the verbal actions such as cooking which are to be construed as the means and therefore, become accomplished (*siddha*), then there would occur a contradiction to such a theory established by the rule *'yeṣām tūtpattau'* etc.

Further, the theory that "the verbal predicates denote the entities which are yet to be accomplished" should not be held as concerning the accomplishability of the productive activity denoted by the endings. For, it has been established, in *Bhāvārthādhikaraṇa,* that a nominal meaning, which is already accomplished (*siddha*), would serve as of a perceptible purpose provided that the same is construed with only the verbal action which is yet to be accomplished and not otherwise. And consequently, suppose the nominal meaning is construed with the activity expressed by the conjugational ending, then the same would not serve as of any perceptible purpose; and hence should be shunned. Thus, it becomes clear that the theory that 'verbal predicates refer to the entities which are yet to be accomplished" is concerned only with the meanings denoted by the verbal roots (i.e. actions and not with the productive activity).

Translation : (P. 28)

***Anvaya* is impossible when verbal action is viewed as instrument**

Moreover, - it should be noted as follows :

Verse 9

When the verbal action, expressed by verbal root, is viewed to be the instrument, the synthactico-semantical relation (*anvaya*) of the instrumentality expressed by the instrumental word *'kāṣṭhaiḥ'* (by woods) in the statement *'kāṣṭhaiḥ pacati'* (he cooks by woods) would become untenable with both the verbal action of cooking, expressed by the verbal root *'pac'*, and also with the productive activity expressed by the conjugational ending *'ti'*. Since the verbal action is considered to be a non-action, i.e. instrument, the instrumentality of woods cannot be construed with the verbal action of cooking. Also, since the productive activity, expressed by conjugational ending, is interrupted by other element, i.e. verbal action which is also an instrument, the instrumentality of woods cannot be construed with the productive activity. Further, since the instrumentality of woods is obtained verbally, i.e. is obtained through third case ending, the woods cannot be construed with the action as the manner or mode of accomplishment.

Note : Verse 9 explains that the instrumentality of the verbal action is not only contradictory to the theory established by the rule *'yeṣām tūtpattau'*, but also is contradictory to the established convention of syntactico- semantical relations as well. When the action such as cooking is viewed as the instrument, the syntactico- semantical relation of the instrumentality of woods expressed by *'kāṣṭhaiḥ'* in *'kāṣthaiḥ pacati'* (he cooks by woods) etc. would become impossible to explain. For, the instrumentality of the woods cannot be explained to be construed with either the verbal action or the productive activity. It cannot be explained to be construed with the verbal action of cooking since the same, being another instrument, ceases to be action. (And the instrumentality of a thing can be construed with only an action). Nor can it (the instrumentality of woods) be explained to be construed with the productive activity since the same, being expressed by the conjugational ending, is interrupted by the verbal action, expressed by the preceding verbal root. Nor, can the instrumentality of woods be explained to be construed with the element of action as the manner or mode of accomplishment (*itikartavyatā*) since the instrumentality of the woods is verbally perceived through the thrid case *'kāṣṭhaiḥ'*.

Translation : (P.29-30)

Explanation of verse 9

IX.1. We shall explain this as follows :

The woods, in 'he cooks by woods' (*kāṣṭhaiḥ pacati*) cannot be explained to have the syntactico-semantical relation with the verbal action of cooking expressed by the verbal root. *'pac'*. Since the verbal action is the instrument, the instruments such as woods, which syntactically expect an action to be related to, cannot be justified in having any contact (i.e. relation) with another instrument (i.e. action of cooking) of dissimilar (i.e. non-action) nature. Again, the same (woods) cannot be justified in having any relation with the productive activity; since the same (relation with) the productive activity is obstructed by some other instrument, namely, verbal action of cooking expressed by the verbal root '*pac*'. Also, the same (wood) cannot be justified in having any relation with the verbal action of cooking in any other way (i.e. as the manner or mode of accomplishment). For, the instrumentality of woods is verbally expressed by the third case ending. Thus, it can be concluded that, when the verbal actions are considered to be instruments, the instruments such as woods can neither be related to the verbal actions, which are now non-actions, i.e. the instruments, nor can be related to the productive activity which is obstructed by another instrument; and so, no relationship of whatsoever can be established, in 'he cooks by woods' etc., between the instruments and also the verbal action.

Translation : (P.30)

Suggestion that instrument can be related indirectly

IX.2. It is possible to establish a relation of the instruments (woods) with the verbal action of cooking indirectly through the productive activity as the same must be implied (assumed) out of the necessity (i.e. a productive activity must be assumed as otherwise the verbal action such as cooking cannot be explained as accomplished and the instruments can be related to the verbal action of cooking through the assumed activity).

Refutation : No, this suggestion is not tenable. Since the instruments are cognized to be related directly (without any interruption) to the verbal action, the relation of them with the action indirectly through the assumed productive activity is not justified.

The two instances of syntactico-semantical relations, i.e. one with an implied activity and another with an expressed action, cannot be considered to be equal. For instance, consider the two statements i) '(he makes) the pot by means of a lump of clay' (*mṛdā ghaṭam*) and ii) 'he cooks by means of the fire woods' (*kāṣṭhaiḥ pacati*)'. However, in the first instance, the relation of the lump of clay is indirect through an implied activity, i.e. making; and therefore, the same requires the implying of an activity; whereas, in the second instance, the relation of fire woods is direct with the action of cooking which is expressed; and hence there is no expectancy for implying of any activity.

Note : The explantory passage of verse 9 establishes that, since the instrumentality of woods etc. expressed by '*kāṣṭhaiḥ*' etc. in '*kāṣṭhaiḥ pacati*' etc. can no way be explained to construe with either the verbal action of cooking etc. or with the productive activity, expressed by conjugational ending, the verbal action such as cooking cannot be held to be the instrument. Further, in this regard, the passage comes up with the suggestion that the instrumentality of woods, in such cases, can be construed with the action of cooking etc. indirectly through the implied activity. The suggestion can be elaborated as follows. When some one cooks rice (*odanam pacati*), the sense cognized is that the rice is to be accomplished through cooking (*pākena odamam bhāvayet*); however, at that time, the cooking itself is not accomplished, and an unaccomplished thing cannot accomplish something else. Therefore, to accomplish cooking, another productive activity must be held to be implied in such cases; and the instrumentality of woods can be construed with the action of such a cooking which is yet to be accomplished through such an implied activity.

Nevertheless, the suggestion is refuted as follows : The synthactico-semantical relation of the instrumentality of woods is expected only directly with the action of cooking in such cases; and not indirectly through the implied activity. The syntactico-semantical relation of instrumentality is expressed to be indirect with the verbal action through the implied sense of the productive activity only in the cases where no predicate is used; for instance, in '(he makes) pot by means of a lump of clay' (*mṛdā ghaṭam*). However, the same relation is expected to be direct with the verbal action where the predicate is used; for instance, in 'he cooks rice by means of woods' (*kāṣṭhaiḥ pacati*). Therefore, since the syntactico-semantical relation of instrumentality cannot be held to be equal (i.e. indirect with the verbal action through the implied sense of the productive activity in cases where the predicate is not used, viz. '*mṛdā ghaṭam'* and also direct with the action in cases where predicate is used, viz. *'kāṣṭhaiḥ pacati'*), the suggestion that the relation of the instrumentality of woods can be held to be indirect with the verbal action of cooking through the implied sense of the productive activity is untenable.

Translation : (P.30)

Refutation of the theory that conjugational ending denotes a separate activity

Verse 10

In the statement such as '(the rice grains) become soft' (*viklidyanti*), and 'they cook (rice grains)' (*pacanti*), the verbal root *'viklid'* refers to the action of becoming soft, whereas the verbal root *'pac'* refers to (the agents resolve to) the cooking. And, since the conjugational endings (*ti*) in both instances refer to the causative, i.e. productive, activity, no distinction between the senses could be explained from the two statements. Also, suppose (to explain the distinction between the senses of the two statements due to the distinction between the agents) the agentship is to be held as the possession of the operation (activity) expressed by the verbal roots, then, since the verbal roots *'viklid'* and *'pac'* themselves express the operation (activity) of becoming soft and also that of cooking respectively, what (i.e. no) distinct sense could be envisaged as the meaning of the conjugational endings ?

Note : Verse 10 refutes the theory that the conjugational ending denotes a separate activity. It does so on the ground that no distinction between the meanings can be explained in the statements *'viklidyanti'* (rice grains become soft) and *'pacanti'* (they cook rice grains) when the activity is held to be the meaning of the conjugational ending. It states that the root *'viklid'* actually refers to the action of becoming soft, whereas the root *'pac'* refers to the action of cooking which is nothing but the agent's resolve. And supposing the conjugational ending is held to refer to the activity, then, in the above instances, the conjugational ending *'ti'* would have to refer to the activity, identical with the operation of the agent; and therefore, no distinction between the meanings conveyed by the two statements would be possible.

Also, the verse refutes the suggestion that the

distinction between the meanings of the two statements can be explained due to the distinction between the agents of the operations expressed by the verbal roots. It states that the agenthood of the rice grains, in the first instance, and also the agenthood of Caitra etc., in the second instance, must be held to be only the possession of the operation such as becoming soft and cooking referred to by the verbal roots *'viklid'* and *'pac'* respectively. And it states further that the causative activity of employing other means accomplishing the action cannot be held to be the agenthood due to the fact that rice grains, being inanimate, cannot possess such a causative activity. Since, therefore, the verbal roots *'viklid'* and *'pac'* themselves refer to such operations of the agents, i.e. the operation of becoming soft and the operation of cooking, which are identical with the agenthood of rice grains and that of Caitra respectively, the conjugational endings cannot be explained to refer to any distinct meaning (in the form of the activity) from that of the verbal roots.

Translation : (P.31-32)

Explanation of verse 10

X.1. Moreover, in your theory, in both the instances, namely, *'viklidyanti'* (rice grains become soft) and *'pacanti'* (they cook rice grains), the conjugational endings (i.e. *'ti'*) refer to the causative activity; and the verbal roots (i.e. *'viklid'* and *'pac'*) refer to the operation of becoming soft (and cooking); and therefore, no distinction would be possible between the meaning(s) of such statements either.

Suggestion that distinction between the meanings is possible due to the distinction between the agents (P.31-32)

X.2. There indeed exists the distinction between the operations (i.e. activities) due to the difference between the agents; and since the conjugational endings can refer to such distinct operations, there could be no difficulty in explaining different senses for the two distinct statements such as *'viklidyanti'* and *'pacanti'*. For instance, the rice grains are the agents in the case of becoming soft (*viklidyanti*); whereas, Devadatta and others are the agents in the case of cooking (*pacanti*).

Refutation (P.32)

We shall ask you here as follows. What have you considered as the characteristic (definition) of an agent in stating that 'distinction between the operations is necessary due to the difference between the agents' etc. ? Suppose you state that you have considered the employment (i.e. controlling) of the means etc. as the agenthood, then how could the agenthood be tenable for the rice grains (since they are inanimate and no inanimate has any controlling power). On the contrary, only Devadatta etc., who are animates, would become the agents of both cooking and becoming soft; and therefore, there would not be any occasion for the distinction between the meanings (due to the difference between the agents). Suppose you state that you have considered the state of being an operation (activity), which is the qualificand and hence is expressed as a non-qualifier, is the agenthood, then you must explain as to what is the meaning of the conjugational endings which you claim to be distinct. For, in that case, since the operation of the agent such as the productive activity has already been expressed by the verbal roots, no distinct meaning would be left to be expressed by the conjugational endings.

Note : The explanation refutes the Siddhāntin's theory that the conjugational endings refer to the activity distinct from the root-meanings. It states that, in such a theory, the distinction between the senses of the statements 'rice grains become soft' (*viklidyanti*') and 'they cook rice grains' (*pacanti*) would become impossible to explain. This is so because, in such cases, both the verbal roots '*viklid*' and '*pac*' refer to the becoming soft of rice grains and the resolve to cook the rice grains; and the conjugational endings refer to the agent's operation, i.e. the activity accomplishing such a cooking. The explanation refutes also the suggestion that the distinction between the operations (activities) can be explained due to the distinction between the agents of such statements; and since the operations can differ, the non-distinction between the meanings of the verbal roots '*viklid*' and '*pac*' would not be an impediment to the explanation of the distinction between the senses of such statements. It holds that the agenthood could be either i) the ability to employ the means of the accomplishment of action or ii) the possession of the operation expressed by the verbal roots. Supposing the first alternative is accepted, then no distinction between the agents could be envisaged in the case of becoming soft and also cooking. For, in both cases, only the animates, i.e. Devadatta etc. could be held to be the agents, since only they can employ the various means such as making the fire etc; and not the inanimates (i.e. rice grains etc.), since they cannot employ any means. On the other hand, supposing the second alternative is accepted, then no distinction of the activity from the action expressed by the verbal roots could be envisaged. For, in both the places, the verbal roots (i.e. '*viklid*' and '*pac*') would themselves express the operation of becoming soft and that of cooking respectively; and hence no distinct activities could be assumed as the distinct meanings expressed by the conjugational endings.

Translation (P.32)

Suggestion that *dhātvarthārtha-vyāpāra* **is** *dhātuvācya* **and** *phalārtha vyāpāra* **is** *pratyayavācya*

X.3. The activities, which have root-meanings (i.e. actions like cooking, offering etc.) as their goal (*dhātvarthārtha-vyāpāra*), are different from the activities which have effects (i.e. becoming soft or heaven etc.) as their goal (phalārtha-vyāpāra). Therefore, the activity or operation, which has root-meanings 'actions' as their goal, is the meaning expressed by the verbal roots *dhātuvācya* and the activity or the operation which has the effect (such as becoming soft or heaven) is the meaning expressed by the conjugational endings *pratyayavācya*. It should be noted that in accomplishing the effects, the root-meanings function as the means with respect to the activity expressed by the conjugational endings.

Note : An attempt is made to explain the distinction between the meanings of the conjugational endings and also that of the verbal roots. According to this suggestion, there are two items to be produced, viz : i) the root-meanings such as the action of 'cooking', 'offering' etc. and also ii) the effects such as 'becoming soft', 'heaven' etc. Now, since both root-meanings and the effects are to be produced (*sādhya*), they need activities that can produce them. Thus, the activity that produces the root-meanings can be considered to be the meaning of the verbal roots and the activity that produces the effects can be considered o be the meaning of the conjugational endings; hence, the distinction of the sense of the conjugational endings from that of the verbal roots is tenable.

Translation (P.32)

Refutation

No, this suggestion is also not essential, i.e. not tenable.

Verse 11

The operation (i.e. activity), which accomplishes the effect (such as 'becoming soft' or 'heaven') and which has the root-meanings (such as the action of 'cooking' or 'offering') as its means, cannot be perceived to be a distinct entity from the verbal actions, the meanings of the verbal roots, and also from the different varieties of effects which too form another aspect of the root-meanings.

Explanation that the activity as distinct from both root-meaning and effect is untenable (P.33)

XI.1. In the case of the *sāṅgrahāyaṇī* offerings, which are separated from (interrupted by) the effects such as the reaching of the village, the activity (such as serving) (which is distinct from both the verbal action of offering and also from the effect such as reaching the village), is perceived to be distinct from the activity which is conducive to offering. However, the same activity must be viewed to be the meaning expressed by yet another root, i.e. '*seveta*'. For, since such an activity is originated from a different effort, the same cannot be considered to be the meaning expressed by the conjugational ending '*ta*' (found occurring after the verb, namely, '*yajeta*' in the statement '*sāṅgrahāyaṇyā yajeta*); and therefore, cannot be considered to be producing the 'offering' expressed by the root '*yaj*' (to offer) found in the verb '*yajeta*'.

Note : Verse 11 refutes the suggestion that the conjugational endings can be considered to express a distinct activity which produces the effects such as the 'becoming soft', 'heaven' etc.; whereas, the verbal roots can be considered to express the activity which produces the verbal actions such as 'cooking', 'offering' etc. It does so on the ground that no activity, which is distinct from both the verbal actions such as 'cooking' or 'offering' and also from the effects such as the 'becoming soft' or 'heaven' is perceived to exist.

Here an objection can be raised as follows :

In the context of 'he offers by means of *sāṅgrahāyaṇesti*' (*sāṅgrahāyaṇyā yajeta*), an activity such as serving (*sevā*), which is quite distinct from both the verbal action, i.e. offering, and also from the effect such as reaching the village, is perceived to exist. And on the basis of such an example, everywhere an activity, which is distinct from both the verbal action and also the effect must be accepted.

However the explanatory passage refutes such an objection. According to this explanation, the activity of serving, perceived in the case of '*sāṅgrahāyaṇyā yajeta*' is the meaning expressed by a different verbal root, namely, '*sev*' (to serve); and therefore, the same cannot be the meaning of the conjugational ending occurring after the verbal root '*yaj*' (to offer) in '*yajeta*'.

Translation (P.33)

Pratyayas **cannot be established to express** '*karotyartha*'

Verse 12

The meaning of the verb '*karoti*' ('performing' or 'making', i.e. productive activity) is invariably concomitant with the *kārakas* such as the grammatical object in '*ghaṭam karoti*' (he makes pot). And, since the synthactico-semantical notion of such a *kāraka* is absent in '*yajeta svargakāmaḥ*' (he who desires heaven should offer), the meaning of the verb '*karoti*' (i.e. activity) is also absent.

Also, since the *kāraka* case endings such as the accusative or instrumental case endings etc. are found to express the sense of the *kārakas* such as the object or the instrument of the activity expressed by the conjugational ending, the absence of the *kāraka* case endings such as the accusative must be admitted due to the absence of the *kārakas* such as the object to be accomplished in the case of *'yajeta svargakāmaḥ'*.

Note : Verse 12 establishes Pūrvapakṣin's objection that the conjugational endings cannot be held to be referring to a distinct sense of the activity, which is the meaning accepted as denoted by the verb *'karoti'* (doing). According to the Pūrvapakṣin, in usages such as *'ghaṭam karoti'* (he makes a pot), the activity, expressed by the verb *'karoti'* (doing), is invariably concomitant with the *kārakas* such as the object; and since the same *kāraka,* i.e. the object, is absent in the case of *'yajeta'* (he must offer), the conjugational endings cannot be held to express the same sense of the activity. Here, when the activity is concomitant with the object *kāraka,* the activity becomes pervaded (*vyāpaka*). And once the pervader, i.e. the object, is absent, the pervaded, i.e. the activity, is also absent. The absence of the pervader, the (object) *kāraka,* should not be doubted in *'yajeta svargakāmaḥ'* either. For, when a *kāraka* is present, the case endings such as instrumental *'ā'* in *'udbhidā yajeta'* ('he must offer by means of *Udbhid*'), which express the same *kāraka* sense of the instrumentality (of *Udbhid*) etc. are always used. It is never the case that a *kāraka* case ending is not used although the *kāraka* sense (i.e. object etc.) is present. Now, since no *kāraka* case ending, such as accusative (*am*), is used in the instance of *'svargakāmo yajeta'* etc., it is established that *kāraka* sense (of object etc.) is absent. Consequently, due to the absence of a *kāraka,* which is to be accomplished, no productive activity, that can accomplish such a *kāraka,* can be assumed to be the meaning of the conjugational ending.

Translation : (P.34-37)

Explanation that activity is not the meaning of the conjugational endings

XII.1. The verb *'karoti'* is always transitive (i.e. is invariably associated with the object *kāraka* such as *'ghaṭam'* in *'ghaṭam karoti'* etc.); and therefore, to cognize the productive activity, the meaning of the verb *'karoti'*, the cognition of the syntactico-semantical relation (i.e. invariable concomitance) of the activity with the object is absolutely necessary. Now, since the syntactico-semantical relation (i.e. invariable concomitance) of the activity with the object is absent in the case of the conjugational endings, we comprehend the absence of the activity, i.e. the meaning of the verb *'karoti'*, in the conjugational endings in *'yajeta svargakāmaḥ'* etc. And this instance is similar to the instance of comprehending the absence of the smoke due to the absence of fire. This phenomenon can be explained as follows The syntactico-semantical relation (i.e. invariable concomitance) of the activity with the object is never seen as the incorrect statements such as 'he should offer the heaven' (*yajeta svargam*), 'he should sleep the comfortableness' (*śayīta svāsthyam*) and 'he should stay the happiness' (*āsīta sukham*) etc. are never made; and hence, we comprehend the absence of the activity in the conjugational endings such as *'ti'* etc. due to absence of the syntactico-semantical relation, i.e. invariable concomitance with the object.

Argument that non-relation is due to the absence of *vibhaktis*

XII.2. You may suppose that the verbs such as *'yajeta'* in *'yajeta svargakāmaḥ'* etc. too are transitive (i.e. are capable of taking objects); however, the non-perception of the syntactico-semantical relation between the objects and the activity is due to the absence of the distinct accusative (and other) case endings that are capable of denoting such syntactico-semantical relations (and not due to the actual absence of the *kārakas* such as the objects). You may explain this phenomenon as follows : The case endings are denotative of only the items functioning as *kārakas* with respect to the meanings of the verbal roots (i.e. verbal actions) (and not the items functioning as *kārakas* with respect to the meaning of the conjugational ending, i.e. the activity); for, such case endings as accusative etc. are not seen (used) in the sense of the object of the activity, the meaning expressed by the conjugational ending, i.e. in the sense of the goal of the person, desiorous of heaven who is to be prompted with respect to the undertaking of the action of offering.

Refutation : However, this argument of yours is untenable. In that case, the genitive case endings, which are enjoined for the sake of denoting the syntactico semantical relations other than that of the object, could have an unrestricted scope for use in all these cases (i.e. in the persons desirous of heaven etc.). Moreover, one would not appreciate this (phenomenon of the unrestricted scope for genitive) as one perceives the instrumental case endings after the words denoting sacrifices such as *'viśvajit'* which are the names assigned to the verbal root-meanings (i.e. actions) which, in turn, are the instruments of the activity expressed by the conjugational endings.

Second argument that relation between the object and the activity exists

Xii.3. There exists indeed the relation between the *kārakas* such as the object and also the *karotyartha* (activity); for, such a relation is perceived (despite the accusative case ending not denoting the objecthood) between the object such as 'heaven' and also the performance, i.e. activity leading the sacrifice, in the statement 'he who desires heaven shall make offering' (*svargakāmo yajeta*).

Refutation : No, this argument is also not tenable. No direct relation can be established between the *kārakas* such as the object 'heaven' and also the performance i.e. the activity leading to the sacrifice, since the same 'heaven' in 'he who desires heaven shall make offerings' (*svargakāmo yajeta*) is perceived as only a distinct qualifier of the person desirous of heaven.

Third argument that the relation between *kārakas* such as the heaven and the activity exists

We can perceive the direct relation between the *kārakas* such as heaven and the performance of the sacrifice in the statement such as 'he shall make offerings for the sake of heaven' (*svargāya yajeta*) etc.

Refutation : No, this argument too is not correct. The relation, between the kārakas such as heaven and the activity in such statements, has the nature of being the relation between the non-object and the activity. Moreover, the absence of the relation between the object and the activity forms the essential cause of assuming the absence of the activity which is the referent of the verb *'karoti'*. (So, other type of relation between the heaven and the *karotyartha* is also not useful). It should be noted that the relation between the non-object and the activity is due to the dative expression in (*svargāya yajeta*) etc. Moreover, it should also be noted that the heaven etc. is perceived to have a relation even with the verbal action of offering expressed by the verbal root in the cases such as 'the offering is for the purpose of heaven' (*svargāya yāgaḥ*) etc.

Note : The explanation reiterates the refutation suggested by the verse 12. It states that the verb *'karoti'* is transitive; and therefore, is found with an object-word. Also since, in the case of *'yajeta svargakāmaḥ'* etc., no word expressing the object such as *'svargam'* is found, we must understand that the *karotyartha*, i.e. the activity, is absent in the conjugational ending. This is so because, the absence of the sense, which pervades (*vyāpaka*) such as the absence of fire, always establishes the absence of the sense, which is pervaded (*vyāpya*) such as the absence of smoke. That is to say that unlike the verb *'karoti'*, in *'ghaṭam karoti'* etc., which is transitive and therefore is associated with the object such as *'ghaṭam'*, the verb *'yajeta'* in *'svargakāmo yajeta'* etc. is intransitive, and therefore, is not associated with any object such as *svargam*. And, since it is not associated with any object, the conjugational ending should not be assumed to denote any activity which can accomplish such an object.

At this stage, an objection is raised which is as follows : The verbs such as *'yajeta'* too are transitive, i.e. are capable of taking objects; however, the non-perception of the syntactico-semantical relation of an object with the (activity) is due to the absence of the accusative case ending that could express such a relation. And the absence of the accusative case ending is explained by the fact that the accusative and other case endings are found after only the words such as *'ghaṭa'* expressing the object (pot), to be accomplished by the action or activity expressed by verbal roots such as *'kṛ'* in *'ghaṭam karoti'* etc.; and not after the words such as *'svargakāma'* expressing the object to be accomplished by the activity expressed by the conjugational endings such as *'ta'* in *'svargakāmo yajeta'* etc.

However, this objection is refuted by the Pūrvapakṣin as follows : Supposing the accusatives are not possible after the objects of the activity, then at least the genitive, which is generally found in the sense of all the remaining syntactico-semantical relations, should have been possible after the same objects of activity. Since, even the genitives are not used in *'svargakāmo yajeta'* etc., it must be held that no object as such exists in such cases; and therefore, the assumption of the activity as the meaning of *pratyaya* is not necessary. Moreover, in the case of the statements such as *'viśvajitā yajeta'* etc., the instrumental case endings are found to be used after the words *'viṣvajit'* etc. expressing the instrument of the activity. Consequently, it cannot be held that no case endings are used after the words which express the *kārakas* with respect to the activity either. Thus, it must be admitted that no object is possible with respect to the activity; and therefore, the conjugational endings should not be accepted to denote any activity that can accomplish an object.

Also, according to the Pūrvapakṣin, no syntactico-semantical relation of an object is possible with the activity. For, in the statement *'svargakāmo yajeta'*, the heaven (*svarga*), which could be held to function as the object, appears as only the qualifier (i.e. modifier) of the person who desires heaven; and therefore, cannot be considered as the direct qualifier of the activity through the relation of being the object. No *kāraka*, which indirectly qualifies the activity, can be considered to be the object of the same activity. Further, even when the heaven (*svarga*) qualifies directly the activity in *'svargāya yajeta'* (one must offer for the purpose of heaven) etc., the same heaven cannot be considered to be the object with respect to the activity, since the heaven is expressed by the word ending in the dative; and whatever is expressed by a word in a dative is certainly not the object as only the accusative is enjoined in the sense of the object.

Lastly, Pūrvapakṣin points out that the dative expression *'svargāya yajeta'* does not establish the heaven (expressed by the word in dative) to be directly qualifying the activity either; for, the same expression can be taken to establish the heaven as qualifying the verbal action of offering as such an expression can be paraphrased as *'svargāya yāgaḥ'* (offering is for the heaven), wherein the heaven is clearly the qualifier of the offering. Thus, it must be admitted that the absence of the syntactico – semantical relation of an object with the activity is the cause that establishes the absence of the need for the conjugational endings to denote an activity.

Translation : (P.37)

Bhāvanā*, having the nature of *kartṛvyāpāra*, cannot be *pratyayārtha

Verse 13

Now, (in the theory, that *kartṛvyāpāra* and *bhāvanā* are one and the same), it would follow that the causative expression such as 'he causes (pot) to become' (*bhāvayati*) and the primitive (non-causative) expression such as 'pot becomes' (*bhavati*) would have the identical (i.e. same) meanings. For, the causative affix (*ṇic*) and the conjugational affix '*ti*' can express the activity in both the cases. Also, suppose it is held that the agent is the one who possesses the operation, which is expressed by the verbal root, (and not the one who possesses the operation expressed by the causative affix), then it could be asked as to what is the separate meaning referred to by the conjugational ending, apart from the operation of the agent.

Note : Verse 13 raises a new difficulty in the theory that the activity, which is accepted to have the nature of the operation of an agent (*kartṛvyāpāra*), be held to be the denoted meaning of the conjugational endings. It states that suppose the activity, having the form of the operation of the agent, is considered to be the meaning of the endings, then the valid distinction between the causative statements such as 'the pot maker causes the pot to become' (*bhāvayati ghaṭam kumbhakāraḥ*) and also the primitive statements such as 'pot becomes, i.e. comes into existence' (*ghaṭo bhavati*) would become untenable. This is so because, while the causative affix (*ṇic*) expresses the (causative) agent's operation of causing something to come into being in the case of the causative usage (*bhāvayati*), the conjugational ending 'ti' could be insisted to be expressing the same agent's operation in the primitive usage (*bhavati*), since the ending is held to be expressing the activity which is nothing but the operation of the agent.

Also, the verse states further, that suppose the agent is held to be the possessor of the operation, expressed by only the verbal root, and not the operation expressed by the causative affix, then no meaning would remain to be expressed by the verbal endings. This is so because, the verbal roots such as *'bhū'* (to be or to exist) can themselves refer to such operations of the agents; and therefore, there would not be any otehr activity left, apart from such an operation, which the conjugational endings could denote.

Translation : (P.38-39)

Explanation of the verse (13) that *bhāvanā* cannot have the nature of kartṛvyāpāra

XIII.1. Now it would follow that like the causative accusative statement 'pot maker causes the pot to become, i.e. to come into being' (*ghaṭam bhāvayati kumbhakāraḥ*), the primitive accusative statement 'the pot becomes' (*ghaṭam bhavati*) should also be made with the inention of perceiving identical syntactico-semantical relations. For, both the statements would have the same meanings. This point can be explained as follows : In the first (causative) statement, the causative affix, i.e. *ṇic*, refers to the operation of the (causative) agent, i.e. the pot maker; whereas in the second (primitive) statement, the conjugational ending *'ti'* refers to the same operation of the agent. Thus, it would follow that the meanings do not differ despite the two distinctly different expressions.

Argument that the distinction between the meanings is tenable

XIII.2. One may hold that, in such statements, the causative operation (i.e. causing some thing to come into being) of the causative agent (pot-maker) is the meaning referred to by the causative suffix (*ṇic*); whereas, the primitive operation of the primitive agent (i.e. coming into being) is the meaning referred to by the conjugational ending. Consequently, the difference between the meanings (i.e. syntactico-semantical items) results in the two statements.

Refutation

No this is not tenable. If one holds so, then he should explain the distinction between the causative agent and also the (primitive) agent in the said statements. Suppose one holds that the agent is the one who employs and also restrains the instruments etc., then it would follow that, in the given statements, only the pot-maker employs and also restrains the instruments; and therefore, he alone is the agent. Now, since both the causative affix and also the conjugational endings refer to the operation of the same agent (pot-maker), the sameness of meanings becomes established in both the statements.

Argument that causative and primitive agents are different

XIII.3. In the above statements, pot is the (primitive) agent of becoming; whereas the pot-maker is the causative agent (who causes the pot to become).

Refutation :

No, this is not tenable. If you hold so, then you must explain as to how the pot (an inanimate entity and so), a non-controlling entity, can have the agenthood (i.e. activity) in the employment as well as in the restraint of the instruments; and thus can transgress (i.e. ignore) the (claim of the) pot-maker for being such an agent (who is capable of such an activity by being animate).

Argument that the agenthood is the possession of the operation

Agenthood can be stated to be the state of possessing the operation which is being referred to by the verbal root as a non-qualifier (*aguṇa*); and hence, is the chief qualificand.

Refutation :

No this is not possible. Suppose such an operation is stated to be the verbal root-meaning, you must explain as to then, what would be the meaning of the conjugational ending, since the operation of the agent is already referred to by the verbal root. Also it is not possible to explain that the two distinct operations are perceived in such instances, so that a distinct division of objects (i.e. meanings) could be possible for the roots as well as for the conjugational endings.

Argument that two distinct operations can be assumed

XIII.4. Instrumentality of verbal action etc. is distinct with respect to the meaning of the causative verbal root and also with respect to the meaning of the conjugational ending. (Therefore, two distinct operations can be assumed as the meaning of the causative verbal root and also as the meaning of the conjugational endings.)

Refutation:

No, this is not tenable either. Since only the verbal action is competent to be the instrument of the causative operation by way of being verbal element, or since only the same verbal action is competent to be the instrument of the primitive operation only in some other way, i.e. by its inherent nature, the instrumentality of the meaning of the verbal root is not distinct (i.e. is one and the same) in both the cases. Consequently, the identity of the meanings (of the roots and also that of the conjugational endings) is impossible to avoid. Thus, it is only appropriately stated that the conjugational endings are not expressive of the operation. For instance, Bhaṭṭa has rightly questioned as to "what element, i.e. verbal root or verbal ending, in the primitive expression *'bhavati'* etc., expresses the sense of the causative derivation of *bhāvanā* (i.e. the causative activity)"

Note : Explanation of the verse 13 suggests that the activity, when regarded as the operation of the agent (*kartṛvyāpāra*), cannot be the meaning of the conjugational endings. It states that since the causative affix *'ṇic'*, in causatives such as *'bhāvayati ghaṭam kumbhakāraḥ'*, and the conjugational ending *'ti'*, in the primitives such as *'ghaṭo bhavati'*, can be denotative of the operation of the agent and also since the verbal root-meaning is the same (action of becoming) in both the cases, the identical cognition of the syntactico-semantical relation of the pot as the object would become necessary in both cases. Such an eventuality, however, cannot be accepted. While, in the causative, the pot is the object, in the primitive, the same (pot) is the agent. Thus, due to the difficulty of the identical cognition, conjugational endings cannot be accepted to express the activity as having the form of the operation of the agent.

Now, an argument is made. While the causative *'ṇic'* expresses the operation of the causative agent, the conjugational ending *'ti'*, expresses the operation of the primitive agent. Thus, cognitions can differ due to the difference between the agent's operations. However, Pūrvapakṣin refutes such an argument as well. He states that no distinction between the causative and the primitive agents can be maintained. According to him, suppose the causative agent is defined as the one who employs the means, i.e. *kārakas,* then such an agent could only be the sentient or animate pot-maker since he alone employs means; thus both *'ṇic'* and *'ti'* would have to denote only the pot maker's operation of causing. Thus, the pot cannot be held to be the primiive agent and the pot-maker to be the causative agent, for, the pot would become untenable for being considered as the agent since the same is inanimate and no inanimate can employ any means.

At this stage, another argument is made. The agent can be held to be the one who possess the operation expressed by the verbal root as a non-qualifier, i.e. as the chief qualificand; and therefore, the pot, which possesses the operation of becoming or existing, is the primitive agent; whereas the pot maker, who possesses the causative operation of causing something to become, is the causative agent. Thus, the primitive and the causative usages, which express the primitive and the causative operations respectively, can be shown to have distinct meanings.

However, Pūrvapakṣin refutes such an argument as well. According to him, in such a theory, since the verbal roots such as *'bhū'* and *'bhāv*ay' etc. are held to be expressing the agent's operation (of becoming and causing to become etc), no distinct activity apart from such an operation can be established as the meaning of the conjugational endings.

Finally Siddhāntin argues as follows :

That the operation of the primitive agent and also that of the causative agent are distinct. For, while the causative operation of the causative agent has the verbal action such as becoming as its instrument, the primitive operation of the primitive agent has something quite different from the verbal action, i.e. axe etc., as its instrument. Thus, due to the difference between the instruments, the causative and the primitive operations can be established to be distinct.

However, Pūrvapkṣin refutes such an argument on the ground that the verbal action is indistinctively the instrument in both the cases : While the verbal action is the instrument with respect to the causative operation by way of being verbal element, the same is the instrument with respect to the primitive operation by its own inherent nature (without being expressed). Consequently, the instrumentality of verbal action cannot be negated in either of the cases. Now, since operations cannot be distinguished due to the difference between the instruments, both causative and primitive usages would become identical in their senses. Therefore, conjugational endings cannot be held to be expressing the activity or operation of the agent.

Translation : (P.39)

In transitives *'pacati'* etc. too, the conjugational endings cannot refer to *bhāvanā*

Verse 14

Moreover, it can be stated as follows :

Even supposing that the activity (*bhāvanā*) is meant to be the operation of the agent, then too, such an activity would become only the activity of putting the pot on fire etc, i.e. cooking etc., in *'pacati'* etc. and not the distinct sense of the activity, expressed by the conjugational endings, as held by you. Thus, such an activity would have only another form of the verbal root-meaning such as cooking etc., in the case of transitive usages such as (*pacati*) etc.

Note : The verse 14 is intended to establish that the conjugational endings, found in transitive primitive usages such as *'pacati'* etc. too, cannot be held to express the activity. According to this verse, suppose the activity is accepted to be the operation of the agent, then such an activity must be analysed to be the activity of putting the pot on fire etc. in the case of the transitive verbs such as *'pacati'* (he cooks) etc. And, since such an activity of putting the pot can be included in the meaning of the root *'pac'* itself, the same is not different from the root-meaning of cooking. Thus, the verse establishes that the activity cannot be established to be a distinct meaning from the root-meaning cooking etc. in transitive usage as well.

Translation : (P.40)

Explanation of verse (14) that activity is included in the reference to root-meanings

XIV.1. Suppose the operation of the agent is the activity

(*bhāvanā*), then such an activity should be analysed as the putting the pot on fire etc. in the context of 'cooking' etc. And naturally, the verbal root 'cook' (*pac*) itself can include such an activity of putting the pot on fire in its reference. Otherwise (suppose the verbal root 'cook' (*pac*) does not include the activity of putting etc. in it's reference then), there will not be any distinction of the meaning of the verbal root 'cook' (*pac*) from the meanings of the verbal roots such as 'accomplish' (*sidh*) and 'become soft' (*viklid*). Also, suppose the verbal root 'cook' (*pac*) does not include the activity of putting etc. in its reference, then too the activity of putting etc. becomes established as only the meaning referred to by the other verbal roots, namely, 'place over' (*adhiśrayati*) etc.; and therefore, the same activity, the sense intended to be expressed by the conjugational endings, does not become different from the meanings of the verbal roots.

Translation : (P.41)

Alternative theory that activity is continuous in its form and hence distinct from root-meanings

XIV.2. Now, an alternative theory can be stated in support of the theory of the activity (*bhāvanā*) as follows : The sense of the activity (*bhāvanā*) is an entity which has the form of being continuous, i.e. which is common to all the undertakings, since it is the object of the cognition of continuity perceived such as 'he performs cooking' (*pākam karoti*) etc. And such a sense is quite distinct from the root meanings (actions), which become the objects of distinct cognitions of discontinuity such as 'he cooks' (*pacati*) etc. in each undertaking.

Translation : (P.41)

Refutation

No, this alternative theory is wrong. In such a theory, since the so-called 'activity', the sense conveyed by the word (*bhāvanā*), incorporates, in itself, the characteristics, which are common to all the distinct undertakings (actions), the same would become only the generality of all the actions expressed by the verbal roots; and not the distinct entity that is not included in the meanings of the verbal roots, i.e. actions.

Note : The explanation points out that the activity cannot be established to be a separate meaning denoted by the conjugational endings in transitive usages such as *'pacati'* (he cooks) etc. as well. It states that suppose the activity is held to be the operation of the agents, then the same operation of the agent must be analysed as the putting the pot on fire etc. in the context of cooking. Now, such an operation, i.e. activity, would be included in the meaning of the verbal root (*'pac'*), i.e. cooking itself or, if not, the same would be regarded as the meaning of the different verbal roots, namely, *'adhisrayati'* (i.e. putting the pot on) etc. However, in both the cases, the activity would not be regarded as the meaning of the conjugational endings such as *'ti'*. Thus, the activity cannot be established as a separate meaning of the conjugational endings.

The explanation also refutes the Siddhāntin's theory that since a cognition of a general activity such as 'he performs' (*karoti*) is produced in all the different instances of undertakings such as 'he cooks' (*pacati*), 'he studies' (*paṭhati*) etc., the same should be taken as an evidence for establishing a separate general activity which is common to all the actions and distinct from all of the verbal root-meanings. It states that the cognition of a general activity, common to all the different instances of undertakings such as studying etc., does not establish the activity as a separate entity as expressed by the conjugational endings. On the contrary, it establishes that the so – called activity is nothing but the notion of generality common to all the different instances of root-meanings such as cooking, studying etc. Thus, there is no need that the activity be accepted as a different entity expressed by the conjugational endings etc.

Translation : (P.42-43)

Second alternative theory that the activity is an effect produced by root-meanings

XIV.3. Now, another alternative theory is stated in support of the separate activity. It is true that the activity incorporates the general characteristics of actions expressed by different verbal roots (i.e. is common to all the actions). However, it does so only as an entity that is produced as the effect of verbal actions; it does not incorporate general characteristics as the generality of all the actions unlike the generality of the cowness etc. which has identical form with the individuals (cow) in which it inheres.This position can be explained as follows : Such an activity (is distinct from the root-meanings because the same) is associated with its own general property as well as the distinct individual characteristics as cognized by each and every one in the expressions such as 'he performs' (*karoti*) (which indicates its general nature of being produced) and 'he performs it quickly' (*s'īghram karoti*) or 'he performs it slowly' (*mandam karoti*) (which indicates its individual characteristics of being produced quickly or slowly). Thus, it becomes established that the general characteristics or nature such as instrumentality, found occurring in the verbal root-meanings, namely, different actions, is quite distinct from the activity; and hence, the same activity is distinct from the verbal actions.

Also, this fact has been stated by scholars as follows : 'The generality of the verbal root-meanings, which is of the form of being the instrument, is quite distinct; and the activity, which has been established as the effect to be produced, is quite distinct.

Note : The explanation introduces the second alternative theory in support of a separate activity. It states that the activity, despite being common to all the root-meanings (actions) and also incorporating the general characteristics of all the actions, is not the same as the generality (*sāmānya*) of all the actions. Unlike the generality such as the cowness, which is common to all the different individual cows, and therefore, is identical with the individual cows, the activity is an entity which is to be produced by the instrumentality of the individual actions and hence is clearly distinct from the individual actions. It also states that unlike the generality, like the cowness, which is inherent in all the cows, the activity is not an inherent property found in all the individual actions. Thus, the activity continues in all the actions only as an entity produced from such actions and not as a generality inherent in all the actions.

Accoring to this explanation, the theory that the activity is an effect produced by the instrumentality of the actions is proved by the usage such as '*karoti*' (he performs) and *'śīghram karoti'* (he performs quickly) etc. Here, in the first instance, the activity is perceived as an entity associated with the general characteristics of performing; whereas, in the second instance, the same is perceived as an entity associated with the specific characteristics of performing, i.e. quickness or slowness. This proves that the activity, as expressed by *'karoti'*, is to be produced by the actions as associated with the general and specific characteristics. Also, the explanation points out that such an activity which is inherent in all the actions continues only as an effect. Thus, it establishes that the *karotyartha* (activity), which is to be produced by the actions, is a distinct meaning expressed by the conjugational endings; and the generality of actions, inherent in all the actions, the instruments, is the generic property of actions.

Translation : (P.44)

Refutation of the second alternative theory

Verse 15

No, this alternative theory is also not tenable. The untenability can be explained as follows : There are no two distinct cognitions, referring to the two distinct forms of generalities, viz. the generality of all the actions to be produced and also the generality of all the actions which are the instruments of producing, which are common to all the distinct actions in statements such as 'he cooks' (*pacati*) etc. Hence, we cannot obtain the two different genralities, namely, an activity to be produced from the actions and also an activity inherent in all the actions that are instruments of producing.

Note : The verse 15 refutes the second alternative theory in support of a separate activity. It states that there is no evidence to prove that there are actually two generalities, viz. an activity which is common to all the actions due to its nature of being produced and also an activity which is inherent in all the actions which serve as the instruments of producing. According to the verse, there arise no cognitions regarding the separate generalities to be identified with an activity to be produced from all the actions and also with an activity inherent in all the individual actions which serve as the instruments of producing. And therefore, an activity, which is associated with the general and specific characterristics of doing (performing), cannot be established as distinct from the verbal root-meanings, i.e. actions.

Translation (P.45)

Explanation of verse (15) that the generality of root-meanings that has the form of an instrument cannot be accepted

XV.1. In the case of the expressions such as 'he cooks' (*pacati*) etc., no congition of the instrumentality such as 'this is an instrument' and 'this is an instrument' is produced with respect to the entity, that is quite distinct from both the instrument (such as woods) and the action (of cooking). Therefore, it would not be possible to assume a generality of root-meanings (i.e. activity of individual actions) as having the nature of an instrument; and therefore distinguished in its form from the actions. Also, in the case of the expressions such as 'he performs it quickly' (*ś'īghram karoti)* and 'he performs it slowly' (*mandam karoti*) etc., only the generality of the actions (which is associated with the slowness and the quickness) is perceived as a sub-division of the generality which is actually the generality of the root-meanings expressed by the verb '*karoti*' (he performs). This instance is, for example, similar to the instances of the redness and the whiteness etc. of a horse which are really nothing but the subdivisions of the generality of horseness.

Note : The explanation states that the position that "the generality of actions is to be identified with the instrumentality of all the actions in producing the activity", is untenable. It points out that no one cognizes the instrumentality of the actions from the statements such as 'he cooks through woods.' One cognizes the instrumentality of only the woods from such statements. Therefore, the assumption of an activity, as the generality of root meanings (actions), which function as the instruments of yet another activity, is totally untenable. Thus, it must be accepted that the generality of the actions has only the form of an activity identical with the actions; and therefore, does not have the form of the instrumentality.

Further, it points out that, in expressions such as 'he

performs slowly' (*mandam karoti*) etc., one cognizes only the subdivision or subvariety of the generality of the root-meanings (i.e. actions) and one does not cognize any separate generality to be identified with the instrumentality of the actions. This point is established by the fact that in expressions like 'red horse is jumping' etc. one cognizes the redness as only a subdivision of the horseness and not as a separate generality of the horses.

Translation : (P.46)

Conclusion that activity cannot be a separate entity

Verse 16

Therefore, it has been stated as follows :

"No effort or operation (i.e. activity), which accomplishes the effects (such as becoming soft 'or heaven') and which has verbal root-meanings as its instruments, can be accepted to have been perceived beyond (besides) the verbal root-meanings (i.e. actions) and also beyond the different effects". Moreover, for maintaining the distinction between the activity (*bhāvanā*) and also the root-meanings, i.e. actions (*dhātvartha*), the distinction between the definitions of the same activity and also the root meanings (actions) must be stated. And, suppose it is stated that the activity is a kind of movement or motion (*parispanda*), then untenability would occur in the case of the verbal expressions such as 'he offers' (*yajati*) etc.

Note : Versee 16 explains the untenability of the separate status for the activity. According to this verse, analysis of the distinct activity as being 'movement' or 'motion' (*parispanda*) is untenable, since, in 'he offers' (*yajati*) etc., the conjugational endings (*ti*) etc. cannot be considered to express any activity that has the form of movement or motion. And, since no analysis of the activity as distinct from the verbal root meanings (actions) is possible, no separate definition of the same activity is possible. Thus, due to the impossibility of a separate definition of the activity, separate status for activity is untenable.

Translation : (P.47)

Explanation of verse (16) that the activity cannot be ***parispanda***

XVI.1. Moreover, the advocate of the theory, that the

activity (*bhāvanā)* and the verbal root-meanings (actions) are mutually distinct from each other must demonstrate the clear distinction between the natures of the same two. It may be maintained that the verbal root-meanings (actions) have the nature of non-movement or non-motion (*aspandātmā*) whereas the activity (*bhāvanā*) has the nature of a movement or motion (*parispanda*). In that case, there would arise a contingency of the absence of the activity in the instances of the verbs such as 'he offers' (*yajate*), 'he knows' (*jānāti*) etc., which have non-moving entities as their agents. Also, there would arise a contingency of considering the verbal root-meanings (actions) as the activity (*bhāvanā*) in the case of verbs such as 'he goes' (*gacchati*) etc. (which have the moving entities as their agents). Also, the possibility of considering the operation of the sentient beings as the activity is refuted earlier.

Note : The explanation points out that, since the analysis of the activity as a distinct entity from the root-meanings (actions) is not tenable, the distinct status for the same activity is unjustified. According to the explanation, the analysis of the activity as movement or motion (*parispanda*) and the analysis of the root-meanings (actions) as non-movement or non-motion (*aspandātmā*) is untenable due to unavoidable omissions and commissions. No activity, in that case, could be explained in the case of the verbs such as 'he offers' (*yajate*), 'he knows' (*jānāti*) etc. since they refer to the non-moving or dormant self such as Caitra, who possess mere volition (desire) for gift (*icchā*) or knowledge of objects (*jñāna*), as their agents. Also, in that case, the root-meanings, i.e. actions such as 'going' (*gamana*), reading (*pāṭha*) etc., could not be prevented from being considered as the activity in the case of the verbs such as 'he goes' (*gacchati*) or 'he reads' (*paṭhati*) etc. since the same actions can be analysed as the movement or motion. The notion of movement or motion is based on the fact that such actions as 'going,'reading' etc. give rise to the effects such as contact, awarness; and since the actions such as 'going', 'reading' etc. give rise to the effects such as contact, awareness, the same (actions such as going) cannot be denied the status of the activity.

Translation (P.48)

Theory that the activity can be established as having the form of movement

XVI.2. One may ask now as to what is this movement or motion (*parispanda*) ? For, such a movement or motion is not perceived to be distinct from the agent who is considered to be the substratum of such a motion (*parispanda*). (However, such an argument is not correct). How is it that the movement (i.e. activity) is not perceived to be distinct from the substratum ? For, in spite of the fact that one has the perception regarding the substratum (i.e. Devadatta), the knowledge of movement such as 'Devadatta moves' (*calati*) is not produced always; rather, it is produced only occasionally at times. And this knowledge must, therefore, be admitted as based on only a movement distinct from its substratum, i.e. as establishing the movement as distinct from its substratum.

Translation (P.49)

Refutation

Verse 17

No, this theory is not sound. (The knowledge such as 'Devadatta moves' (*calati*) may be accepted as based on something distinct from its substratum (the agent Devadatta etc.). Nevertheless, there is no ground to accept that the same knowledge is based on the motion or movement. The knowledge of movement such as 'Devadatta moves' may be based on the effects such as the separation from the region left behind and also the contact with the region following. For, no distinction of the moving entity, (i.e. Devadatta etc.) from the stationary (i.e. the effects such as 'contact' and 'separation') is perceived by any one.

Note : Now, a theory is proposed as follows : The activity, which has the form of movement or motion, must be accepted as a distinct ertity from its substratum, namely, Devadatta etc. For, inspite of the perception of the substratum such as 'Devadatta, the knowledge such as 'Devadatta moves' etc. is not always produced. And this occasional perception proves that the motion or movement is an entirely distinct entity from its substratum. This instance is similar to the instance of a qualifier being distinct from its qualificand. For instance, inspite of the perception of the qualificand such as a person, the cognition of the qualifier, namely, 'staff' (*daṇḍa*) such as 'staff-holder is a person' (*daṇḍī puruṣaḥ*) is produced only occasionally; and therefore, the same cognition proves that the qualifier, i.e. staff, is a distinct entity from its qualificand, i.e. person. Thus, the cognition such as 'Devadatta moves' (*calati*) must be accepted as establishing a separate movement or motion, which can be identified with the activity. However, Pūrvapakṣin refutes such a theory. According to him, the cognition such as 'Devadatta moves' (*calati*) may be accepted as based on something different from its substratum, such as Devadatta etc., nevertheless, the same cannot be accepted as based on the movement. That is to say that the cognition such as 'Devadatta moves' can be accepted as establishing soemthing different from mere substratum; nevertheless, the same need not be accepted as establishing the movement. For, the cognition 'Devadatta moves' is actually based on the effects such as contact and separation which are produced by moving. Thus, the cognition does not refer to any movement as such which is supposed to be producing the effects contact, separation etc. On the other hand, the same refers to the effects such as contact and separation.

Also, it should be noted here that no 'moving' entity, i.e. movement or motion, is separately cognized from the 'constant' entity, i.e. 'contact' or 'separation', which is produced from moving ; thus, the assertion that the cognition such as 'Devadatta moves' refers to the movement or motion as distinct from the effects 'contact' 'separation' etc. is untenable.

Translation (P.50-51)

Explanation of the verse (17) that *calati pratyaya* must be based on effects

XVII.1. The motion or movement, (*parispanda*), when becoming an object of perception (i.e. of eyes), is accepted to have the separation from the region left behind and also the contact with the region following as its effects. Therefore, such knowledge of movement as 'Devadatta moves' should be held to refer to only the effects such as 'contact' and 'separation'. The person, unless comprehending the effects, i.e. the leaving of the region behind and also the reaching of the region next, would not be able to comprehend the knowledge of the motion or movement such as 'Devadatta moves' (*calati*) etc. The scholars, though carefully examining the knowledge such as 'Devadatta moves', do not perceive any distinction of the moving entity, (i.e. Devadatta eyc.) from the stationary (except possessing the effect 'contact' and 'separation').

Translation (P.50-51)

Objection that '*calati pratyaya*' cannot be based on merely effects

XVIII.2. (It may be held that the knowledge of movement such as 'he moves' (*calati pratyaya*) is based on the effects 'separation', 'contact' etc. and not on the distinct movement; however, such a theory is not correct.) Since the person 'Devadatta' etc., who has remained motionless after making a certain movement, is indeed the abode of the effects such as contact, separation etc., the same person 'Devandatta' etc. would have to be perceived as 'moving'. However, such a motionless person is never perceived as 'moving'. Moreover, when effects, such as contact and separation, are produced from the activity of one of the two items (i.e. from the bird out of the bird and also a post), the contingency of perceiving the activity as occurring in both places (i.e. in the bird as well as in the post) would arise, since the effects, on which such a knowledge is based, are binary (i.e. are related to both the bird as well as to the post).

Translation (P.51)

Argument that *calati pratyaya* is based on both the effects together

You may argue as follows :

The post and the *śyena* bird, in the context of the bird flying out of a post, possess only the separation and not the contact. And, since, the effects such as contact and the separation, as occurring together, are the cause of such a knowledge of movement (i.e. 'it moves' etc.), no contingency of perceiving such a knowledge (as 'it moves' etc.) would ever arise under such a situation.

Translation (P.51)

Refutation

No, this argument is not tenable. When the two effects, namely, the contact and also the separation, are produced by the two different *śyena* birds in one (post), the incorrect knowledge of movement such as 'the post moves' would become a necessity. That is to say that when the post is being contacted by one bird (hawk) and also is being separated by another bird (hawk) (i.e. when one bird sits on the post and another bird flies out of the same post), the knowledge, namely, 'post moves', would become a necessity (since the post can be claimed to possess both the effects, contact and separation, together).

Translation (P.51-52)

Second argument that the effects occuring in a particular order forms the basis

The effects such as separation and also the contact, which occur in a particular order (i.e. first separation from the region left behind and then the contact with the region next) only can be considered to be the basis (i.e. the cause) of such knowledge as 'post moves' etc.

Translation (P.52)

Refutation

No, this argument too is not tenable. There occurs no such knowledge as 'he moves' etc. when the post has the separation produced by the action of flying of a bird, which contacted the post earliar, which inn itself precedes the contact produced by the action of sitting of another bird.

Note : The explanation of the verse 17 points out the objection of the Siddhāntin that the cognition such as 'Devadatta moves' (*calati*) cannot be stated to be based on only the effects 'contact' and 'separation'; but rather, the same should be accepted as based on a distinct motion or movement which can be identified with the activity. According to the Siddhāntin, unless the cognition 'Devadatta moves' is accepted as based on the movement, the same becomes necessary even when a person has stopped after having made a movement, since he possesses the effect 'contact' and 'separation' even after stopping from the movement.

Moreover, in accepting the cognition as based on the effects, even the statements such as 'the bird moves' and 'the post moves', wherein the movement is seen in both the bird and the post, would become necessary, since the effects 'contact' and 'separation' produced by the movement of the bird is found occuring in both the bird as well as the post.

Now an argument is made as follows : The statement 'post moves' can be prevented even in the theory that the cognition 'he moves' is based on the effects. For, the effects separation and contact can together be accepted as forming the basis of such a cognition of movement. And, since the post does not possess the effects separation and contact together, the cognition 'post moves' can be avoided.

However, Siddhāntin refutes such an argument on the basis that even the post can be shown to possess both the effects 'separation' and 'contact' when a bird comes to the post and sits on it following another bird which leaves and flies out of it. Thus, since post can be shown to have both the effects 'separation' and 'contact' together, the statement 'post moves' becomes impossible to prevent in the theory that the cognition 'he moves' is based on simply such effects.

Here, another argument is made in support of the theory that the cognition 'he moves' etc. is based on the effects. According to this argument, the cognition can be insisted to be based on only the effects 'separation' and 'contact' occuring in that particular sequential order. And since, in the case of one bird coming and sitting on the post and then another bird leaving and flying out of it, the effects occur in the order of contact and then separation (and not in the order of separation and then contact), no such statement as 'post moves' can be insisted. Thus, the cognitions of movement can be based on the effects rather than on the movement.

However, Siddhāntin refutes such an argument as well. He states that the post can possess the effects 'separation' and 'contact' in that particular sequential order when a bird, sitting earlier on the post, leaves and then another bird comes and occupies it. And, under such circumstances, the statement 'post-moves' can never be prevented in the theory that the cognition 'he moves' etc. is based on merely the effects. Thus, the cognition of movement such as 'he moves' must be admitted to be based on the movement or motion.

Translation : (P.52)

Reply to the objection that cognition cannot be based on effects

Here we reply as follows :

Verse 18

(Neither simply the effects such as contact and separation nor any other entity such as motion or movement are the basis of the cognition such as 'he moves' etc.) However, only the effects such as the contact and separation, delimited by the particular points of location (*deśaviśeṣa*), which are produced without any break (i.e. which are produced in continuity of one after another) are to be considered as the object, i.e. the basis, of such a cognition. And the 'sky' (*ākāśa*) is considered to be the particular point of location of the entities.

Note : Verse 18 replies to the objection of the Siddhāntin that the effects such as contact and separation cannot be the basis of the cognition 'he moves' etc. According to this verse, neither simply the effects, such as contact and separation, nor any other entity, i.e. movement or motion, are the basis of the cognition. However, the effects separation and contact as delimited by the particular location – points of space (*des'a*) are the basis of such a cognition. And the points of location, which delimit such effects are those of the sky (and not those of the post etc), since only the sky is conventionally known as the location–points of space of all the entities in the world. Thus, in the theory that such effects as contact and separation, delimited by the points of location, i.e. sky, are the basis of the cognition of movement such as 'he moves', the statements 'Devadatta moves' ('*devadattaḥ calati*') (when Devadatta has stopped after making a movement) and 'post moves' (*sthāṇuḥ calati*) (when a bird sits on the post following another bird flying out of it) cannot be imposed since such a basis, i.e. the effects 'separation' and 'contact' delimited by the particular points of location of sky, is absent.

Translation (P.52-53)

Explanation of verse (18) that effects which are continuous and delimited by the location – points form the basis of *calati pratyaya*

XVIII.1. The knowledge of movement such as 'he moves' is not based on mere effects such as the separation and the contact. However, the same is based on the succession of the effects such as separation and contact which are produced without any break. Thus, in the case of the stationary (i.e. the agent who has stopped after moving), no such knowledge (as 'he moves') is produced (since such effects are absent in him). Also, the knowledge of movement such as 'it moves' is based on the effects delimited by the location – points of space. The effects such as separation and contact, which merely occur in the post, cannot be claimed to be the objects, i.e. effects delimited by the particular location – points of sky; and therefore, the post, which merely possesses the effects such as contact with birds (but does not possess the same effects as occurring in particular points of location, i.e. the sky), cannot be considered to be possessing the effects delimited by the location – points of space. The scholars, who are well-versed in worldly affairs, do not regard the two birds (hawks), coming into contact with the post and separating from the same, as functioning as the location – points of the post. Therefore, we recognise only the sky or either (*ākās'a*), in which all the entities occur, to be delimiting points of location of all the entities that can be delimited by the points of location. Consequently, only the effects such as contact and separation delimited by the points of sky form the basis of such a knowledge as 'it moves'. And, since such effects are absent in the case of the post, the contingency of making the statement 'post moves' does not occur.

Note : The explanation points out that the undesired contingency of making the statements 'Devadatta moves' and 'post moves' can be avoided by accepting that the effects, which are continuous and also delimited by the particular location – points, are the basis. In the case of the person who has stopped after making a movement, the statement 'Devadatta moves' can be avoided, since he does not possess the effects contact etc., which are continuous. Also the explanation points out that the statements such as 'post moves' etc. can be avoided when the effects which are delimited by the location – points of space, i.e. sky, are considered as the basis of the cognition of movement such as 'it moves' etc. This is so because, the post, despite possessing the effects 'separation' from and 'contact' with the birds (hawks), cannot be considered as possessing the effects delimited by the location – points of sky. And consequently, the statements such as 'post moves' can be avoided due to the lack of the basis for making such statements, i.e. the lack of the effects separation and contact delimited by the location – points of sky in the post.

Translation (P.53)

Objection that the cognition of movement cannot be based on effects

XVIII.2. Certainly, since the sky is imperceptible, the effects such as separation and contact of the bird etc. from and with the sky are not justified in being considered as the objects of perception, which is a product of sense organs. This is so because, such effects as separation and contact of the bird etc. from and with the sky are not related to the senses (i.e. are not sensual) due to their non-occurrence in the perception, i.e. in sense organs. And this instance is similar to the instance of the separation and contact of a tree, from and with the wind which are imperceptible due to the imperseptibility of wind. (Now, since the knowledge such as 'it moves' is produced from the sense-perception, the same cannot be considered as based on such effects as separation from and contact with the imperceptible sky).

Note : Here an objection is raised as follows :

The sky is held to be the delimiting points of location, i.e. location of all the entities; and the effects separation and contact, as delimited by such points of sky, are held to be the basis of the cognition of movement such as 'It moves', etc. However, the sky, due to the absence of form etc., is imperceptible; and therefore, the effects such as separation and contact, as delimited by such points of sky, should also be imperceptible. Now, since the cognition 'it moves' etc. is established to be perceptible, the same should not be accepted as referring to such imperceptible effects as contact and separation.

Reply that effects such as separation and contact need not be imperceptible

No, certainly, it is not proper (to consider that such effects as separation and contact of the bird etc., from ad with sky are imperceptible). For otherwise -

Verse 19

Suppose the effects such as separation and contact of the bird etc. from and with the sky are beyond the reach of the sense perception, then how could the fixed location (i.e. delimiting points) of the separation and the contact of the moving bird be cognized ?

Note : This verse provides a reply to such an objection. It states that, despite the sky being imperceptible, the effects 'separation' and 'contact', delimited by the points of sky, must be admitted to be perceptible. According to the verse, otherwise the location of the moving birds which is fixed in the sky on the basis of the effects 'separation' and 'contact' would become impossible to perceive. The location of the moving bird is perceived in the form that the bird has reached such and such point in the sky etc. Since the effects delimited by the location–points of sky should be admitted as perceptible, the same can be considered as the basis of the cognition of the movement such as 'It moves' etc.

Translation (P.54)

Explanation of the verse (19) that effects must be perceptible

XIX.1. Suppose the effects such as the separation and the contact of the bird from and with the sky etc. are held to be imperceptible, then how could the knowledge of the different locations, namely, the different points of sky, be possible in the event of a flying (i.e. moving) bird.

Translation (P.54)

Argument that location –points of sky can be inferred

It may be argued that the activity (i.e. movement), which forms the cause of the effects such as contact and separation, can function as the inferential cause (*liṅga*) of the inference of such effects as the contact and separation (and hence, the inference of the different location – points of sky is possible).

Reply : No, this is not tenable. For, the perception of the definite points of location is necessarily obtained. And the knowledge regarding the definite points of location such as 'here (in the sky) it (i.e. bird) has reached, but not there' cannot be deemed to be possible in the event of the non-perception of the (effects) such as contact etc. with the particular points of location in the 'sky'.

translation (P.54)

Argument

XIX.2. The knowledge, i.e. perception, regarding the definite points of location such as "here it has reached, but not there", etc. is rendered possible due to the difference between the multitudes (i.e. ranges) of lights which pervade the different points of sky.

Translation (P.54)

Reply :

Supposing such different multitudes (i.e. ranges) of lights are the objects of the knowledge of definite points of location such as 'here the bird has reached, but not there; then the same (lights) can be considered to be the points of location in the sky; and therefore, the effects such as the contact and also the separation, which occur in the sky, also become perceptible (due to the perceptibility of the lights). (Thus only the effects such as contact and separation, which occur in the multitudes of lights of sky, should be the basis of the cognition of movement).

Morever, only the assumption of the perceptibility of the effects such as the contact and the separation, that are already established by other means, as existent, is proper (i.e. justified) in spite of the fact that the same (effects) may occur in entities that are either perceptible or imperceptible. However, the assumption of the perceptibility of the cause of such effects, namely, the movement or motion, which is not yet established as existent by any means, is not justified.

Note : The explanation of the verse 19 points out that despite the imperceptibility of the sky, the effects 'contact' and 'separation', delimited by the sky, must be regarded as perceptible. Otherwise, if the effects are imperceptible, then the perception of the different points of location such as 'the moving bird has reached such and such points of sky' would become untenable.

The explanation refutes, at this juncture, the Siddhāntin's argument that the knowledge of the points of location can be obtained through the inference of the effects such as the contact and the separation, which have the activity i.e. movement or motion as their inferential cause and hence, there is no need to perceive the effects as such. According to the explanation, the knowledge of definite points of location such as 'the moving bird has reached here (this point of sky,) but not there, the other point of sky', cannot be explained unless the perception of the effects 'contact' and 'separation' with and from the particular points of sky is obtained.

The explanation refutes also another argument that since the different multitudes or the ranges of lights in the sky are perceptible, the knowledge of definite points of location that 'the moving bird has reached here this point of sky, but not there, the other point of sky' (i.e. 'contact occurs here but not there'), can also be explained.

According to the explanation, such an argument is counterproductive. For, suppose the different multitudes or the ranges of lights are the objects of the knowledge of location – points such as 'the moving bird has reached here this point, but not there the other point', then the same should be accepted as the points of location of sky; and, since such points of location are perceptible, the effects such as contact and separation, which occur at such points of location, too become perceptible.

The explanation, further, points out that only the effects such as contact and separation, which are already established as existent, are justified in being assumed as perceptible; and therefore, the assumption of the perceptibility of the movement or motion which is yet to be established as existent, is not justified.

Translation : Siddhāntin's objection that movement can be infered due to its effects

XIX.3. Now, it may be stated as follows : We intend to infer (i.e. establish) the existence of the movement, i.e. the activity, through the very effects such as contact and separation. This theory can be explained as follows : The entities that are incidental, i.e. that are produced, cannot be held to have been accomplished without any cause (*hetu*). Also, since the effects such as contact and separation are incidental, the same cannot be considered to have been produced without any cause, i.e. they cannot be produced merely through their own locus; they need yet another cause to accomplish them. Thus, movement can be established through the effects.

Note : It should be noted here that, at this stage, the Siddhāntin wants to infer the existence of the movement or motion, i.e. the activity, through the existence of the effects 'contact' and 'separation'. Siddhāntin argues that since no incidental entity, i.e. product, can come into existence without a producing cause, the effects contact and separation, which are incidental, cannot come into existence without a producing cause, i.e. movement or motion. Also, he argues that since the effects contact and separation are incidental, the same cannot be established as being produced merely on account of their locus, i.e. substratum, but rather, they need a separate producing cause. That is to say that despite the existence of the locus, the incidental entities are seen sometimes occuring and sometimes not occurring; and this proves that the same require another cause, besides their locus, for their production. Thus, the movement or motion can be inferred on account of the effects contact and separation which require such a movement.

Translation (P.56)

Refutation of Siddhāntin's objection that movement can be inferred

No, this is not tenable (i.e. logical). For, you intend to

establish the movement, i.e. the activity, on the basis of effects 'contact' and 'separation'. However,

Verse 20

Suppose, the movement is eternal, then the effects such as contact and separation would always need to be produced; and, on the other hand, suppose the movement is non eternal, then, the cause of itself (i.e. of movement), can be considered to be the cause of the effects as well. So, why to assume, in between, an intermediate entity such as movement as the cause of the effects such as contact and separation ?

Note : Verse 20 seeks to refute the Siddhāntin's claim that the existence of movement can be inferred through the effects, namely, contact and separation. It states that the movement, which is intended to be inferred, can be either eternal or non-eternal. And, suppose the movement is held to be eternal, then the effects 'contact' and 'separation' would need to be produced always since the producing cause, namely, the movement is ever present. On the other hand, suppose the same movement is held to be non-eternal, then the cause, that produces such a movement, could itself be accepted as the producing cause of the effects 'contact' and 'separation' as well. Thus, since the effects can be explained as being produced through the producing cause of the movement itself, the assumtion of a separate entity, namely, the movement or motion for the sake of explaining (i.e. producing) the effects, becomes unnecessary.

Translation (P.56-57)

Explanation of verse (20) that effects can be produced by the cause of movement

XX.1. Now, according to the Siddhāntin, the movement or motion *(karma)* should be inferred through the effects 'contact' and 'separation' as either eternal or non-eternal. However, suppose such a movement is held to be eternal, then the effects 'contact' and 'separation' would have an undesired contingency of being produced always due to the ever-presence of the required cause (i.e. the movement) and also due to the non-requirement of any other cause. On the other hand, suppose the same movement is held to be non-eternal, then the movement should itself be accepted as needing a separate producing cause (for its production); and therefore, the effects could also be established, i.e. produced, by means of the producing cause intended to produce the movement. Thus, what is the need for accepting a separate intermediate movement which is not profitable or useless.

Argument that movement *'karma'* is the cause (P.57)

XX.2. Some one, i.e. Siddhāntin, may hold here as follows :

Since the activity such as movement (*karma*) is both eternal (non-deviating) (i.e. is invariably found to have been associated with the effects such as contact) and immediate or essential (i.e. occurring in the same locus as the effects), the same (movement) must be accepted as the cause of the effects such as contact and separaton. And, since the effort (*prayatna*), etc. is a deviating cause (i.e. is not invariably found to have been associated with the effects 'contact' etc.) and is non-immediate (unessential) (i.e. is not occurring in the same locus as that of the effects 'contact' etc.), the same effort (*prayatna*) could not be conceded to be the cause of the effect 'contact' and 'separation'. This position can be explained as follows : The faculty of impulse (*saṁskāra*) such as velocity, and effects 'contact' and 'separation' are found inhering in the very things (i.e. hand, feet etc.) in which the activities such as movement are inherent. Also, when the movement, i.e. the activity, is present, the effects such as contact and separation invariably containue to exist, i.e. come into being. The cause, which is inferred on account of (the production of) the effects, cannot be established otherwise to be existent by any valid means when the same effects are not produced. (Thus, the movement, i.e. the activity, cannot be a deviating *hetu* in the establishment of the contact and separation).

On the other hand, the effort occurs in the self (i.e. in the locus different from that of the effects). Also, despite the presence of the effort in the self, only one out of many limbs of body, which are associated with the self, possessing the effort, reaches a different region (place) due to the effort. (Thus such a deviating effort cannot be the cause of the effects.).

Note : The later part of the explanation reestablishes the position of the Siddhāntin that only the movement, i.e. the activity, must be conceded as the cause of the effects. According to the explanation, only the means, which is neither deviating nor is non-immediate (non-essential), could be accepted as the cause of some effects. And since, out of the two means (i.e. movement and effort), only the movement is both non-deviating (i.e. it invariably produces the effects 'contact' and 'separation') and is immediate (i.e. it occurs in the limbs 'hand', etc. wherein the effects 'contact' and 'separation' are produced), the same should be accepted as the cause of the effects. On the contrary, since the effort is neither non-deviating (i.e. it does not produce the effects in all limbs despite the same being associated with the self) nor is immediate (i.e. it does not occur in the limbs where the effects occur), the same could not be considered as the cause of the effects.

Translation (P.58)

Reply

Verse 21

The Siddhāntin, who thinks that the movement, i.e. the activity, alone is the cause, should be replied as follows : You, Siddhāntin, hold that only the entity, which is already established by other means to exist, should be considered to be the cause of some effect due to its eternality (i.e. due to its non-deviation) and also due to its immediacy (i.e. due to its occurrence in the locus of its effects); and therefore, you also hold that the entity, which is different from such an established entity, should not be considered to be the cause (i.e. is a non-cause). However, in that case, how can the movement, i.e. the activity, be considered to have been produced from such an effort since the same effort too is neither eternal nor immediate ?

Note : The verse 21 refutes Siddhāntin's argument that only the movement, i.e. the activity, which is eternal, i.e. non-deviating, and immediate, must be regarded as the cause of the effects. It does so by pointing out that suppose an entity, that is non-eternal and non-immediate, is not allowed to be the cause, then effort too cannot be considered to be the cause with respect to the (production of the) movement (activity). For, the effort is both non-eternal and non-immediate with respect to the production of the movement as well.

Translation (P.58-59)

Explanation of verse (21) that effort cannot be the cause of even the movement

XXI.1. In the event of the presence of many entities (instruments), only the entity, that has already been established to be existing, would be established as the cause of the effects to be produced due to the eternality and the immediacy. Therefore, the entity, that has not been already established to be existing, cannot be assumed, i.e. established, to be the cause due to the eternality and the immediacy.

However, the entity such as effort, that is opposite in its nature (i.e. deviating in its nature by being non-eternal and non-immediate), is totally unjustified in being considered as the cause of something,; and therefore, only the movement, i.e. the activity, can be assumed to be the cause of the effects due to its non-deviating nature in producing the effects despite not being already established by other means to be existing. Thus, in the case of such a theory, alas, even the effort would become the non-cause of the activity (i.e. of the movement) due to its deviating nature in producing the effects.

Translation (P.59)

Alternative theory that effort can be explained as the cause of movement

XXI.2. Now, an alternative theory can be as follows : The effort, despite its occurrence in a locus (i.e. the self), which is different from that of the effects, can be considered to be the cause of the movement (the activity), since the same is perceived to have a relation with the movement which is found in the body. Also, the effort, despite the perception of its deviation from the movement (the activity), can be considered to be the cause of the same movement (the activity), since the deviation of a cause can be explained away due to the obstruction of its potentiality to produce an effect at times. Therefore, the effort should be the cause of the movement (the activity).

Translation (P.59-60)

Establishment of the theory that effort can be established as the cause of the effect and movement

In that case, we shall ask, what offence have the effects 'contact' and 'separation' committed ? For, due to which offence, leaving aside the (claim of the) well established cause such as the effort, the unestablished entity such as the movement (activity) is searched for (as the cause of producing the effects 'contact' and 'separation'.). Also, usually, the effort, which produces the movement (the activity), is found to have the same locus (i.e. body or bodily parts) as that of the effects contact and separation. And that is a point to be pondered over.

Note : The explanation seeks to point out that the movement (the activity) need not be assumed as the cause of the effects 'contact' and 'separation'. It states that despite the effort being a deviating cause in producing the effects 'contact' and 'separation', the same cannot be denied the status of the 'cause'. For, the effort needs in any case to be considered as the cause of the activity (i.e. movement) so that the same can facilitate the production of the effects. And since, the effort, despite deviating, needs to be considered as the cause of the activity, there is no harm in considering the same as the cause of the effects as well. Thus, instead of assuming an unestablished entity such as movement (activity) as the cause of the effects, the sanctioning of the status of the cause for the effort, which has already been established as the cause of the movement (activity), is much more logical. Also, the effort can be explained to exist indirectly in the body or bodily parts wherein the effects 'contact' and 'separation' are produced. Therefore, the argument that since the effort exists in the self and the effects are produced in the body, the effort is a deviating entity is also not really correct. Thus, the movement (the activity) need not be accepted as the cause of the effects 'contact' etc.

Translation : (P.60)

Movement (activity) cannot be inferred through effects

Verse 22

Existence of a cause is inferred through its effects in the time prior to the production of the effects. However, the cognition of movement such as 'he moves' (*calati*) refers to the movement (the activity) as belonging to the present time (wherein the effects exist as already produced). Therefore, it cannot be accepted that the cause, i.e. the movement (the activity), is obtained, i.e. inferred, due to the effects 'contact' and 'separation'.

Note : Verse 22 seeks to refute the position of the Siddhāntin that the movement (the activity) can be inferred through the effects 'contact' and 'separation'. It states that only the existence of the cause prior to the production of the effects (and not the existence of the cause at the present time wherein the effects exist as already produced) can be inferred through the effects. However, the cognition of the movement such as 'he moves' (*calati*), which is held to be the evidence establishing the existence of the movement (activity), refers to the activity as only belonging to the present time, wherein the effects occur as already produced. Thus, the activity, which occurs at the same time as the effects 'contact' and 'separation', cannot be accepted to be inferred from the effects.

Translation : (P.60-61)

Explanation of the verse (22) that movement cannot be inferred

XXII.1. Only the existence of the cause, at the time, preceding the time of the origination of the effects, is conducive to the origination of the effects. However, the existence of the same (cause), at the same time as that of the effects, is not conductive to the origination of the effects; for, the effects are already accomplished at that time (and hence, no use in considering such an existence as conducive to the origination). Therefore, the person intending to infer the cause due to the effects, infers actually (the existence of) the cause as belonging to the time preceding the time of the origination of the effect. However, he does not infer the same cause as belonging to the present time (wherein the effects exist as already produced). Thus, the cognition of the movement (the activity) such as 'he moves', is accepted as referring to the movement (the activity), which is assumed of its existence (origination) through the inferential cause, namely, the effects 'contact' and 'separation', as belonging to the time preceding the time of the origination of such effects, and therefore, would not be accepted to refer to the movement (the activity) as belonging to the present time wherein the effects exist as already produced.

Note : The explanation states that the movement (the activity) cannot be expected to be inferred through the effects 'contact' and 'separation'. It emphasizes the point that only the existence of the cause prior to the effects is conducive to the production of the effects and not the existence of the same cause at the present time, since the effects have already been produced at that time. Thus, the effects can infer only the existence of the cause prior to the origination of themselves. Now, since the cognition of the cause, namely, the movement (the activity), is to be obtained through the *calati pratya*ya such as 'he moves', the same must have a reference to the movement (activity) as belonging to only the time preceeding the time of the origination of the effects. However, in actuality, the cognition of the movement (the activity) such as 'he moves' refers to the activity as belonging to only the present time. Thus, due to the impossibility of *calati pratyaya* to refer to the movement as belonging to the past time, the movement, i.e. activity, cannot be accepted as inferred through the effects.

Also, it cannot be argued that since the cognition of movement such as 'he moves' referes to only the effects ,'contact' and 'separation' (which belong to the present time), the form of such a cognition as referring to the movement belonging to present time is not contradictory. For, no separate cognition beyond 'he moves', which can refer to the movement (activity) as belonging to the past time, is found. Thus, the movement, i.e. activity, cannot be accepted as being inferred through the effects.

Translation (P.62)

Movement cannot be inferred through either of the effects Moreover -

Verse 23

How can the movement (the activity), which lasts only upto the origination of the effect 'contact', be inferred from the same effect 'contact' as existing at the present time ? Also, on the other hand, when the movement (the activity) is being inferred through another of the effects, namely, the separation, there would occur an undesired contingency of the occurrence of the same movement (the activity) even on the post (since the post too possess the separation from the bird).

Note : The verse 23 tries to establish that the movement (the actvity) cannot be inferred through either of the two effects, i.e. 'contact' and 'separation'. It states that suppose the movement (activity) is intended to be inferred through the effect 'contact', then the same can be inferred only through the effect 'contact' which is produced. However, in that case, the activity, is not possible to be established as existing at the present time. For, the inference based on the effect 'contact' can be had only in the second moment of the origination of the contact; and since, by that time, the movement (the activity) is lost, the contact can establish the movement (the activity) as belonging to only the past time.

On the other hand, suppose, the movement (the activity) is intended to be inferred through the other effect, namely, separation, then the same movement (activity) can be established as belonging to the present time, since the movement (activity) lasts upto the origination of the separation preceding the contact. However, the difficulty is that such a movement (activity), inferred on the basis of the effect 'separation', would have to occur even on the post, since the post too possesses the separation from the bird when the bird flies out of it.

Translation (P.62)

Explanation of the verse (23) that movement cannot be the object of 'he moves'

XXIII.1. The movement (the activity), lasting only upto the origination of the effect 'contact', and being inferred at the time (i.e. moment) following the moment of the knowledge of the origination of the effect 'contact', cannot be held to exist at the present time (i.e. at the moment wherein the effect 'contact' exists). However, the effects such as contact and also the separation are found occurring at the present time only. (And therefore, the movement (activity) cannot be the object of the cognition such as 'he moves', which refers to the activity as existing only at the present time).

Also, the objects i.e. matters have only a form congenial to (i.e. in conformity with) their form of the cognition involving (referring to) themselves; and they do not have the form opposite, i.e. in contrast, to their form of the cognition. Thus, only the effects 'contact' and 'separation', which exist at the present time, and not the movement (the activity) (which does not exist at the present time), can be the objects of reference of the cognition such as 'he moves'.

Translation (P.63)

Alternative theory that movement can be inferred from 'separation'

XXIII.2. Now it can be proposed as follows :

That since the movement (the activity) is to be inferred from the (production of the) separation (from the earlier region), the same movement (the activity) can be held to produce the separation first, and then to continue to stay (i.e. exist) upto the production of the other effect, namely, the contact (with the next region). Therefore, we can infer the movement (the activity) as existing at the present time (wherein the effect 'contact' too exists).

Refutation (P.63)

No, this alternative theory too is not tenable. For, in that case, the movement, i.e the activity, would have an occasion to be inferred even on the post. This is so because, the separation has equality with the contact in its occurrence on the post

Translation (P.63-64)

Conclusion

XXIII.3. Thus, it should be concluded that the action (*kriyā*), referred to by the verbal root, is nothing but a particular type of quality such as contact or separation. And the meaning referred to by the term 'verb' (*kriyāpada*) does not have a nature that is quite distinct from the qualities (i.e. that of being some movement or activity). Consequently, since there is nothing like an activity, the same cannot be considered as either the meaning denoted by the verbal root or that denotd by the verbal ending.

Note : The explanation tries to establish the

Pūrvapakṣin's theory that the cognition of movement such as 'he moves' refers to only the effects such as 'contact' and 'separation' and not to any separate activity as such. It states that the activity lasts only upto the production of the effect 'contact', and therefore, the same, inferred on account of the 'contact', can only have the form belonging to the past time. And, since the cognition 'he moves' refers to the entities as belonging to the present time; and the effects 'contact' and 'separation' belong to the present time, only the effects 'contact' and 'separation' must be regarded as the objects of such a cognition and not the activity. It should be noted here that the objects of a cognition have the same form as that of their cognition; and therefore, the activity, which has the form as belonging to the past, cannot be the object of the cognition ,'he moves', which has a form as belonging to the present by referring to the entities belonging to the present.

Also, the explanation points out that the activity cannot be inferred through the other effect, namely, separation. According to this explanation, despite the presence of the activity at the time of separation (it lasts upto the production of the contact which follows the separation), the inference of the same activity as existing at the present time due to separation is untenable. For, in that case, the activity would need to occur on the post since the separation from the bird occurs there. Thus, it concludes that no activity, distinct from the qualities, i.e. the effects 'contact' and 'separation', can be accepted as tenable; and therefore, nothing like the activity can be the meaning of the verbal roots. On the other hand, only the qalities, i.e. the effects such as 'contact' and 'separation', are tenable; and therefore, the same must be accepted as the things meant by the term *'kriyā'*. Also, since no activity can be established as tenable, the question of ascertaining as to whether such an activity is the meaning of verbal roots or that of the conjugationl endings does not arise.

Translation (P.64)

Reassertion of the inference of the existence of activity

XXIII.4. And, now as regards the inference, i.e. assumption, of the activity : Inspite of the fact that all the necessary *kārakas* such as instrument etc. are present, the cognition involving a reference to the continuous activity, such as 'he cooks' (*pacati*) is produced only occasionally at times under certain conditions; (and therefore, an entity like the activity, which is distinct from the *kārakas*, must be posited as the basis of the cognition)

Translation (P.65)

Refutation

We shall state, however, that such an inference is not possible.

Verse 24

Since the cognition such as 'he cooks' (*pacati*) can be established on the basis of (i.e. explained away as advocating) the existence of only the particular qualities (i.e. *vikledana* etc.), the inference of a separate entity, namely, an activity is not tenable to assume.

Note : Kriyāvadin reasserts the inference in support of the existence of a separate activity. He states that the cognition such as 'he cooks' (*pacati*) is not produced merely because that all the *kārakas* are present. It is produced only sometimes, i.e. occasionally, when the activity of cooking is continuous. This fact suggests that the cognition 'he moves' is based on something other than merely *kārakas*. And the basis for such a cognition, therefore, must be the continuous activity since such a cognition is produced only in the event of such a continuous activity. Thus, on the basis of such a cognition, a separate activity must be admitted.

However, verse 24 refutes such a proposition. According to the verse, Kriyāvādin must state as to whether, he wants to establish something other than all the *kārakas* or the activity as the basis of the cognition 'he cooks' (*pacati*). Suppose only a mere basis other than all the *kārakas* is meant to be established by such a cognition, then *siddhasādhana doṣa* occurs, since the qualities such as (*vikledana*), which are different from all the *kārakas*, have already been established as the basis of such a cognition by everybody. On the other hand, suppose a distinct activity is meant to be established as the basis of such a cognition (due to the untenability of any of the specific qualities to be the basis), then 'example' would become difficult to be established, since the Kriyāpalāpin (grammarian) has never accepted such an activity, anywhere earlier. Thus, the inference of a separate activity as distinct from the qualiies, cannot be established.

Translation : (P.65)

Explanation of verse (24) that qualities, and not the activity, are the basis

XXIV. 1. And, the distinct qualities, characterised by the loosening of contact and the separation, which are found to occur in the parts of rice grains (and fire), are produced only occasionally at times in spite of the all the *kārakas*. Therefore, the cognition such as 'he cooks' (*pacati*) must be admitted to occur due to the existence of such qualities. Thus, it is not justified that a separate activity, which is distinct from such qualities, be inferred as the object of such a congnition.

Translation (P.65-66)

Argument that activity is the cause of qualities

XXIV.2.Now, it may be argued that there exists a separate activity due to such occasional distinct qualities. (For, the qualities like separation and contact are produced only due to the activity by means of cooking; and so, without the activity, the qualities cannot be explained). Otherwise, such a quality of separation and contact would have an occasion (to be produced) in the case of the presence of mere *kārakas* as well.

Translation (P.66)

Refutation

No, this argument is not tenable. Suppose an activity is inferred to facilitate the production of the qualities like the separation and the contact, then a second activity would have an occasion to be inferred with respect to the first activity as well. (For, the first activity also would not result in the presence of mere *kārakas*). And such an occasion of inferring activities, would lead to further occasions of inferring the activities; and thus the infinite regression would occur.

Also, it cannot be argued by Kriyāvādin that suppose the activity is not inferred, then the particular quality like contact would become necessary to be produced at the mere presence of all the *kārakas*. For, the contact of the fire with the parts of rice grains comes into being gradually, and then gets increased in its intensity. Therefore, the same contact, which functions as the cause of the separation (of the parts of rice grains from the fire), need not have the existence, i.e. origination, at the mere presence of all the *kārakas*.

Translation (P.66)

Argument that activity is the cause of contact

Now, it can be argued as follows : In that case, it can be accepted that the activity is the cause of the same contact (of the fire with the parts of rice grains).

Translation : (P.66)

Refutation

No, this argument is also not tenable. The conscious effort etc., which are considered as the cause of the activity, can be considered as the cause of such effects like contact as well. (Thus, there is no need to infer an activity from such cognition as 'something moves' or as 'he cooks' etc.)

Note : The explanation of verse (24) establishes that the activity cannot be inferred due to the cognition such as 'he cooks'. It argues that the qualities, like the separation and the loosening of the contact of the parts of rice grains, are produced only at times and not always in spite of the fact that all the *kārakas* are present. Therefore, the cognition such as 'he cooks' must be admitted to have been based on the occasional things, namely, the qualities and not on the *kārakas*. Thus, a distinct activity need not be inferred as the basis of such a cognition.

At this juncture, Kriyāvādin (i.e. Bhāvanāvādin) puts forth another of his arguments that the activity should be established as the cause of such qualities since the same qualities must be explained as produced from such an activity; and otherwise (i.e. if the qualities are produced from the presence of mere *kārakas* alone, then) the same would have an occasion to be produced always during the presence of the *kārakas*.

However, the explanation refutes such an argument as well. It states that suppose the activity is inferred on the ground that the qualities are not produced by the *kārakas* and also on the ground that they need an activity to produce them, then the activity would need, further, another activity to produce itself, since the same too is never produced by the *kārakas* alone. Thus, there occurs an occasion for infinite regression of activities. Also, it refutes the Kriyāvādin's argument that suppose the activity is not accepted as the cause of the qualities, then the same would have to be produced at the mere presence of the *kārakas*. It states that the contact of the fire with the parts of rice grains, which is the actual cause of the loosening of the contact of the rice grains, is gradual, and therefore, the qualities need not be produced suddenly always due to the presence of the *kārakas*.

Lastly, the explanation refutes the Bhāvanāvādin's argument that the activity can be accepted as the cause of the contact of the fire with the grains, sicne otherwise the gradual production of the same cannot be explained. According to the explanaiton, since the Kriyāvādin accepts an effort *(prayatna)* as the cause of the activity, the same (effort) can be considered as the cause of the effcts such as 'contact', 'separation' etc. as well. Now, since all the three arguments for establishing the activity are untenable, the activity cannot be established.

Translation (P.67)

Establishment of Niyogavādin's theory

Thus, as explained, there exists no activity which is distinct from the action of offering (*yāga*); and therefore -

Verse 25

The sense 'one shall accomplish the heaven by means of the offering through the activity,' (*yāgena svargam bhāvayet*) is merely an unreal assumption of the explanation of the statement 'he who desires heaven shall offer' *(svargakāamo yajeta*). And the actual sense, understood in such statements, is the compulsory duty (*niyoga*) of the offering which is imposed for the person desirous of heaven.

Note : The verse 25 establishes the Niyogavādin's theory that only the compulsory duty' (*niyoga*) is the sense understood by the verbs (*yajeta* etc.) by refuting the existence of a separate activity. It states that, since there exists no distinct activity as such, the explanation of the sense such as 'one should accomplish the heaven by means of the offering through the activity', wherein the activity has the heaven as its object and offering as its means, is mere assumption.

Translation (P.67)

Explanation of verse (25) that only compulsory duty and not the activity is the sense of '*svargakāmo yajeta*'

XXV.1. Only in the event of the existence of an activity, distinct from actions, the action such as offering (*yāga*) could be explained as the instrument with respect to such an activity. Then, since an activity has syntactical expectancy for a grammatical object, the desired heaven, which actually functions as the qualifier of the person (in the phrase '*svargakāmaḥ*'), can be ascertained to be the object in the syntactical expectancy for the object; and such an ascertainment could be made possible owing to the semantical competency of the heaven to be the object of the activity. However, in the event of the non-existence of an activity, distinct from the action of offering etc., the given analysis of the sentence-meaning, namely, 'one should achieve the heaven by means of offering through the activity', (wherein the activity is perceived distinctly from the action of offering), will have to be concluded as caused by the mere conceptualization, i.e. figment of imagination, so that the dull witted people can easily be deceived. Thus, it should be accepted that the statement 'he who desires heaven shall offer' (*svargakāmo yajeta*) enjoins merely the compulsory duty of a particular person (who is desirous of heaven) towards the offering.

Translation (P.70-71)

Untenability of '*yāgena svargam bhāvayet*' as *vākyārtha*

XXV.2. Also, the effect (i.e. the object or goal) such as heaven can be explained to be accomplished by itself (without any means) or through some menas other than the offering, when the offering is actually performed. Or, as an alternative, it may be suggested that such an effect like heaven is never accomplished at all. Nevertheless, it is not tenable to accept that the meaning such as 'one shall accomplish the heaven by means of the offering through the activity' (*yāgena svargam bhāvayet*) is conveyed by the statement 'he who desires heaven shall offer' (*svargakāmo yajeta*).

Translation

Argument of Bhāvanāvādin that *'svargakāmaḥ'* is not the qualifier

XXV.3. The phrase 'he who desires heaven' (*svargakāmaḥ*), in the statement 'he who desires heaven shall offer; (*'svargakāmo yajeta'*), cannot be considered as the qualifier of the person at all. For, none of the three established purposes of a qualifier, namely, i) the avoidance of non-application (*ayoga vyavaccheda*), ii) avoidance of application with something else (*anyayoga vyavaccheda*), and iii) avoidance of complete non-application (*atyantāyoga vyavaccheda*) can be distinguished, i.e. accomplished.

Also, since there exists no generic property like "the state of being the one who desires heaven" (*svarga-kāmatva*), the phrase 'he who desires heaven' (*svargakāmaḥ*) cannot be considered to be syntactically or semantically connected with the person through the generic property.

Translation (P.71-72)

Reply :

XXV.4. In that case (i.e. when *'svargakāmaḥ'* cannot qualify the person), the heaven cannot be claimed to be something that is to be accomplished by means of the offering through the activity as well. For, in the statement *'svargakāmo yajeta'*, the heaven is not stated (indicated) in that way, i.e. as the object to be accomplished with an accusative ending.

Also, it cannot be held that the heaven is related to the activity as the object to be accomplished due to its inherent competency. For, only the heaven, which functions as the qualifier of the person, is to be accepted as syntactico-semantically related to the activity as something to be accomplished indirectly by implication, and hence the same lacks the competency.

Again, the qualifying status for the desire for the heaven occurring in the person is not contradictory to the other, i.e. to the Niyogavādin, who postulates compulsory duty towards the offering for the person.

Note : The explanation gives a detailed account of the advantages and disadvantages of the theories of both Bhāvanāvādin and Niyogaavādin before establishing Niyogavādin's theory. First of all, the explanation states that, since no activity can be established apart from the actions and effects, the analysis of the sense of the statement '*svargakāmo yajeta*' as 'one should accomplish the heaven by means of offering through the activity' (*yāgena svargam bhāvayet*) is untenable. (In such an analysis, the heaven is construed as the object to be accomplished through the activity; and the verbal root-meaning, action of offering (*yāga*), is construed as the means of the activity). Therefore, the contention of Bhāvanāvādin that the heaven, despite being a qualifier to the person, should be perceived as the object to be accomplished through the activity due to the syntactico-semantical expectancy of the activity for an object stands refuted. Thus, the Niyogavādin establishes his theory that, in statements like '*svargakāamo yajeta*', the compulsory duty (*niyoga*) towards the undertaking of the offering (*yāga*) is assigned for the person, who is qualified by the desire for acccomplishing the heaven.

At this juncture, the explanation refutes Bhāvanāvādin's argument that unless the heaven is considered as the object to be accomplished through the activity, the accomplishability of the heaven, due to the lack of desire to accomplish the same, becomes untenable. It states that the accomplishability of the heaven can be explained by itself without any cause or by some other unknown cause (by apūrva or the force of the assigning of the compulsory duty ?). Also, if without the cause, the accomplishment of the heaven is contradictory and the cause cannot be traced beyond the activity, then, the Niyogavādin holds that, the heaven need not be accepted as the object accomplished at all; and therefore, by all means such an analysis of the sense, namely, "one should accomplish the heaven by offering through the activity" is wrong.

Now, the explanation points out Bhāvanāvādin's argument that the desire for the accomplishment of the heaven (*svargakāmatva*) cannot be considered to be the qualifier of the person. According to the Bhāvanāvādin, the qualifiers are meant to distinguish (*vyavaccheda*) the qualificand. And the distinction is due to either : i) avoidance of non-application, (*ayogavyavaccheda*), or ii) avoidance of complete non-application (*atyantāyogavyavaccheda*) or iii) avoidance of application with something else (*anyayogavyavaccheda*).

Here, avoidance of the non-application means the heaven is to be desired and not 'not to be desired;' avoidance of complete non-application means the heaven is to be desired by all means and not 'not to be desired by any means,' and avoidiance of application with others means only heaven is to be desired and not anything else. However, none of the three above avoidances are possible here. Avoidance of non-application is untenable since no individual, who is always desiring heaven can be traced; avoidance of complete non-application is untenable since no individual, who is never desiring heaven can ever be traced; avoidance of application with other things is untenable since no individual, who is not desiring anything else (like food etc.) can be traced.

Finally, the explanation provides the reply of the Niyogavādin, who considers the (desire for the) heaven to be the qualifier of the person. According to the Niyogavādin, the accomplishability of the heaven, accepted by Bhāvanāvādin, is also equally untenable. He states that since the 'heaven' (*svarga*) is not used with an accusative ending, that can denote the accomplishability, such accomplishability can not be perceived. Also, Niyogavādin points out that the heaven cannot be perceived *to* have the accomplishability due to its inherent competency to function as the object either. Only (the desire for) the heaven, that qualifies the person, can be accepted to have the relation with the activity; and therefore, unless the same (desire for the) heaven is accepted to have the qualifying status, the accomplishability would not be tenable. However, since Bhāvanāvādin does not accept (the desire for) the heaven to be the qualifier, the accomplishability of the heaven is untenable.

Translation : (P.72)

Observation of Bhāvanāvādin that even Niyogavādin cannot consider '*svargakāmaḥ*' as the qualifier

XXV.5. You (Niyogavādin) cannot consider (the desire for) the heaven as the qualifier of the person. For, suppose the (desire for the) heaven is viewed to be the qualifier of the person, then the same heaven would have an occasion to be considered as either an effect or a cause. (However, when the same heaven is considered to be the effect, your own theory gets contradicted, since you have never accepted the eventuality of considering the heaven as an effect). Also, suppose the desire for the heaven is considered to be the cause, then the same desire for the heaven would have to be construed either as combined, or as non-combbined, i.e. separate, qualifier *(upasamhāra anupasamhāra)* with the rest of the sentence. However, in the case of the construction of the phrase 'one who desires the heaven' (*svargakāmaḥ*) as a combined qualifier, the phrase 'for ones entire life' (*yāvajjīvam*) would become redundant in the combined construction of the statement 'one who desires the heaven shall make Agnihotra offerings for one's entire life' (*yāvajjīvam agnihotram juhuyāt svargakāmaḥ*) (since the sense of living is already conveyed through the phrase 'he who desires the heaven' *svargakāmaḥ*). On the other hand, in the case of the construction of the phrase' one who desires the heaven' *svargakāmaḥ*) as a separate qualifier, the same would become redundant (since the phrase 'for one's entire life' (*yāvajjīvam*) would have conveyed the sense of the person who desires heaven as well).

Translation (P.73)

Refutation

XXV.6. The observation of Bhāvanāvādin that the (desire for the) heaven cannot be construed as the cause of offering, holds good only in so far as the daily or obligatory duties *(nitya karma)* are concerned; however, the same (observation) cannot hold good as far as the duties done with a motif, i.e. optional duties (*kāmya* or *anitya karmas*), are concerned. (For, in such cases, the question of construing the phrase 'one who desires heaven' (*svargakāmaḥ*) as a combined or a non-combinned qualifier with the phrase 'for one's entire life' (*yāvajjīvam*) does not arise, and therefore, redundancy cannot be imposed).

Also, it should be noted that just because redundancy would occur for the phrase 'one who desires heaven' (*svargakāmaḥ*) in construing the same phrase 'one who desires heaven' as a non combined, i.e. separate qualifier, a non-meaning (such as the heaven being the effect to be accomplished by means of offering) cannot be comprehended by the phrase 'one who desires heaven' (*svargakāmaḥ*).

Moreover in spite of the fact that the statement 'one who desires heaven shall make Agnihotra offerings for one's life' (*yāvajjīvam...'*) can prescribe the performance of the Agnihotra rite for everyone, another statement such as *'agnihotram juhuyāt svargakāmaḥ'* is made for teaching the performance of the Agnihotra rite again. And, since the phrase 'one who desires heaven' is used in such statements again, the same phrase should not be considered meaningless. Thus, it is certainly possible to explain the meaningfulness (non-redundancy) of the phrase 'one who desires heaven' (*svargakāmaḥ*).

Note : Bhāvanāvādin makes an observation regarding the qualifying status of *'svargakāmaḥ'* as follows : The Niyogavādin cannot consider that (desire for) the heaven is a qualifier. He states that when the (desire for) the heaven is accepted to be a qualifier, the same, i.e. heaven, would need to be considered as either an effect or a cause, since the qualifiers are either effects or a cause. For instance, the qualifier, namely, health, is an effect in the statement 'he who desires health should eat limitedly' (*ārogyakāmo mitam aśnīyāt*) and the qualifier, namely, 'burning' is the cause in the statement 'he who burns the house withers away'. However, since heaven is not acceptable for Niyogavādin as an effect accomplished through the activity, the same cannot be construed as the qualifier from the view point of an effect. On the other hand, when the qualifier 'the desire for the heaven' is regarded as a cause, the phrase 'one who desires heaven', must be construed as either a combined or a non-bombined, i.e. separate, qualifier. However, neither of the two options are tenable. For, suppose 'one who desires the heaven' (*svargakāmaḥ*) is construed as a combined qualifier, then the phrase 'for one's entire life' (*yāvajjīvam*) in the statement *'yāvajjīvam agnihotram juhoti'*, which is read combinedly with *'svargakāmaḥ'*, becomes redundant since the idea of offering Agnihotra rites 'for one's entire life' (*yāvajjīvam*) can be obtained as a qualification of the person through the phrase 'one who desires the heaven' (*svargakāmaḥ*) by implication. On the other hand, suppose the phrase 'one who desires the heaven' is construed as a non-combined, i.e. separate, qualifier, then the same phrase would become redundant since the idea of 'the desire for the heaven' can be obtained through the general statement 'for one's entire life' (*yāvajjīvam*) by implication (i.e. a heaven-desiring individual can be covered by the general category of living beings). Thus, the phrase 'one who desires heaven' cannot be construed as the qualifier from the view point of cause either.

However, the Niyogavādin refutes such an observation. He states that the qualifier 'one who desires the heaven', is redundant only in the case of the statements prescribing the obligatory rites such as *Agniṣṭoma,* and not in the case of the statements prescribing the optional rites such as *Jyotiṣṭoma* etc. In the case of the statements prescribing the optional rites, such as *'svargakāmo jyotiṣṭomena yajeta'*, the question of combining or non-combining the qualifier 'one who desires the heaven' with the phrase 'for one's entire life' does not arise. This is so because, such optional rites are never performed for one's entire life; and hence, the phrase 'for one's entire life' (*'yāvajjīvam'*) is never used in such cases; thus the phrase *'svaryakāmaḥ'* cannot be claimed to be redudant. Also, Niyogavādin states that despite the phrase *'svargakāmaḥ'* becoming redundant in the case of the statements prescribing the obligatory rites, the same phrase *'svargakāmaḥ'* cannot be analysed as referring to the object 'heaven' which is to be accomplished, since a wrong idea cannot be accepted as a meaning under any circumstances. Finally, Niyogavādin explains that even the so-called redundancy can be avoided. According to him, the very fact that the phrase *'svargakāmaḥ'* is used again in addition to the phrase *'yāvajjīvam'* suggests that the same phrase is meaningful. And the meaning suggested in such a case is that the person desirous of heaven must perform the Agnihotra again and again for one's entire life. Thus, the Niyogavādin establishes that the assumption of a separate activity, in addition to the qualities etc., to explain the sense of the statement *'svargakāmo yajeta'* as 'one must accomplish the heaven by means of the offering through the activity' (*yāgena svargam bhāvayet*), is untenable.

Translation (P.74)

Citing of Bādari in support of the position that activity, distinct from action, cannot be accepted

Verse 26

The blessed sage Bādari, knowing the fact that the activity, as distinct from the action (or quality), cannot be justified, has ruled as follows : The things such as the effects 'heaven' etc., which are distinct from the refining (*samskāra*) such as pounding, quality (*guṇa*) such as tawniness and substances (*dravya*) such as rice grains, cannot be accepted to have the subsidiaryness (subordination) to the action of offering, etc.

Note : Niyogavādin cites Bādari for supporting his theory that no activity, distinct from the effects (qualities) and actions (cooking etc.) can be accepted as the meaning of the conjugational endings. According to Bādari, only things, namely, substance (*dravya*) like rice grains, quality (*guṇa*) like tawniness of a calf and refining (*samskāra*) like pounding of paddy etc. function as the subordinates (*śeṣa*) to the action of offering an oblation, or to the action of performing a sacrifice etc. However, the trio, namely, the action of offering (*yāga*), the effect (*phala*) and the person (*puruṣa*), are not subordinates to each other, i.e. the action of offering is not subordinate to the effect, the effect is not subordinate to the person, and the person is not subordinate to the object due to the difference in the ability of the effect etc. Thus, the offering (*yāga*) cannot be construed as an instrument *kāraka* with respect to the so – called activity.

Translation (P.74-75)

Explanation of the verse (26) that only *dravya*, *guṇa* and *saṁskāra* are subsidiaries

XXVI.1.

Substance (material) (such as rice grains) and quality (such as tawniness) are understood to have subordinate status with respect to the action of offering (or buying). They are understood so on account of their inherent capacity, i.e. ability (to bring about such actions), and also on account of the fact that they are used with the *kāraka* (i.e. instrumental) case endings in such statements as *vrīhibhir yajeta* or *aruṇayā gavā somam krīṇāti*. etc. Also, the refinining such as cleaning of cups and pounding (of rice grains) can be found to have subordinate status with respect to the action of offering. Such a refining is syntactically or semantically related to the object (such as the cups or rice grains) through either accusative word (in '*graham sammārṣṭi*' and '*vrīhīn avahanti*') or through their inherent capacity. And in such cases, once the refinement obtains the subordinate status to the object, it can obtain the same (subordinate status) to the action of offering etc. through the object (i.e. cups, rice grains etc.)

Translation (P.76)

Explanation that others, excepting *dravya, guṇa* and *karma* are not subordinates

XXVI.2. The action of offering (*yāga*) (which is considered to be a subordinate to the effect 'heaven' by Bhāvanāvādin) is, by its own nature, devoid of any object (i.e. is intransitive); and hence cannot have heaven as its object. Also, suppose the same (offering) is held to have an object (i.e. to be transitive), then too, it can have only the deity (such as Indra) as its object (i.e. as recipient). Thus, either way, how could the action of offering be related to the heaven (i.e. the offering cannot be subordinate to the effect 'heaven'). (In the same way, effect (*phala*) and also person (*puruṣa*) are also untenable for being considered as the subordinates). Moreover, even supposing that the effort (activity) exists, then too, the action of offering can have a relation with the heaven, only indirectly through the activity, since the same heaven is the object to be produced through the activity. Thus, considering that such an activity does not exist, apart from the root-meanings such as the action of offering etc., the blessed sage Bādari has held that the subordinate status rests only in the material, the quality and also the refinement.

This concludes the section on the prima facie view (Pūrvapakṣa).

Note : Niyogavādin (Pūrvapakṣin) quotes Bādari's view to establish his theory that no activity distinct from the action and the effect can be accepted. Bādari holds that substance such as rice grains and quality such as tawniness are considered to be subordinates to the action of offering (an oblation) and buying a calf respectively. And they are considered so on account of their nature of being accomplished (*siddhatva*), which is an inherent capacity to accomplish the action, and also on account of their nature of possessing *kāraka*, i.e. instrumental, case endings in *'vrīhibhir yajeta'* and *'aruṇayā gavā-somam krīṇāti'* which refer to the status of being the most efficient means of the *dravya*, i.e. rice grains, and *guṇa*, i.e. tawniness, respectively.

Also, he holds that the refinement (*samskāra*) (such as the cleansing of the *camasa* cups and the pounding of the rice grains etc.) is considered as subordinate to the action of offering. And it is considered so on the basis of its relation with the objects, i.e. cups and the rice grains, respectively. For instance, the refinement is considered to be subordinate to the offering on account of its natural ability, i.e. capacity, to take an object such as *camasa* cups or rice grains. Also, the refinement is considered to be subordinate to the action of offering on account of its possessing *kāraka*, i.e. accusative case endings in *'graham sammārṣṭi'* and *'vrīhīn avahanti* expressing their *kāraka* relationship of the objecthood. Thus, the refinement becomes subordinate to the action of offering indirectly through the objects to which it is related.

However, things, apart from *'dravya'*, *'guṇa'*, and *'samskāra'*, namely, the trio of *'yāga'*, *'phala'* and *'puruṣa'*, cannot be considered to be the subordinates to anything. This is so because, the offering (*yāga*) is not expressed to be connected with the effect, namely, the heaven by any word. Also, the same, being intransitive (offering is merely the mental resolve to abandon the oblation), cannot inherently have any object. Similarly, the effect and person cannot be connected with any thing and therefore, are not subordinates to anything.

Moreover, supposing that the effort (activity) does exist, then too the heaven can be considered to be what is to be accomplished (*bhāvya*) through the activity due to its syntactico-semantical expectancy for an effect. Consequently, the action of offering must be connected with the effect 'heaven' through only the activity. Thus, the action cannot be considered to be a subordinate to the effect 'heaven' directly. However, since the activity does not exist as a distinct entity from the actions, Bādari has stated that the subordinate status rests only in the trio of *dravya, guṇa* and *samskāra*. And, since the activity cannot be established to be the meaning of the conjugational endings, in finite verbs, as distinct from root-meanings (actions), the assumption 'one should accomplish the heaven by means of offering through the activity' (wherein the offering is construed as a means subordinate to the activity) *'yāgena svargam bhvayet'* as an explanation of 'he who desires heaven shall offer' *'svargakāmo yajeta'* is untenable. This is the essence of the Pūrvapakṣin's theory.

SIDDHĀNTA

Translation : (P.77)

Statement of reasons for accepting the accomplishing (productive) activity

Here, we state the following reasons for accepting a distinct accomplishing (productive) activity.

Verse 27

A distinct sense of accomplishing (productive) activity (*bhāvanā*) must be inferred in the conjugational endings in the case of the verbs *'pacati'* (he cooks) etc. due to the fact that there exists grammatical agreement (i.e. syntactico-semantical coreferentiality) between the verbs *'pacati'* etc., on the one hand, and the verb *'karoti'*, on the other. Also, a distinct activity must be assumed, since the assumption of polysemy is unjustified for the verb *'karoti'*.

Note : Verse 27 marks the beginning of the *Siddhānta*. At the very outset, Siddhāntin states his reason for assuming a distinct sense of accomplishing (productive) activity apart from the root-meanings (*dhātvartha*). According to him, the verb 'karoti' (he does or makes) has grammatical agreement, i.e. syntactico-semantical coreferentiality, with the verbs *'pacati'* (he cooks) etc. in question and answer series like *'kim karoti'* (what does he do) - *'pacati'* (he cooks) etc. And this fact must be taken as an evidence for accepting the verbal (conjugational) endings as having a reference to the activity as distinct from the verbal root-meanings, namely, actions and effects. Also, since polysemy, i.e. reference to different meanings in different usages, is not justified, the verb *'karoti'*, which is found, in isolation, to be expressing the productive activity, must also be held as expressing the same productive activity in usages along with the verbs *'pacati'* (he cooks) etc. as well. And once the identity of meanings is accepted for the verb *'karoti'*, in different usages, the conjugational endings *'ti'* etc. in *'pacati'* etc. would automatically get established as referring to the general sense of productive activity, since otherwise semantical coreferentiality of *'pacati'* with *'karoti'* cannot be explained.

Translation (P.79-80)

Explanation of the verse (27) that the productive activity must be accepted

XXVII.1. In statements such as 'he makes a pot' (*ghaṭam karoti*) etc., the verb *'karoti'* (he makes) refers to the productive activity (*bhāvanā*), which is the object of expressions like 'he produces' (*janayati*), 'he causes' (*utpāduyati*) etc. Such a verb as *'karoti'*, which is used in grammatical agreement (i.e. in semantical co-referentiality) with the verbs *'pacati'* (he cooks), cannot be accepted to have a denotation in the sense different from the activity (*bhāvanā*), i.e. in the sense of the root-meanings (actions). For, suppose the verb *'karoti'* is accepted to have several denotations in several root-meanings, then it would amount to accepting the same *'karoti'* as having no certain denotation in any particular meaning. Consequently, due to the untenability of the ascertainment of any particular meaning to be denoted, the established convention regarding the proper usage of the verb *'karoti'* in the sense such as the activity would itself become untenable. Also, when the proper usage of the verb *'karoti'* is tenable in accordance with the potentiality to denote some meaning, (i.e. the activity), ascertained already in some particular instances, the assumption of another potentiality to denote some other meaning (i.e. the actions in general) is totally unjustified.

Also, (suppose we assume another potentiality to denote the actions in general, then) the earlier recognized potentiality of the verb *'karoti'* to denote the activity (*bhāvanā*) would be contradicted; and again it would amount to assuming yet another potentiality that has not been already recognized.

Moreover, since only the meaning, which has already been recognized as the meaning of a word in an earlier usage, is accepted as the meaning in the subsequent usages as well, the verb *'karoti'* cannot be assumed to have another potentiality to denote some other meaning, i.e. the sense of the actions in general.

Translation : (P.81)

'karoti', in agreement with 'pacati', denotes bhāvanā :

XXVII.2. Also, the verb *'karoti'* conveys the sense of the productive (accomplishing) activity (*utpādanā*) everywhere. We understand the sense of the productive (accomplishing) activity from the expressions such as 'what does he do ?, - he cooks' (*kim karoti-pacati*) (wherein the word *'karoti'* is used in agreement with *'pacati'*) like we do it from the expressions such as 'he makes a pot' (*ghaṭam karoti*).

Now, since the verbal (conjugational) endings (*ākhyātapada*) such as *'ti'* in *'pacati'* ('he cooks') etc. are found to have been used in the language in grammatical agreement (i.e. in semantical coreferentiality) with the verb *'karoti'* (he) cooks, which refers to the activity everywhere, the same (verbal endings such as *'ti'* in *'pacati'* etc,) would be inferred to have the denotion in the sense of the particular activity of producing the action of cooking etc.

Note : The explanation of the verse 27 establishes the activity as the meaning of the conjugational endings. It states, at the outset, that the verb *'karoti'* expresses the productive activity, in *'ghaṭam karoti'* (he makes a pot) etc., which is usually expressed by the explanatory term *'janana'*, *'utpādana'* etc. In such cases, the pot, being something to be accomplished, needs an activity that can accomplish, i.e. produce, it. And, since the verb *'karoti'* is established as expressing the productive activity in *'ghaṭam karoti'* etc., the same must be accepted as expressing the productive activity in other cases such as *'kim karoti'* - *pacati* (what does he do ? - he cooks) etc. as well. Otherwise, since the verb *'karoti'* becomes polysemous by expressing the root-meanings (such as actions and effects) in general, the proper usage of the same verb *'karoti'* with a fixed denotation in a fixed sense would become untenable.

At this juncture, an argument is made as follows : That the words such as *'akṣa'*, despite being polysemous, have been accepted as the proper means of communication of the fixed sense of eye etc. due to the possibility of determination of the sense by the context etc. Similarly, the verb *'karoti'*, despite being polysemous, can be accepted as the proper means of communication of the sense of the activity due to the possibility of the determination of the sense of the activity. However, the explanation refutes the agrument on the ground that only the word *'akṣa'* etc., which cannot be explained with a single denotation, should be accepted as polysemous; and the words *'karoti'* etc., which can be explained with the recognition of a single denotation, should not be accepted as polysemous; and therefore, the words *'karoti'* etc., which can be explained with the recognition of a single denotation in all cases of usages, are not justified in being considered as polysemous. This is so because, no valid reason could be ascertained as to why different denotations must be accepted for the verb *'karoti'* in different usages as single denotation would suffice in all cases of usages. Also, when a new potentiality for denoting a different sense is assumed for the verb, the potentiality recognized earlier for the same verb would become contradicated; and thus, an unnecessary potentiality for the denotation of another sense would be established. Moreover, since, in different usages of a word, the sense recognized as the word-meaning in the earlier usages, is usually cognized, the assumption of the new potentiality for the denotation of another sense would necessarily contradict the earlier potentiality. In the case of the usage *'kim karoti'* too, only the productive activity, which is cognized as the meaning in *'ghaṭam karoti'*, is cognized. Thus, conjugational endings such as *'ti'* in *'kim karoti - pacati'* etc. must be accepted as expressing the sense of the particular activity of producing the root-meanings, i.e. the action of cooking etc., since the same is found used in agreement with *'kaorti'*.

Translation (P.82-84)

Argument that conjugational endings cannot denote particular activity

XXVII.3. It is indeed true that affixes (*pratyaya*) such as verbal endings, due to their non-distinct nature everywhere, are not sufficient enough for (i.e. are not competent to produce) the knowledge of the sense of the particular activity of producing the cooking etc. (*bhāvanāviśeṣa*). However, the finished words, i.e., the words associated with their endings such as *pacati*, which are distinct due to the difference between the bases, are competent to produce the knowledge of the sense of the particular activity of producing the cooking etc. Consequently, the finished words such as *'pacati'* etc. can produce the knowledge wherein the sense of the activity in particular, expressed by the verbal ending (*ti*), may be perceived to be the chief qualificand, i.e. nucleus of semantical relations by being connected with the actions, such as cooking expressed by the verbal bases such as (*'pac'*).

Translation (P.82-84)

Maṇḍana's justification that conjugational endings can refer to the particular activity

Also, the conjugational endings, being common to all the verbal forms, can produce only the cognition of the activity in general. The same endings are not independent in denoting their sense like the finished words. However, the same conjugational endings such as *'ti'*, while referring to the sense of the activity, as haiving syntactico-semantical expectancy for the verbal base-meanings (such as the action of cooking), can convey the sense of the activity particularized as the activity conducive to the cooking etc. by sacrificing their own meanings (of general activity) due to the fixed order of precedence of the bases and their own succession.

It has been established, now, by all means, that the finished words like *'pacati'* etc. are used in the sense of the particular activity (conducive to the cooking etc.). Therefore, the finished words, such as *'pacati'* etc. have a denotation in the activity which, although intrinsically distinct, i.e. particularized, needs the support of verbal base meanings (i.e. syntactico-semantical relation with different actions) to manifest the distinction clearly. Thus, the reference (by the conjugational endings etc.) to the activity (particularized as the one being conducive to the action of cooking etc.) is not contradictory in the instance of *'pacati'* etc.

Note : Now, the Siddhāntin refutes the Pūrvapakṣin's argument that since the conjugational endings such as 'ti' etc. are identical in all instances, the same cannot have denotations in different particular activities. According to the Siddhāntin, although the conjugational endings are identical in all cases, and therefore, are not competent to denote the particular activities by themselves, the finished words such as *'pacati'*, etc,. which differ due to the difference between verbal bases, are certainly competent to denote the same particular activities. Since the finished words are associated with the variety of verbal bases and the same (bases) have different denotations in different verbal actions, the finished words can denote the particular activities as conductive to the different actions such as cooking etc.

Also, according to the Siddhāntin, the conjugational endings can be accepted to have different denotations in the particular activities dueto their fixed order of occurrence. That is to say that the conjugational endings and the verbal bases have a fixed order as far as their occurrence is concerned. The verbal bases occur prior to the endings, whereas the endings occur after the bases. The fixed order of occurrence cannot be explained unless the conjugational endings are held to denote particular activities as conducive to the different verbal base-meanings, i.e. actions. Words like *'gām'*, which have no fixed order of occurrence in *'gām ānaya'* or *'ānaya gām'*, etc., can be accepted to have a denotation in the generality of the cowness. However, the endings, which have a fixed order of occurrence after the bases, must be explained as conveying their sense of the activities particularized as conducive to the verbal base-meanings, i.e. actions. Thus, the conjugational endings, despite having a denotation in the activity in general, produce the cognition of the particular activities due to their nature order of occurrence and sacrifice their own meaning in accordance with the verbal root-meanings.

The activity is intrinsically distinct, i.e. particularized as individual activity. Nevertheless, the same needs the verbal root-meanings (actions and effects) to manifest, i.e. to bring out, its distinctive nature. Therefore, the verbal root-meanings function as the *upādhis* that manifest the distinctive nature of the activity. And thus, helped by the association of the verbal root-meanings, the activity manifests itself as distinct and becomes conducive to the different actions and effects. Also, since the finished word has its denotatin only in the particular activity, the reference of the conjugational endings to the particular activity, conducive to the action of cooking etc., is not contradictory in the case of *'kim karoti - pacati'* etc.

Translation : (P.85-86)

***'karoti'* and *'ti'* can have** *sāmānādhikaraṇya*

XXVII.4. Now it may be doubted as follows :

Verbal endings such as *'ti'* are intended to have the denotation in the sense of the activity in general; and therefore, how could it be that the two phrases such as *'karoti'* and *'ti'* in 'what does he make' (*kim karoti*) and 'he makes cooking' (*pacati*), both of which have the potentiality to denote the activity in general, are used in grammatical agreement with (i.e. in semantic coreferentiality to) each other. However, we shall make the following statement (in justification of such usages).

Verse 28

(It is not correct to state that the two phrases, which have potentiality to denote the activity in general, cannot have grammatical agreement). The grammatical agreement (lit. non-distinct statement) is found even in the case of words expressing the generality and also the generality qualified by the distinction. For instance, the statements such as 'which king is coming' (*ko rājā yāti*) - 'King of the *Pāñcālas* is coming' (*pāñcālarājaḥ*) (which express the generality of king and also the generality of king as qualified by the royalty of Pāñcālas') have grammatical agreement.

Note : In spite of the fact that the conjugational endings can convey the particular activity, the same are actually found to have a denotation in the general activity alone. Also, the verb *'karoti'* is found to have a denotation in only the general activity. Therefore, pūrvapakṣin, argues that, since both the conjugational endings such as *'ti'* and the verb *'karoti'* are found to denote only the general activity as such, the grammatical agreement, i.e. syntactico-semantical coreferentiality, between the two phrases, namely, *'karoti'* and 'ti' of *'pacati'* in usages such as *'kim karoti - pacati'*, becomes untenable. And, to avoid such an untenability, one must accept the view that the verb *'karoti'* is expressive of the general activity and that the verbs such as *'pacati'* are expressive of the particular activity leading to the actions such as cooking etc.

However, Siddhāntin refutes such an argument by verse 28. The grammatical agreement between the words such as *'taruḥ'* and *'vṛkṣaḥ'*, expressing merely the general notion like the treeness may be untenable; however, the grammatical agreement between the phrases such as *'karoti'* and *'ti'* of *'pacati'*, expressing the general activity and also the general activity qualified by a particular *upādhi* such as 'conduciveness to the cooking', is not untenable, since one phrase expresses the general notion of the activity, and the other expresses the same as qualified by the *upādhi*. This is explained by the fact that the two phrases such as 'k*o rājā yāti'* (which king is coming) *'pāñcālarājaḥ'* (king of the Pāñcālas is coming), which express the general notion of king and also the king as qualified by the royality of Pāñcālas, are used in grammatical agreement. Thus, the grammatical agreement between the phrases *'karoti'* and *ti* of *'pacati'* expressing the general notion is not untenable since one of them expresses the general activity and the other expresses the same as qualified by the conduciveness to the cooking. And so, the verbs such as *'pacati'* need not be held to be expressing the particular activity leading to cooking.

Translation : (P.87)

Explanation of verse (28) that words expressing the general notion can agree with each other

XXVIII.1. The statements, i.e. the words of answer, which have general notions delimited by the particularities as their objects of reference, are observed to have been used in grammatical agreement with the words of question which express the general notion without any delimitations, i.e. qualifications. For instance, the statement, i.e. the word of answer such as 'the king of the Pāñcālas *(Pāñcālarājaḥ)* is observed to have the grammatical agreement with the word of question such as 'which king is coming' *(ko rājā yāti)*.

Translation (P.87-88)

Words expressing general notion must be mentioned in the answer

Also, it is quite justified that the word *(rājan)*, which expresses the sense of the king in general *(sāmānya)*, is specifically mentioned, i.e. is included, in the statement of answer as well. Otherwise (i.e. suppose the word *'pāñcāla'*, which refers to the sense of the king particularized as the royality of the *Pāñcāla* regions, alone is included and the word *'rājan'* expressing the general sense of the king is not included then) such a word, i.e. *'rājan'*, occurring in the question, would have been required to be implied so that the general sense of the king could have been qualified by the royalty of the Pāñcālas.

Especially, the mentioning, i.e. the inclusion of the word, referring to the activity in general, is justified in the statement of answer such as *'pacati'*, since the sense of the activity is one which has no particular word recognized as indicating its distinct characteristics; and therefore, has its clearly distinctive nature (characteristics) manifested due to only the snytactico-semantical association with some other sense, i.e. verbal action. Consequently, in the establishment of the sense of the activity, particularised as conducive to the action of cooking etc., there occurs neither the fault of establishing (i.e. denoting) the sense that has already been established *(siddhasādhana)*, nor the fault of establishing the sense contrary to what is to be established *(viparyayasādhana)*, nor the fault of the untenability of any example *(dṛṣṭāntābhāva)*.

Note : The explanation illucidates the point that the grammatical agreement between the statements (words), expressing the general notions, is not untenable; and therefore, the same grammatical agreement between *'karoti'* and *'ti'* of *'pacati'* in the question and answer series *'kim karoti'* - *'pacati'* is justified. Here, the question refers to the general activity as such and the answer refers to the same activity as qualified by the conduciveness to the cooking. The explanation substantiates further this point by illustrating the grammatical agreement between *'rajā'* and *'pāñcālarājaḥ'* in *'ko rājā yāti* - *'pāñcālarājaḥ'*. Here, the word 'rājā' in the question, refers to the general notion of king, whereas the word *'pāñcālarājaḥ'* in the answer refers to the same as qualified by the royalty of Pāñcālas. Nevertheless, the words *pāñcālarājaḥ* and *'rājā'* agree in case number and gender. Thus, similarly, agreement between *'karoti'* and *'ti'* of *'pacati'* is not grammatically untenable.

Now, an objection is raised as follows : That the answer must consist of only the word expressing the particular notion and it must not consist of any word expressing the general notion; for, the general notion is *asiddha;* and also that the person, who questions, has an intention to know only about the particular notion, i.e. the distinctive characteristics. However, this objection is refuted as follows. Supposing the answer does not consist of the word expressing the general notion, and consists of only the word expressing the particular notion, then the answer such as *'pāñcālaḥ'* would require the implying of the word *'rājā'* expressing the general notion of king as otherwise the person belonging to Pāñcālas could not be recognized as a particular type of king. Also, similarly the answer regarding the activity must consist of a word expressing the general notion of activity, since no other word, which expresses the activity as conducive to the cooking, is available; and therefore, the same activity must be understood as particularized due to its association with the verbal root-meanings. Thus, in spite of the fact that, in question and answer series like *'ko vṛkṣaḥ'* - *'śimśapā'*, the answer consists of only the word expressing the particular tree of *śimśapā*, the answer, regarding the activity, must cosnsit of a word (i.e. ti) expressing the activity in general as well.

Now, Siddhāntin concludes that the establishment of the distinct activity, on the basis of the grammatical agreement, does not invovle the difficulty of *siddhasādhana*, since the conjugational ending is newly established to be expressing the activity; also he states that the establishment of the activity does not invovle the difficulty of *viparyayasāadhana* and *dṛṣṭāntābhāva*, since neither the denotation of merely the sense of the verb *'karoti'*, which is contrary to what is to be established, is resorted to; nor the establishment of the activity on the basis of mere inference, which is devoid of any known example, is resorted to.

Translation :

Reply to Pūrvapakṣin's objection that 'karoti' cannot be bhāvanāvacana

Verse 29

It is not correct to state that the usage of the verb *'karoti'* is observed both ways in the sense of the activity (*bhāva*), and also in the absence of the activity (*abhāva*) (due to the absence of an object to be accomplished and also due to the absence of the word expressing the activity). The activity must be accepted as existent, since verbal root-meaning is ultimately recognized as the object to be produced through the activity and also since the *ghañanta* words such as *'pākaḥ'*, expressing the root-meanings, are held to be indicating the same activity.

Note : This verse is a reply to the objection raised by Pūrvapakṣin in verse 3. The objection was that, since *'karoti'* is found used even in *'kim karoti ghaṇṭā' - 'dhvanati'* etc., wherein no object to be accomplished can be traced, the same *'karoti'* need not be accepted as expressing the activity. However, this verse refutes such an objection on the ground that, even in such cases as *'kim karoti ghaṇṭā' - dhvanati'* etc., the root-meaning, i.e. ringing or sounding, is produced (*bhāvya*); and therefore, *'karoti'* needs to express a producing agency, namely, the activity. Also, another objection was that, in *ghañanta* usages such as *'kā kriyā'- 'pākaḥ'* etc., the activity is absent since no word, i.e. conjugational ending etc. that can denote such an activity, is found. However, the verse refutes such an objection on the ground that, in the *ghañanta* usages such as *kā kriyā' 'pākaḥ'* etc. too, the same *ghañanta* words should be held to be indicating the activity, since otherwise the cooking, which is to be produced, cannot be explained as accomplished.

Translation (P.90)

Explanation of the verse (29) that *dhātvartha* is *bhāvya*

XXIX.1. In the instances such as 'bell rings (sounds)' (*ghaṇṭā dhvanati*) the activity, distinct from the action of ringing, is stated (by the Pūrvapakṣin) to be absent due to the absence of any effect (object) to be produced from such an activity. (However, this argument is not tenable.) Every verbal root-meaning produces some effect which does not exist before. And the ringing (sounding) too produces the effects such as happiness, sorrow or awareness. Or otherwise, the action of ringing (sounding) itself would ultimately become the effect to be produced through the activity.

Note : The explanation of verse 29 first points out that the objection of the Pūrvapakṣin that, in intransitive usages such as *'kim karoti ghaṇṭā' - 'dhvanati'*, no perceptible effect such as becoming soft of rice grains etc. is produced; and therefore, the activity, which is supposed to produce such an effect, need not be presumed. However, it refutes such an objection by holding that even the intransitive root-meaning such as ringing (sounding) produces an effect such as happiness, grief or awarness. Supposing the awareness etc. cannot be considered as the effect to be produced due to the lack of speaker's intention for cognizing the same as the meaning, then the explanation suggests that the verbal root-meanings, namely, the ringing, (cooking etc.) must themselves be considered as the effects to be produced through the activity; and therefore, the verb *'karoti'*, in *'kim karoti ghaṇṭā'* etc., is also not used in the absence of the activity.

Translation : (P.90)

Refutation of the objection that *dhātvartha* is only *karaṇa*

XXIX.2. Also, it cannot be argued that the root-meaning (i.e. the action of cooking etc.) *dhātvartha* functions as only the instrument (*karaṇa*) everywhere with respect to the activity; and hence, the action of ringing (sounding) cannot function as the object to be produced with respect to the activity. For, in some instances, where the mere production of the root-meaning, i.e. the action, is intended, (and therefore), no distinct effect is intended to be produced (from the activity), the same root-meaning, 'action', functions as the 'object' (*karman*) to be produced with respect to the activity.

Note : In *'agnihotram juhoti'* (he offers Agnihotra oblations), the root-meaning' 'offering' functions as only the object (*karma)* to be produced with respect to the activity, since no distinct object as such is expected to be produced from the activity; and also, the root-meaning 'offering' cannot be claimed to be the instrument *(karaṇa*) with respect to the production of some effect, since no distinct effect (object), apart from the root-meaning, is to be produced. Similarly, in *'ghaṇṭā dhvanati'* (bell rings), the root meaning 'ringing' functions as the object with respect to the activity, since no distinct effect (object) such as happiness is expected to be produced from the activity; and also, the action of ringing cannot be claimed to be the instrument with respect to the production of the effect (happiness etc.), since no such distinct effect (object) apart from the root-meaning is expected to be produced.

Translation (P.96)

Activity is present in '*kā kriyā-pākaḥ*' etc.

XXIX.3. Also, in *ghañanta* instances like '*kā kriyā*' (what is the action) '*pākaḥ*' (cooking is the action), the activity is very much present. For, 'word-meaning' (*śabdārtha)* is of two types due to the distinction between the heard (i.e. denoted) (*śrauta)* and the indicated (*lakṣyamāṇa*) meanings. And, since the *ghañanta* word 'cooking' (*pākaḥ)* is meant to have an indication in the sense of the activity, particularized as conducive to the cooking, the absence of the same activity cannot be due to the absence of any word referring to such an activity.

Note : Siddhāntin refutes the objection that, since *ghañantas* such as *pākaḥ* etc. do not denote the activity, the same is absent. He states that even in the question and answer series involving *ghañantas* such as 'what is the action' (*kā kriyā)* and 'cooking is the action' (*pākaḥ)* etc., where no words, expressing the activity through denotation, are found, the activity is referred to by the words 'cooking' (*pākaḥ*) etc. through a separate indication assumed in the sense of the activity; for, otherwise, the action of cooking etc. are not possible to be explained as produced from the activity. Hence, the indication must be accepted for the words 'cooking' (*pākaḥ)* etc. Also, since the words are of two types; namely, denotative (*śrauta)* and indicative (*lakṣya)*, no difficulty can be envisaged in accepting the indication for the word '*pākaḥ*' etc. in the sense of the activity. Thus, the words 'cooking' (*pākaḥ)* etc. themselves indicate the sense of the activity; and hence, Pūrvapakṣin's argument that 'the activity is absent in such instances as *ghañanta* usages due to the absence of the words referring to such an activity' is not tenable.

Translation :

Pūrvapakṣin's objection that the activity would become indicated meaning in *tiṅantas* as well

(Suppose, the activity is accepted to be the indicated meaning in the *ghañanta* usages such as '*kā kriyā-pākaḥ*' etc. by assuming an indication in the sense of the activity, then) it can be argued that the activity should be accepted as an indicated meaning in the case of the finite verbs (*tiṅantas*) such as 'he cooks' (*pacati*) etc. as well.

Note : Pūrvapakṣin states now his objection as follows : Suppose, the activity is considered to be an indicated meaning, by assuming an indication for the *ghañanta* words '*pākaḥ*' etc., in it, then the same activity can be considered to be an indicated meaning in the case of the finite verbs such as 'he cooks' (*pacati*) etc. as well. Consequently, the position that "the activity is a meaning to be denoted by the verbal ending '*ti*' due to it's semantical coreferentiality with '*karoti*' cannot be maintained.

Refutation

No, this is not correct. For, -

Verse 30

Who (which person) can deny the distinction between the concepts of 'accomplsihed' (*siddha*) and 'yet to be accomplished' (*sādhya*) arising out of the *ghañanta* usages such as 'cooking' (*pākaḥ*) and *tiṅanta* usages such as 'he cooks' (*pacati*). Also the objecthood (*bhāvyataā*) of the root meanings (action of cooking etc.) cannot be established without their association with the activity which is capable of producing such actions.

Note : Siddhāntin refutes Pūrvapakṣin's objection as follows :

Despite accepting the activity as an indicated meaning in the case of '*ghañanta*' usages such as (*pākaḥ*), the same activity can be considered to be the denoted meaning in the case of the usages of the finite verbs such as 'he cooks' (*pacati*) etc. For, the root-meaning such as the action of cooking is perceived as 'accomplished' (*siddha*) in the case of *ghañanta* usages; whereas, the same root-meaning (the action of cooking) is perceived as 'yet to be accomplished', (*sādhya*) in the case of finite verbs. And such a distinction between the actions can be explained only by accepting a denotation for finite verbs in the activity which can produce such an action.

Translation (P.93)

Explanation of the verse (30) that the activity must be accepted as denoted meaning in the finite verbs

XXX.1. Since you have been asked, you may kindly elaborate on the following point : Does or does not the meaning of the verbal root (*dhātvartha)* such as the action of cooking, differ between the *ghañanta* usages such as 'cooking' (*pākaḥ*) and also the usages of the finite verbs such as 'he cooks' *(pacati*) etc. And also, who could deny the clear, i.e. manifested, distinction between the cognitions produced from such usages. This can be explained as follows : In the case of the usages of finite verbs such as 'he cooks' (*pacati),* the root-meaning (the action of cooking etc.) is perceived (i.e. obtained) as something yet to be accomplished (*bhāvya*). However, in the case of *'ghañanta'* usages, such as 'cooking' (*pākaḥ*), the same is not perceived as of that nature, i.e. as something yet to be accomplished (*bhāvya).* Hence the root-meaning (action of cooking) is perceived as already accomplished (*siddha*). This is so because, the *'ghañ'* affix is enjoined in the sense of the action which is already accomplished; and therefore, only the root-meaning 'action', which is not associated with any *kāraka* relations or accomplishability etc., is stated to be the sense conveyed by such *ghañanta* words by the Nirukta passage such as "Only the root-meaning, which is not qualified (i.e. not associated with any *kārakas)* and is without any attributes (i.e. is not to be accomplished), is called action".

Note : Earlier, Pūrvapakṣin had raised the objection that the activity could not be the denoted meaning of the conjugational endings in the usages of finite verbs since, in *'ghañanta'* usages such as *'pākaḥ'*, the same activity is accepted to be merely an indicated meaning. However, Siddhāntin refutes such an objection by reasoning as follows:

The root-meaning such as the action of cooking is referred to as something already accomplished (*siddha*) in *ghañanta* usages; whereas the same action of cooking is referred to as something yet to be accomplished (*sādhya*) in the usages of finite verbs. The Nirukta passage, namely, "Only the root-meaning, which is not qualified (i.e. not associated with any *kārakas*) and is without any attributes (i.e. not to be accomplished'), is called action" establishes that in *ghañanta* usages such as *'pākaḥ'* etc. only the action, which is already accomplished, is the root-meaning; whereas, in the usage of finite verbal forms, the action, which is yet to be accomplished, is the root-meaning. Thus, in order to explain the accomplishment of the action of cooking etc., the conjugational ending *'ti'* etc. must be assumed to denote the activity in finite verbs.

Translation (P.94)

Siddhāntin's conclusion that the activity is the denoted meaning

XXX.2. Now, since the objecthood (i.e. the state of being what is yet to be accomplished) of the action is due to its association with the activity, the same (activity) should be regarded as the denoted meaning of the conjugated verbal forms (i.e. of the conjugational endings in verb forms). Also, suppose the activity is accepted to be merely what is implied or understood in both the cases, then the cognitions of the activity would not have differed between the case of the *'ghañantas'* and the case of finite verbalforms; for, in both cases, the activity, being merely what is to be implied or understood, does not differ, i.e. is same.

Note : Siddhāntin states that despite that the action of cooking, expressed by the verbal root, is by nature, accomplished (*siddhasvabhāva*); and therefore, does not require any activity to produce it, the same, when found co-referred to by finite verbal forms (i.e. when verbal roots refer to the action and the conjugational endings refer to the activity), would become what is to be yet accomplished (*sādhya*). Consequently, the same action requires the activity to produce it; and such an activity must be held to be the denoted meaning of the conjugational endings. Otherwise, suppose the activity is considered to be merely implied or understood in both the cases, i.e. in *ghañantas* and also in finite verbal forms, then the difference beween the cognitions produced from such words would become difficult to explain.

Translation : (P.95)

Refutation that *buddhibheda* is due to *sādhanasambandha*

XXX.3. Also, the difference between the cognitions of the actions produced from *ghañanta* and finite verbal forms *buddhi bheda* cannot be said to be caused by the (difference between the) association and also non-association with the *kārakas;* for, in that case, the cognitions from passive (transitive) and impersonal (intransitive) verbs, such as 'it is gone to' (*gamyate*) and 'it is stayed at' (*sthīyate*) would also need to differ.

Note : Siddhāntin wants to point out that the difference between the cognitions produced from the *gañantas* and the finite verbal forms is due to the association of the action with the activity, and not therefore, due to the association of the action with the *kārakas* (such as object, agent etc.). It is possible that in cases like '*pacati*' (he cooks), the action of cooking etc. could be explained to be the entity yet to be accomplished due to its association with the *kartṛ* (agent) *kāraka*, and thereby to explain the Nirukta statement *dhātvarthaḥ kevalaḥ śuddhohbhāva ity abhidhīyate*. However, such a position would contradict the established convention that 'The root-meanings (actions) are cognized to be what are yet to be accomplished (*sādhya*) in both passive (*karmaṇi*) and impersonal (*bhāve*) statements such as 'it is gone to' (*gamyate*) and 'it is stayed at' (*sthīyate*) since, in the first instance, the root meaning (action) is associated with the object (*kāraka*), whereas, in the second instance, the same root-meaning is not associated with any object (*kāraka*).'

Translation (P.96)

Explanation of the meaning of finite forms such as '*pacati*' etc.

Verse 31

Scholars, who know the functional relation, i.e. signification, of words, explain the meanings of the finite form of verbs such as '*pacati*' (he cooks) distinctly as '*pākam karoti*' (he makes or performs cooking). However, such a method is not resorted to by the scholars for the explanation of the meaning of the verbal roots in *ghañanta* forms such as '*pākaḥ*' etc.

Note : Siddhāntin wants to point out that the finite forms of verbs such as '*pacati*' are explained to have two separate denoted meanings : i) namely, the action of cooking (*pāka*) and ii) the activity (*karotyartha* or *bhāvanā*) by analysing the same ('*pacati*') as '*pākam karoti*'; whereas the *ghañanta* forms such as '*pākaḥ*' are explained to have only one denoted meaning, namely, the action of cooking etc. (*pākaḥ*) since the same are not analysed as '*pākam* karoti' etc.

Translation (P.97)

Explanation of verse (31) that only finite verbs are analysed as referring to the action and the activity

XXXI.1. One explains the meanings of the finite forms of verbs such as *'pacati'* (he cooks) distinctly as *'pākam karoti'* (he makes or performs cooking). Here, such an explanation is resorted to only after perceiving the two-fold division of the meanings quite well; and therefore, it is not correct to state that one has done so without perceiving the two-fold division of the meanings. On the other hand, one does not explain the meaning of the verbal forms distinctly as *'pākam karoti'* in the case of *ghañanta* forms such as *'pākaḥ'* (cooking) etc.; for in such cases, cognition of difference between the meanings is absent. Now, we understand that the action of cooking etc. are the verbal root-meanings and the activity is the meaning of the conjugational endings in finite forms, whereas the action of cooking etc. are the denoted meanings of the *ghañanta* words and the activity is the indicated meaning of the same in *ghañanta* forms.

Note : Siddhāntin wants to state that the scholars analyse the finite verbs such as *'pacati'* distinctly with two separate words as *'pākam karoti'* etc., since they know that the finite verbs denote two separate meanings. However, they do not analyse the *ghañanta* forms so with two separate words as *'pākam karoti'*, since they know that the *ghañanta* forms denote only one meaning, namely, the action such as cooking (i.e.becoming soft of parts etc.). Thus, since the activity is found to be cognized only in the presence of the conjugational endings and not otherwise, it becomes established that the activity (*bhāvanā)* is the denoted meaning and not the indicated meaning of the conjugational endings in the case of finite verbs.

Translation (P.97-98)

Objection that explanation of two distinct meanings is mere assumption

XXXI.2. Now, one may object here as follows : The explanation of the meanings distinctly as the action and activity in the case of finite forms of verbs is only due to the assumption of the distinction between the meanings which do not exist. For instance, consider the explanation of the meanings of the same verb *'pacati'* as *'pākasya abhinir vartanam karoti'* (he performs the accomplishment of cooking). (Here, in such an explanation, the accomplishment (*abhinirvartana)* does not amount to any new thing which is substantially different from 'the activity' (*karotyartha*). Nevertheless, by assuming the distinction between the *karotyartha* and *abhinirvartana,* such an explanation is resorted to).

Translation : (P.98)

Refutation

No, this objection is not tenable. Suppose such is the case, then there should have been the explanation of the meanings of *ghañanta* forms such as *'pākaḥ'* also distinctly with two separate words by assuming the distinction; however, we do not find any such explanation of the meanings of the *ghañanta* forms in two–fold ways.

Note : Siddhāntin refutes Pūrvapakṣin's objection that ' in finite forms of verbs too, the explanation of the meanings distinctly as *'pākam karoti'* etc. is only due to the assumption of unreal distinction'. According to the Siddhāntin, suppose the distinction between the meanings is unreal and is like 'performing (*karaṇa*) and 'accomplishing' (*abhinirvartana*) of cooking (*pāka*) in *'pākasya abhinirvartanam karoti'* etc., then such an explanation of the unreal two meanings should have been possible in the *ghañanta* usages as well; however, since such an explanation is not found there, the explanation is not due to the mere assumption of the distinction; but rather, is due to the reality of the distinction between the meanings.

Translation (P.98)

Second objection that distinction between the meanings is assumed due to the distinction between expressions

It may be again objected as follows :

The distinction between the meanings, in the case of the finite verbs too, is assumed due to the distinction between the expressions, i.e. the references, of the finite verbs as *'pākam karoti'* etc. (and not due to the reality of the two meanings).

Refutation

Suppose you object so, we shall answer as follows : Let the distinction be established first between the meanings due to the distinction between the expressions, i.e. the references; and then, we could explain such a distinction later between the objects, i.e. between the meanings as well.

Note : Siddhāntin refutes again Pūrvapakṣin's objection that ' the distinction between the meanings in the finite verbs too is incorrect and the assumption of such a distinction is merely due to the two fold expressions, i.e. the refereces; of the finite verbs'. Siddhāntin states that let the distinction be accepted at the word level due to two fold analysis of the verbs; and once such a distinction is accepted at the word level, the same distinction could be explained at the object level, i.e. at the meaning level, as well. By this, Siddhāntin has refuted effectively the objection that *'karoti'* is used both ways in the sense and absence of the activity (*bhāvābhāve prayogaḥ syāt* etc.) and hence *karotyartha* cannot be *bhāvanā*'.

Translation (P.99)

Objection that assumption of the activity involves infinite regression

XXXI.3. Now, in this way, suppose the action is perceived to be something yet to be accomplished (*sādhya*) due to its association with the activity (*bhāvanā)*, then, the activity too can be perceived as having the nature of something yet to be accomplished (*sādhya rūpa*) (due to its association with another activity); and hence, yet another activity would become necessary to produce the activity. And further, in the same way, yet another activity would become necessary, and thus, non-finality (infinite regression) would result (in the assumption of the activity).

Note : Pūrvapakṣin wants to raise the objection that suppose the action of cooking etc. is accepted, in verbs, to be something which is yet to be accomplished (*sādhya*) due to its association with the activity, then the activity too can be insisted to be something yet to be accomplished due to its association with another activity. And such an activity can be insisted to be accomplished due to yet another activity and so on; and thus, the assumption of the activity involves the infinite regression of the activity.

Translation (P.99)

Solution - the alternative theory

One may try to solve the difficulty by proposing the following theory :

That the activity is nothing but an operation; and the very nature of such an activity is such that the same is produced, i.e. accomplished, independent of any other (activity). Consequenly, since the activity can be established to be 'what is yet to be accomplished' (*sādhya)* due to its own inherent nature, the same (establishment of the activity) is not dependent on the association of yet another activity. (Thus, the assumption of the activity does not involve the infinite regression of the activity).

Note : Siddhāntin wants to solve the problem of non-finality (infinite regression) of the activity by proposing that the very nature of the activity is such that the same is accomplished independent of any other activity; and therefore, it does not require any other activity to accompllish itself. Thus, there is no difficulty of assuming another activity to produce the first activity and yet another activity to accomplish the second activity and so on.

Translation (P.100-103)

Rejection of the alternative theory

XXXI.4. In that case, let even the root-meanings, i.e. the action of cooking etc., be accepted as of such nature, i.e. as of what are yet to be accomplished independent of an activity. And this can be explained as follows : The action of cooking etc., being what are yet to be accomplished by their own nature, or if not so by their own nature, then by being imposed of such a nature on themselves on account of the usages of the roots in such a sense, are perceived (i.e. grasped) as of the nature of 'operation' (*vyāpāra)*. Consequently, relations of the syntactico-semantical items (*kāraka sambandha*) can be explained to be possible with the actions expressed by the verbal roots in the case of the *ghañanta* usages such as 'The cooking of rice is effected by Devadatta in the bowl' (*devadattena sthālyām odanasya pākaḥ*) etc. as well. Otherwise, since the relations of the syntactico-semantical items are not tenable with the non-operation (*avyāpāra*), the items such as Devadatta, bowl etc., which are related to the non-operation, i.e. the action, cannot be considered as the *kārakas*, or the syntactico-semantical items. And this is explained by the fact that the *kāraka* nature of the same syntactico-semantical items is caused by their relation with the operation (*kriyā* or *vyāpāra*) which is to be accomplished.

Now, as regards the distinction between the cognition of the action such as cooking as something which is already accomplished and the cognition of the action such as cooking as something which is yet to be accomplished. The distinction is explained on account of the dominance, i.e. obstruction, of the objecthood (accomplishability) of the action of cooking by the accomplishedness (*siddhabhāva*) that is obtained due to the *ghañ* suffix in the case of the *ghañanta* words (*pākaḥ*) and also (is explained) on account of the non-dominance, i.e. non-obstruction, of the objecthood of the action of cooking by the accomplishedness due to the absence of the same suffix in the case of the finite verbal forms (*pacati*) etc. Moreover, scholars demonstrate, i.e. explain, such a form or nature of the action as something yet to be accomplished (*sādhya*) which is not overcome (by the *siddhabhāva*) due to its association with another operation, since the same nature cannot be explained in any other way; and this explanation is similar to the explanation of the same nature of the accomplishability of the activity as due to its association with another operation. Further, it should be noted that the reference to the state of being what is already accomplished and also to the state of being what is yet to be accomplished (of the action of cooking etc.) by one and the same word such as *pākaḥ* cannot be held contradictory; for, the reference to the two different states is to be obtained through the different parts of the word '*pākaḥ*', i.e. base (viz. *pac*), and also the suffix (viz. *ghañ*). This instance is similar to the instance of the reference to the two different ideas, i.e. to the difference of cow individuals and also to the non-difference of the cowness by the base 'go' and also by the suffix '*tva*' respectively in the case of the word '*gotva*' etc.

Also, for the scholars, who desire to establish a distinct activity in the case of the conjugated forms, i.e. finite verbs, as the meaning expressed by the conjugational endings, by cognizing the root-meanings (the actions of cooking etc.), as having only the nature of what are yet to be accomplished and also by demonstrating the same as distinct from the activity, the root-meanings would have the undesired contingency of functioning as only the objects with respect to the activity. Thus, for them, the root meanings would not function as the instruments with respect to the activity.

Thus, it should be concluded that the root-meanings (i.e. the actions of cooking etc.), which have the nature of being the operations inherently in themselves, are referred to by the very words, i.e. the roots such as *'pac'*. Also, the root-meanings (actions), which have the nature of being the operations, can be considered to be either the activity (*bhāvanā*) or actions (*kriyā*) depending upon whether the same are perceived to be competent in producing an effect or whether the same are perceived to have the nature of being what are accomplished. Thus, everything is fine (tenable).

Note : Pūrvapakṣin wants to establish his own theory that the activity is not a distinct entity from the root-meanings, i.e. the actions. He states as follows : Suppose the activity has the state of being what is yet to be accomplished independently, by its own very nature, then the actions of cooking etc. too can be accepted to have the same state of being what are yet to be accomplished by their own very nature or due to the imposition of such a nature on them. Thus, the actions of cooking etc. can be explained to be an operation (*vyāpāra*) that is yet to be accomplished. Now, since the actions of cooking etc. are established to be what are yet to be accomplished by their own (very) nature, independently (without the association of an activity), the same can be explained to be an operation that is the qualificand of the syntactico-semantical relations (*kāraka sambandha*). In statements such as *'devadattena kāṣṭhaiḥ sthālyām odanasya pākaḥ'* etc., the *ghañanta* word *'pākaḥ'*, expressing the action of cooking, is used in relation to various *kārakas* such as the agent 'Devadatta', the instrument 'fuel woods' etc.; and such a usage becomes tenable only when the actions, expressed by the *ghañanta* words, are accepted to have the nature of an operation (*vyāpāra*) that is yet to be accomplished. This phenomenon can be explained as follows : Only the items related to an operation, which is yet to be accomplished, are considered as the *kārakas*. And, various items like *'Devadatta'*, 'fuel woods' etc. are indeed used as *kārakas* in such statements. Thus, in order to facilitate the *kāraka*-hood for Devadatta etc., the actions of cooking etc., which are referred to by the root *'pac'* etc., must be conceded as an operation that is yet to be accomplished.

Now, as regards the distinction or differcnce between the cognitions of the actions produced from the usages involving *ghañanta* and also the finite verbs. The action of cooking is cognized to be what is already accomplished *(siddha)* in the case of the usage involving *ghañanta* words since the objecthood, i.e. the nature of being what is yet to be accomplished (*sādhyatva*) of the action has been obstructed or dominated by the sense expressed by the *'ghañ'* affix; whereas the same action is cognized to be what is yet to be accomplished (*sādhya*) in the case of finite verbs since the same nature has not been obstructed or dominated by the sense expressed by the *'ghañ'* affix. Thus, it is not contradictory that one and the same action is cognized as both and *'siddha' 'sādhya'* in *ghañanta* and finite verbs respectively.

Now, as regards the explanation of the nature of being what is yet to be accomplished (*sādhyatva)* of the action of cooking etc. Such a nature of the action of cooking etc. can be explained due to its mere association with another operation (*vyāpāra*) as well; and thus, such a nature does not require the postulation of the existence of yet another operation. This instance is similar to the instance of explaining the nature of being what is yet to be accomplished of the activity due to the mere association with another activity without postulating the existence of yet another activity.

Pūrvapakṣin wants to state, further, that the reference to the nature of being what is yet to be accomplished and that to the nature of being what is already accomplished etc. by the root *'pac'* and *'ghañ'* affix in the word *'pākaḥ'* etc. are not contradictory with respect to the action of cooking etc. According to him, such distinct natures are explained by the fact that one is expressed by the verbal base *'pac'* etc. and the other is expressed by the *'ghañ'* affix. This instance too is similar to the instance of the reference to the cow individual (*govyakti*) and to the cowhood (*gojāti)* by the nominal base 'go' and the abstract suffix *'tva'* respectively in the word *'gotva'* etc.

Further, Pūrvapakṣin wants to point out that in the Siddhāntin's theory that conjugational endings refer to an activity *(bhāvanā)*, which is distinct from the action of cooking etc. expressed by the verbal root *'pac'* etc., the root-meanings (actions) would have to be considered as only the objects with respect to the activity, since the same (actions of cooking etc.) are cognized to be only the objects to be accomplished and not the instruments. Thus, Pūrvapakṣin concludes that due to the impossibility of accepting a distinct activity, apart from actions, only the action of cooking etc. should be accepted to be the meanings of finite verbs (i.e. *pacati* etc.) and the same root-meanings, which have the form of an operation as well, are called the activity *(bhāvanā)* or the action *(kriyā)* depending upon whether the same are perceived to be what are competent to produce an effect or perceived to be what are accomplished.

Translation : (P.103)

Refutation of Pūrvapakṣin's view

Such a position, as stated by Pūrvapakṣin, is, however, improper.

Verse 32

When the distinction between the objects, i.e. an activity and also an action, is being actually cognized, the position that such a distinction is mere (assumption of) word-reference is not desired (tenable). Also, only upon the establishment of the root-meanings as being what are yet to be accomplished *(sādhya)*, the dominance or the obstruction of such a nature by the meaning of the *'ghañ'* ending, i.e. by the nature of what is already accomplished (*siddhabhāva*), could be held as appropriate.

Note : Now, Siddhāntin refutes the Pūrvapakṣin's position that the finite verbs express mere verbal root-meanings (actions) which have the nature of being both an activity, in view of their ability to produce an effect, and an action, in view of their nature of being the objects to be produced. According to him, since the distinction between the meanings of the verbal ending (i.e. activity) and of verbal root (i.e. action) is cognized vividly, the positon that they are mere assumptions of word-reference; and hence, have no reality as such, is not tenable. Also, according to him, the position that 'the accomplishability (*sādhyatā)* of the root-meanings (action of cooking etc.) is dominated (obstructed) by the state of being what is already accomplished (*siddha-svabhāva)*, expressed by the '*ghañ*' suffix in '*ghañanta*' usages', is not tenable, since the accomplishability of the same has not been established by the Pūrvapakṣin in the case of finite expressions.

Translation (P.104-5)

Explanation of verse 32

Refutation of the claim that the activity as distinct from the root-meanings (actions) is assumption of word-reference

XXXII.1. It will be shown, i.e. demonstrated by us, Siddhāntins, that the activity is different from the root-meanings (qualities or actions), which are of the form of non-operation. Therefore, it is not correct to hold that such a theory of the distinction between the activity and the actions is mere manifestatin (i.e. assumption of the unreal things) through the power (lit. competency) of words (i.e. word-reference). And, such an argument of mere word-reference could have been possible provided that we have assumed the two distinct entities in the absence of the real existence of such two entities in the outside world.

Also, since the words are used with the intention of conveying the syntactico-semantical relations between the referents, i.e. the *kārakas* and the activity, that exist, the same words cannot be assumed to have the power of manifestation for the establishment of the existence (i.e. production) of the unreal things through *kārakas*. Now, as regards the obstruction of the nature of what is yet to be accomplished (*bhāvayatā)* of the action of cooking etc.: The statement that such a nature of the action is dominated or obstructed by the meaning of the '*ghañ*' affix in '*ghañanta* words is tenable, i.e. justified, only when the reference to such a nature of what is yet to be accomplished through the verbal roots is already ascertained. However, since such a reference to the accomplishing nature of the actions has not been ascertained, i.e. is not established due to the lack of any means for ascertaining such a reference, such a statement is not valid. Also, since the syntactico-semantical relations of *kāraka* items can be explained with respect to the activity that is to be understood, i.e. implied, as well, we shall assume an implication in the sense of the activity in *ghañanta* usages despite the non-reference to the same activity by words. In instances such as 'part,i.e division, by a pair of scissors' (*śaṅkulayā khaṇḍaḥ)* such a relation of the instrumental *kāraka* (i.e. pair of scissors) is established with the implied activity. (Therefore, in *ghañanta* usages such as '*pākaḥ*' too, we can explain the *kāraka*-relations with respect to the activity by implying the same).

Note : Siddhāntin states that since, the activity would be demonstrated as being quite distinct from the root-meanings (i.e. since the activity would be demonstrated as synonimous with movement or operation *spandavyāpāra paryāya* and also, since the root-meanings would be demonstrated as identical with the quality or action), the root-meanings cannot be accepted to be both action and activity depending on whether the same are viewed to be operation to be accomplished or a productive force. Thus, Pūrvapakṣin's claim that "the activity, as distinct from the root-meanings 'actions', is mere assumption of word-reference" stands refuted.

Also, the claim of mere assumption of word-reference would be tenable provided that the activity and the actions are unreal entities; however, since such is not the case (i.e. since they would be established to be real), such a claim is unjustified. Again, since words are used with the intention that the expressed meanings (i.e. the existing *kārakas)* be cognized as syntactico-semantically related to the activity; and also, since they are never used with the intention of establishing the non-existing entities through the *kārakas*, the statement that the root-meanings (actions) can be established as having the dual nature of the activity and the action to be accomplished is untenable.

Further, Siddhāntin refutes the claim of Pūrvapakṣin that the '*ghañ*' affix refers to the nature or state of being what is already accomplished (*siddhatva)* of the actions; and therefore, the nature of being what is yet to be accomplished (*sādhyatva)* of the actions becomes dominated or obstructed by the accomplishedness in *ghañanta* usages. Siddhāntin states that, since the reference to such a state of the actions is not yet established by any means, the same cannot be held to dominate or prevail over the accomplishability of the actions. Also, it is possible to explain *ghañanta* usages such as *'kāṣṭhaiḥ pākaḥ'* (cooking is by means of woods) despite the absence of the denotation of the activity by the *ghañanta* word *'pākaḥ'*. For, the *kārakas* such as woods could relate, as instruments, to the activity which is understood by implication. And this usage is similar to the usage 'part by a pair of scissors' (*śaṅkulayā khaṇḍaḥ*) which is meant to convey the sense of 'part produced through a pair of scissors' (*śaṅkulayā kṛtaḥ khaṇḍaḥ)* by implying the activity that produces such a part through a pair of scissors.

Translation (P.106)

An activity distinct from root-meanings (actions) must be admitted

Verse 33

Suppose only a root-meaning (action) is referred to by finite verbs such as *pacati* etc., then no distinction between the cognitions produced from the statements such as 'rice grains cook' (*viklidyanti*) and 'Devadatta etc. cook' (*pacanti*) would be tenable. Also, suppose there exists no distinction between the operations (activities) referred to by such finite verbs (as *'viklidyanti'* and *'pacanti'*), then, why should the distinction between the agents be accepted in such finite usages ?

Note : Siddhāntin points, further, the difficulties in not accepting the activity as distinct from the root-meaning (action). Suppose only a root-meaning (action) is referred to by finite verbs and also suppose there exists no distinction between the activity and the action, then both the statements *'viklidyanti'* and *'pacanti'* would have to refer to only the 'becoming soft' (*viklitti)* of rice grains. And, hence, both the statements would have to produce only identical cognitions. Also, different cognitions could not be explained on the basis of two different agents, namely, 'rice grains' in the case of *'viklidyanti'* and 'Devadatta etc'., in the case of *'pacanti'*. For, since the activities (operations) do not differ, the question of accepting two different agents do not arise in such usages.

Translation (P.107)

Explanation of verse 33

Distinct activity is necessary to explain distinction between the cognitions from *'viklidyanti'* and *'pacanti'*

XXXIII.1. Indeed in finite verbs, mere root-meaning cannot be cognized to have the nature of being both an operation, i.e. activity, and an action as well. For, since the root-meaning (i.e. the action of becoming soft) does not difer between the sentences such as 'rice grains become soft' (*viklidyanti*) and 'Devadatta etc. cook' (*pacanti*), the contingency of the non-distinction between the cognitions would be unavoidable in the case of such sentences. Also, it cannot be claimed that such a contingency would not arise due to the difference between the agents of such sentences. For, without the difference between the activities (i.e. operations), the difference between the agents would not be tenable. Also, the difference between the agents cannot be explained due to the difference between the characteristics of such agents. For, suppose the distinguishing characteristic of the agentship is defined to be the state of controlling, i.e. employing different syntactico-semantical items (*kārakas*), then only animates such as Yajñadatta etc., who can control or employ the *kārakas*, and not inanimates such as rice grains, would become agents; and suppose the distinguishing characteristic of the agentship is defined to be the state of having the operation referred to by the verbs, then only the rice grains, which have the operation of becoming soft referred to by the finite verbs *'viklidyanti'* and *'pacanti'*, (and not Yajñadatta), would become agents. From this, (the difficulty in explaining) the distinct cognitions, from the finite verbs such as *'bhinatti'* (divides into parts), *'dalati'* (splits or 'bursts' open), *'chinatti'* (cuts), *'dvaidhībhavati'* (makes or becomes into two) etc. become(s) commented upon. Therefore, it becomes absolutely clear that an activity (lit. operation), which is distinct from the root-meanings (i.e. actions, quality etc.), should be accepted as the meaning of conjugational endings so that the distinction between the cognitions of the meanings of finite verbs and thereby the distinction between the agents of the two different finite verbs would become tenable.

Note : Siddhāntin reiterates that the root-meanings cannot be considered to have the form of an operation (i.e. activity) and of an action as well. For, suppose, in finite verbs, root-meanings are held to have the form of an operation and also the fom of an action, then the different cognitions, which are perceived from the finite verbs *'viklidyanti'* and *'pacanti'*, would become untenable, since the operation of becoming soft of rice grains is identical in both the cases. Also, different cognitions cannot be explained due to the different agents in the usages with such finite verbs. For, suppose an agent is held to be the one who controls or employs different *kārakas,* then only the animates like Yajñadatta, and never the inanimates like rice grains, can be considered to be the agents of *'viklidyanti'* and *'pacanti'*, since only the animates control *kārakas*. On the other hand, suppose an agent is held to be one who has his operation referred to by finite verbs, then only the inanimates such as the rice grains, and never the animates such as Yajñadatta, can be considered to be the agents, since only the inanimates have their operation, i.e. 'becoming soft', referred to by such finite verbs. Thus, the root-meaning cannot be accepted to have the from of both an action and an activity.

Translation (P.108)

Alternative explanation of the distinct activity :

XXXIII.2. It may be objected now as follows : The theory that "the operation (i.e. the activity) is cognized to be distinct from the root-meanings (i.e. actions or quality)" could hold good only in the case of those finite verbs such as *'viklidyanti'*, *'pacanti'* etc., which refer to an action inherent in the objects such as rice grains; and therefore, how could such a theory of distinct activity hold good in the case of the finite verbs such as *'yajati'* (he offers), *'āste'* (he is) etc., which refer to the actions that are inherent in the agents such as the persons etc.? However, we answer as follows : "without the distinction between the operations (activities) referred to by verbs, why should the distinction between the agents be accepted". An agent is one whose operation (activity) is denoted as the non-qualifier (i.e. as the chief qualificand of all *kāraka*-relations) by the verbs; and therefore, the priests (*ṛtviks*) and the sacrificer (*yajamāna*) are the agents respectively in the statements such as 'priests make oblations' (*ṛitvijo yajanti)* and 'the sacrificer performs a ritual' *(yajate yajmānaḥ*) etc. However, since a particular type of determination (resolve to perform a ritual), which is denoted by the verb *yajati'*, is considered to be the activity of the sacrificer, the statement such as 'the officiating priests make oblations' (*yajanti yājakāḥ)* becomes untenable, when an activity, which is distinct from an action of offering is not conceded to be the meaning of the verbal endings. On the other hand, in the event of accepting the operation (the activity), which is distinct from the root-meaning (action of offering), as the chief qualificand of syntactico-semantical relations, such a statement becomes tenable.

Note : Pūrvapakṣin holds the theory that the activity, as distinct from the action, is found only in the case of finite verbs wherein verbal roots refer to an action inherent in the objects; for instance, in *'viklidyanti'*, *'pacanti'* etc. (Here, the verbal roots *'viklid'* and *'pac'* refer to the action of becoming soft which inheres in the rice grains and hence the activity is distinct). However, in the cases where the action is inherent in the agent himself, the activity does not differ from the action. For instance, in *'yajati yajamānaḥ'*. (Here, the action of performing or offering (i.e. resolve) is inherent in the agent, i.e. sacrificer, and hence the activity is not distinct). However, Siddhāntin wants to refute such a theory. According to him, unless the distinction between the activity and the action is accepted, the distinction between the different agents such as *'yajamāna'* and *'ṛtvik'* becomes untenable. For instance, in the statement *'yajate yajamānaḥ'*, the sacrificer is the agent with respect to the root-meaning, i.e. resolve to perform a ritual. However, in the case of the statement *'yajanti yājakāḥ'*, the priest, cannot be regarded as the agent with respect to the root-meaning, i.e. 'resolve to perform the ritual'. He can be the agent of only the activity which causes such a resolve to perform the ritual. Thus, unless the activity is accepted to be distinct from the action, such distinct statements with distinct agents become untenable; and therfore, the activity must be held to be different from the action.

Translation (P.109)

Argument that 'yajati' need not refer to distinct activity

XXXIV.3. It may be argued now as follows : Despite the finite verb *'yajati'* not denoting the distinct operation (activity), and also despite the same denoting merely the resolve to perform a ritual (i.e. the resolve to offer the oblation material), the distinction between the agents, namely, the *'yajamāna'* and *'ṛtvik'* is tenable to explain. For, due to the distinction between the syntactico-semantical expectancies for the independence (of different agents), the distinction between the agents becomes tenable. This instance is similar to the instance of the distinction between the means (instruments) due to the distinction between the syntactico-semantical expectancies for the excellence (i.e. the effectiveness to produce an effect).

Note : Pūrvapakṣin argues again as follows :

The distinction between the agents, namely, *'yajamāna'* and *'ṛitvik'* can be explained despite the distinction between the activity and the action. The distinction between the agents can be explained due to the distinction between the syntactico-semantical expectancies for the independence of the agents. That is to say that both *'yajamāna'* and *'ṛtvik'* possess their respective actions such as resolvidng to perform a ritual and making of oblations. However, when the *'yajamāna'* is expected to have the independence in his action, the same *'yajamāna'* becomes the agent; and when the *'ṛtvik'* is expected to have the independence in his action, the same becomes the agent. And this instance is similar to the instance of considering the axe or the hand as the most effective means (*karaṇa*) due to the excellence (i.e. due to the effectiveness they possess) in producing the action of cutting. Thus, there is no need that the finite verb *'yajati'* must be accepted to denote the activity as distinct from the action of others.

Translation (P.111)

Refutation of the argument

What is this independence of agents ? Suppose you state that the independence means the controlling of the syntactico-semantical items (*kārakas)*, then, how is it that the usages, such as 'woods etc. cook' (*kāṣṭhādīni pacanti)* etc. are tenable ? For, since there exist no *kārakas* apart from woods etc. that the woods etc. could control, such usages cannot be explained with the expectation of controlling the *kārakas.* Therefore, it should be accepted that the independence means the state of having a reference to the activity of the agent, which functions as the qualificand of all the syntactico-semantical relations. Thus, in support of such a position, it is stated (in Mahābhāṣya) that "vessel is independent when the operation (i.e. activity) belonging to the same vessel is being referred to."

Note : Siddhāntin refutes the Pūrvapakṣin's argument that agents can differ due to the distinction between the levels of independence in their actions. He states that suppose the independence is defined as the ability to control other *kārakas,* then the statements such as 'woods etc. cook' (*kāṣṭhādīni pacanti)* etc. would become untenable, since all the *kārakas,* namely, woods etc., are considered as only agents, and thus, no *kāraka*s, that can be controlled, exist. Therefore, it has tobe accepted that the independence means the reference to the activity of the agent as the chief qualificand of all syntactico-semantical relations. And that is why in Mahābhāṣya Patañjali also supports such a view by stating that when the activity belonging to the vessel is being referred to, the vessel is independent.

Translation (P.112)

Second argument that the verbal roots can refer to the activities

XXXIII.4. Allright, let it be accepted that there does exist distinction between the operations (activities) of different agents. Nevertheless, such operation (activity) must be conceded to be referred to by the verbal root only. Now, since the root '*pac*' (to cook) refers to the activity of (the animate) Devadatta etc. (i.e. placing the vesel on fire etc.), and also since the root '*viklid*' (to become soft) does not refer to the activity of Devadatta (it refers to the activity of the inanimate 'rice grains'), the distinction between the references to the meanings (i.e. operations) as well as the distinction between the agents can be explained in the statements such as 'Devadatta etc. cook' (*pacanti*) and 'rice grains become soft' (*viklidyanti*).

Also, the root '*yaj*' (to offer), which is actually referring to the *yajamāna's* activity, i.e. resolve to perform a ritual, can be held to refer to the operation (activity) of the *ṛtviks* (i.e. the making of the oblations) due to the fact that the same *ṛitvik's* activity is meant to be conducive to the *yajamāna's* activity. Thus, the *ṛtviks* can be explained to be the agents in '*ṛtvijo yajanti*' due to the reference to the activity of making oblations. And, in support of this theory, it has been stated as follows : The activity of commissioning and that of soliciting etc., are undertaken with the intention of accomplishing the activity of cooking; and therefore, all of them are justified in being considered as the meanings of the root '*pac*' itself.

Note : Pūrvapakṣin concedes that 'Devadatta' and 'rice grains' possess two different kinds of activities in '*devadattaḥ pacati*' and '*taṇḍulāḥ viklidyanti*'. However, he insists that there is no need to accept that the conjugational endings refer to such distinct activities. According to him, such different activities too can be held to be referred to by the verbal roots such as '*pac*' (to cook) and '*viklid*' (to become soft). Now, since the root '*pac*' refers to the activity of the animate 'Devadatta' (i.e. the activity of putting the vassel on fire etc.) and the root '*viklid*' refers to the activity of the inanimate 'rice grains' (i.e. the activity of becoming soft), the distinction between the verbal references as well as the distinction between the agents in the usages of finite verbs '*pacati*' and '*viklidyanti*' can be explained. Thus, there is no need that the conjugational endings must be held to refer to the operations (activities) to facilitate the distinction between the verbal references and also between the agents. Pūrvapakṣin maintains also that the root '*yaj*' (to offer), which actually refers to the activity of the *yajamāna*, namely, the activity of resolving to perform a ritual, be taken to refer to the activity of the '*ṛtvik*' (namely, the activity of making oblation) as well, since the same activity of making the oblation is meant to accomplish the activity of the *yajamāna*. Consequently, the *'ṛtviks'* can be considered to be the agents with respect to the verb *'yajanti'* in the usages *'ṛtvijo yajanti'* etc. Thus, there is no need that the conjugational endings be held to denote the activity, which is distinct from the root-meaning, to facilitate the use of *'ṛtvijo yajanti'*.

Translation (P.113-114)

Refutation of the theory that roots refer to the activity

Verse 34

No, this argument is not sound. The roots *'pac'* (to cook) and *'yaj'* (to offer) are dependent on, i.e. have reference to, mere action of 'becoming soft' and 'a particular type of resolve to perform a ritual'. And, since the roots, *'pac'* and *'yaj'* in their *'ghañanta'* as well as *'tiṅanta'* forms, have been perceived to have the same sense of 'becoming soft' and 'particular resolve to perform a ritual, respectively, they cannot be considered to be denotative of any other sense, i.e. the activity of the agents, namely, Devadatta and the *ṛtvik*.

Translatin (P.114-116)

Explanation of the verse 34

XXXIV. 1. The roots *'pac'* (to cook) and *'yaj'* (to offer) denote, in their respective *'ghañanta'* forms such as 'cooking' (*pākaḥ*) and 'offering' (*yāgaḥ*), mere action of 'becoming soft' (*viklitti*) and action of offering, i.e. 'resolve (*saṅkalpa*) to perform a ritual'. And therefore, they do not denote any activity found in the agents which is distinct from such root-meanings. And, this must be conceded to be so because, the *'ghañanta'* words such as *'pākaḥ'* (cooking), unlike the finite forms such as *'pacati'* (he cooks), have never been explained as 'the activity of cooking' (*pākasya kriyā*) (which could have supported a distinct sense of the activity for roots).

Note : Siddhāntin refutes the view that the roots *'pac'* (to cook) and *'yaj'* (to offer) etc. refer to both the action and also the activity. For, according to him, the roots, in *'ghañanta'* forms, refer to simply the action of becoming soft (*viklitti*) (found in the rice grains) and also to the action of offering, i.e. the resolve to perform a ritual (which is found in the *yajamāna).* However, they do not refer to the activity such as *adhiśrayaṇa* etc. (found in the agent 'Caitra') or to the activity such as making *yajamāna* offer etc. (found in the *ṛtvik).* Also, according to him, the roots, in their finite (*tiṅanta*) forms too, are perceived to refer to the same sense of the action(s); and hence, cannot be considered to have a denotation in any distinct sense, i.e. the activity. Siddhāntin observes that the '*ghañanta*' forms such as '*pākaḥ*' (cooking) and '*yāgaḥ*' (offering) are known to denote only the action of becoming soft and a particular type of resolve (found in the rice grains and also in the *yajamāna* respectively); and therefore, they cannot be held to denote any different sense of the activity. He, also, observes that the '*ghañanta*' words such as '*pākaḥ*' have never been explained as 'the activity of cooking' (*pākasya kriyā*) unlike the finite verbs like '*pacati*' in the language. Therefore, the roots can never be considered to denote the activity as well.

Translation (P.116-117)

Verbal roots in finite forms cannot refer to the activity

XXXIV.2. Also, in the same way, the roots '*pac*' and '*yaj*', in the quasi-passive usages (*karmakartari)* such as 'rice grains are cooked by themselves' (*pacyante taṇḍulāḥ svayameva*) and active usages (*kartari*) such as 'the sacrificer offers' (*yajate yajamānaḥ*), refer to mere actions of becoming soft and offering, i.e. resolve to perform a ritual; and therefore, in such cases, merely such actions are accepted to be the operations (activities) of the agents, namely, 'rice grains' and 'sacrificer' respectively. Therefore, in the statements 'Devadatta cooks' (*devadattaḥ pacati*) and 'the priests make oblations' (*yajanti yājakāḥ*), the roots '*pac*' and '*yaj*', which are perceived as referring to merely the becoming soft and to the offering, i.e. resolve to perform a ritual, are not justified in being considered as having a reference to some different sense, i.e. the activity that can bring about such actions.

Note : Siddhāntin refutes the idea that the roots '*pac*' and '*yaj*' etc. can at least in finite forms, denote both the action and the activity. According to him, such roots, in *karmakartari* and *kartari* statements such as '*pacyante taṇḍulāḥ svvayameva*' and also '*yajate yajamānaḥ*', are accepted even by Pūrvapakṣin, to denote merely the action of becoming soft of the quasi-object, and also the action of offering (resolve) of the agent. And, further, such actions themselves are visualized to be the operations, i.e. the activities since no separate activity can be envisaged in such cases. Consequently, it is not justified that the roots *'pac'* and *'yaj'* etc. should be held to have a further reference to the separate activity which may bring about such actions.

Translation (P.117-118)

Statement that roots must be held to denote merely the actions

XXXIV.3. Also, merely the things amounting to the actions constitute the verbal root-meanings. For, such an alternative does not involve any deviation (of the use of the verbal roots from such meanings). And, things amounting to more than the actions cannot constitute the verbal root-meanings. For, such an alternative involves deviation. Further, the reference to the activity is due to the (use of) another word (i.e. the conjugational ending such as *ti*). Thus, the activity of the agent, which is perceived as referred to only upon the use of the conjugational endings, is the meaning of only the same conjugational endings (and not that of the verbal roots). Again, chief qualificands (i.e. center or uncleus of syntactico-semantical relations) are mostly the meanings referred to by the conjugational and other affixes. And, since the activity too is the chief qualificand (of the syntactico-semantical relations) of the *kārakas* and actions, the same acquires the status of being only the meaning of the conjugational endings.

Note : Siddhāntin refutes the argument that the verbal roots can be considered to denote the actions such as cooking and offering which have a further reference to the activities of the agents (such as *adhiśrayaṇa* in the case of cooking and making *yajamāna* offer in the case of offering). According to him, such a position is not tenable, since the roots are used invariably in the sense of only the actions, and not in the sense of the activities that produce them. Also, only those entities are established as word-meanings which never deviate from word-reference. Since the roots are seen to have been used without a reference to the activity, the same (activity) cannot be the root-meaning. Siddhāntin points out further that, since the reference to the activity is due only to the use of the other words, namely, the conjugational and other affixes, the same can be the meaning of only the conjugational and other affixes. Again, since the chief qualificand (i.e. nucleus of the syntactico-semantical relations) is always the meaning of the affix, and the activity is the chief qualificand, the same should only be regarded as the meaning of the conjugational affix.

Translation (P.119-120)

Explanation of the activity in intransitive '*asti*' etc.

XXXIV.4. It may be argued now that there occurs a deviation of the conjugational endings from the reference to the activity in the case of the intransitive verbs such as '*asti*' (to exist) etc. However, such an argument is incorrect. (For, in the case of the intransitive finite verbs such as '*asti*' etc. too, the accomplishing activity is, in reality, cognized as accomplishing the state of existence of the agent by the use of the word, i.e. conjugational ending.) For, in spite of its apparent absence of referennce, in reality, the activity is cognized due to the (use of) words, i.e. the conjugational endings (ti) etc. in such cases. Otherwise, suppose the refeence to such an activity is not accepted in the case of the intransitive finite forms such as '*asti*' etc., then, the finite expressions such as 'something exists' (*asti*), and also the expressions of action and abstract nouns such as 'becoming' (*bhāva*) and 'being' (*sattā*) would have an identical reference.

Note : Pūrvapakṣin argues that the position that the conjugational endings invariably refer to an activity is not tenable. According to him, the conjugational endings found after intransitive roots such as '*as*' (to exist) in '*asti*' etc. cannot be claimed to refer to any activity, which accomplishes something, since in the case of intransitives, nothing can be stated as 'being accomplished' (*bhāvya*). However, Siddhāntin refutes such an argument. According to him, even in the case of the intransitive finite usages, such as '*asti*' etc., the conjugational endings can be accepted to refer to an activity. This is in spite of the fact that, in such cases, no separate object (effect) such as becoming soft or heaven is actually accomplished. He states that when someone or something is perceived as existing, the agent of existece can be visualized to attain a particular state of existence (*sattā),* and thus, an activity, which is conducive to such a state of existence of the agent, can be accepted. Also Siddhāntin points out that unless a reference to an activity is accepted in the case of the usages such an *'asti'* (to exist) etc., the expressions of finite verbs such as *'asti'*, wherein the verbal base is associated with the conjugational endings (*ti* etc.), and also the expressions of action nouns, such as *'bhāva'* and abstract nouns such as *'sattā'*, wherein the verbal bases are not associated with any conjugational endings, cannot be differentiated as producing the different cognitions of the root-meanings as what is yet to be accomplished (*sāddhya*) and also as what is already accomplished (*siddha).*

Translation (P.121)

Objection that *sattā* itself is referred to as *sādhya* by the verbal roots

XXXIV.5. The cognition of the state of existence (*sattā)* as something yet to be accomplishd, in the usages of finite verbs such as *'asti'* (he exists), is due to the fact that the verbal roots such as *'as'* refer to the same state of existence as something yet to be accomplished. And the cognition of the same state of existence as something yet to be accomplished is not due to the fact that the conjugational endings refer to any accomplishing activity in such cases. The state of existence (*sattā)* and the state of becoming (*bhāva)* etc. are cognized as having the form of things which are already accomplished on the ground that the roots *'as'* (to be) and *'bhū'* (to become) refer to such a state of existence as something already accomplished in the abstract noun and *ghañanta* usages such as 'being' (*sattā)* and 'becoming' (*bhāva).* However, the same state of existence (*sattā*) etc. are not cognized so on account of the fact that the conjugational endings do not refer to the activity in such cases.

Note : Pūrvapakṣin raises the objection again that the difference between the cognitions from the expressions of finite verbs such as *'asti'* etc. and also the cognitions from the expressions of abstract nouns such as *'sattā'* etc. can be explained without resorting to the view of the expression of the activity by the conjugational endings. According to him, the verbal root *'as'* can itself refer to the state of existence (*sattā*); and it refers to the *sattā* as some thing yet to be accomplished in the expression of finite verbs such as *'asti'*, whereas the same refers to the *sattā* as something already accomplished in the expressions of abstract nouns such as *'sattā'* etc. Consequently, it can be held that the difference between the cognitions from the finite verbs and also the cognitions from the abstract nouns is due to only the expressions of the *sattā* as something yet to be accomplished and also as something already accomplished by the verbal roots; and not due to the expression or non-expression of the activity by the conjugational endings.

Translation (P.121)

Refutation of the objection

XXXIV.6. (No, this objection is not tenable). In the case of the transitive finite verbs such as *'pacati'* (he cooks) etc , the accomplishability of the root-meaning, i.e. cooking, has been ascertained as caused by only the association of the activity. (Thus, in the intransitives *'asti'* etc. too, the accomplishability of the root-meaning, i.e. *sattā* (the state of existence), must be accepted as caused by the activity). However, it may be objected as follows : Suppose you Siddhāntin establish the deviation of the verbal roots such as *'yaj'*, *'pac'*, from the reference to the activity in the case of the active statements such as 'sacrificer offers, i.e. resolves to perform a ritual' (*yajate yajamānaḥ*)' and also in the case of the quasipassive statements such as 'rice grains cook by themselves' (p*acyante svayam eva taṇḍulāḥ),* then we would also establish the deviation of the conjugational endings from the reference to the activity in the same cases. Also, suppose another activity apart from the action of offering, i.e. resolve to perform a ritual, in the case of *'yajate yajamānaḥ'* and the action of becoming soft (i.e. cooking) in the case of *'pacyante svayam eva taṇḍulāḥ'* is accepted as having been referred to by the verbal roots, so that the deviation from the reference to the activity is avoided, then only the non-deviation of the verbal roots (from the reference to the activity) would become established.

Nevertheless, this objection too is not tenable. For, the reference to the activity, accomplishing the action of 'offering' and 'cooking', has been accepted as caused by only the conjugational endings in such cases. Also, since the reference to the activity is due only to the presence (i.e. use) of the conjugational endings, the same (reference to the activity) gets established even without the use of transitive verbal roots such as '*yaj*' and '*pac*', in intransitive finite forms such as '*asti*' etc.

Note : Siddhāntin refutes the Pūrvapakṣin's theory that 'the accomplishability of *sattā* is due to the expression of the same as something yet to be accomplished by the verbal roots, and not due to the reference to the activity by the conjugational endings'. He states that, in '*pacati*' etc., the accomplishability of the cooking is ascertained as only due to the reference to the activity. Also, he refutes the Pūrvapakṣin's position that, in the statements such as '*yajate yajamānaḥ*' and '*pacyante svayam eva taṇḍulāḥ*', the verbal roots themselves should be accepted as referring to another activity apart from the offering, i.e. resolve to perform a ritual, and becoming soft etc. so that the deviation of the verbal roots from the reference to the activity can be avoided. He states that only the conjugational endings, and not the verbal roots, are accepted to have a reference to the activity in such statements. Also therefore, no deviation of the conjugational endings, from the reference to the activity, can occur in such cases as well.

Translation (P.123)

Establishment that conjugational endings alone refer to the activity

Also, since there occurs deviation (of the roots from the reference to the activity) in the case of the *ghañanta* usages such as 'cooking' (*pākaḥ*) etc., verbal roots cannot be held to have a reference to the activity. Again, since in such '*ghañanta*' usages, the activity of the agent is not demonstrated to be distinct (from the action of becoming soft etc.), the two distinct meanings cannot be cognized from the verbal roots. On the other hand, since, in other cases, i.e. in finite expressions such as '*pacati*' etc., the activity is established to be distinct from the root-meanings as evidenced by the analysis such as *pākam karoti* etc., the establishmentof the theory that the conjugational endings and also the verbal roots have two distinct meanings becomes absolutely necessary.

Now, since the entities, belonging to the general and the particular categories, are never found to function as what is to be accomplished (*sādhya*) and also as what is the means of accomplishment (*sādhana*), the activity and the action cannot be held to be the general and the particular meanings of the roots. Moreover, since never a general entity can be considered to be what is to be accomplished, the activity cannot be considered to be the generality of actions conveyed by the verbal roots. Further, since neither the verbal roots nor the conjugational endings can be admitted to refer to the generality of actions, there would arise an undesired contingency of non-reference to the activity in the view that activity is a generality of actions.

Note : Siddhāntin concludes that the activity, which is totally distinct from the root-meanings (action of cooking etc.), should be considered to be referred to by only the conjugational endings. He states that, since in *'ghañanta'* usages such as *'pākaḥ'* etc., the verbal roots (*'pac'* etc.) deviate from the reference to an activity, and also, since in such cases the activity of the agent (Caitra etc.) is never recognized as a distinct meaning referred to by the verbal roots, the activity cannot be the meaning of the verbal roots (*'pac'* etc.). He states also that the position that the verbal roots *'pac'* etc. refer to an activity which is quite distinct from the action of becoming soft etc. is not tenable, since in the usages of finite verbs such as *'pacati'* etc. (which are to be explained as *'pākam karoti'* etc.), the activity of the agent has been shown to be a distinct meaning expressed by the conjugational endings from the root-meanings 'becoming soft' etc. Siddhāntin refutes further the Pūrvapakṣin's view that, since the action like cooking is a particular entity and the activity is a general entity, acceptance of both of them as verbal root-meanings can help to maintain a distinction between the two meanings. According to him, since nowhere the general and the particular entities are found functioning as what is to be accomplished and also as what is the means of accomplishment, such a view is untenable. Also, since the activity is always perceived as what is yet to be accomplished, the activity cannot be considered to be the generality of actions expressed by the verbal roots that are never accomplished. Further, in the theory that the activity is a generality of actions, the difficulty of non-reference to the activity would become unavoidable since, neither the verbal roots nor the verbal endings are admitted to refer to such meanings. Thus, the verbal roots and the conjugational endings must be held to refer to the actions and the activity respectively.

Translation (P.127)

View that the activity must be held to be distinct from the actions

Verse 35

Moreover, one and the same entity (i.e. the root-meaning) cannot be assumed to function as its own means and also (as) its own object. Therefore, scholars state that the activity is distinct from the root-meaning (action of cooking etc.)

Note : Siddhāntin points out that, since one and the same entity cannot function as both its means and object, the root-meaning (cooking etc.) cannot be held as its own means and also as its own object to be produced. Thus, an activity, which is quite distinct from the action, should be held as the means of accomplishing the action (of cooking etc.); whereas the action (of cooking etc.) must be held as the object to be accomplished through the activity. Siddhāntin, therefore, has held that the activity, which accomplishes such an action, must be viewed to be a distinct entity referred to by the conjugational endings.

Translation (P.127)

Explanation that the activity as distinct from the action must be conceded in view of '*yajeta aśvamedhena*' etc.

XXXV1. In the theory that the activity is identical with the action (of cooking etc.), expressed by the verbal root, the syntactico-semantical relationship of the instrumentality and the objecthood of the action (of offering etc.) would become untenable with the activity as manifested in the statements such as 'One should offer by means of Aśvamedha sacrifice' (*yajeta aśvamedhena)*, 'I shall offer by means of many sacrifices' (*īje bahubhir yajñaiḥ*), 'He offers his own sacrifice' (*svam yajñam yajati*). Also, the distinction between the activity and the action as the generality of the root-meanings (i.e. actions), and also as the particularity of the root-meanings, expressed by the verbal roots, is not competent to explain the syntactico-samantical relationship of the instrumentality etc. of the action (of offering etc.) with the activity. For, since a generality is never something to be accomplished by anything, the same can never be considered as the activity that accomplishes the root-meanings (actions).

Also, when there exists the relationship of the qualifier and also the qualified (i.e. chief qualificand) between the action and also the activity, the instrumental ('*ena*') and the accusative ('*am*') *kāraka* cases found after the verbal derivations (*avśvamedhena* and *yajñam)* would become contradicted.

Note : Siddhāntin points out that suppose the verbal roots are accepted to refer to the action and also to the activity as identical with each other, then the syntactico-semantical relationship that exists between the action of offering etc. and also the activity could become impossible to explain. For, in '*yajeta aśvamedhena*', '*īje bahubhir yajñaiḥ*' and '*svam yajñam yajati*' the verbal derivatives '*aśvamedhena*', '*yajñaiḥ*' and '*yajñam*' are found with the *kāraka* case endings (instrumental '*ena*' and accusative '*am*') expressing the syntactico-semantical relationship of the instrumentality and also the objecthood of sacrifice (i.e. the action of offering) with the activity. And, such a relationship would become untenable if the action is considered identical with the activity. Therefore, the action expressed by the verbal roots, must be held as distinct from the activity, the meaning of the conjugational endings or '*karoti*'.

Also, he points out that even by conceding the distinction between the activity and also the action of offering etc. as the generality and the particularity of the verbal root-meanings, such a syntactico-semantical relationship is not tenable to explain. For, according to him, the generality is not something that is to be accomplished; and therefore, the same cannot be considered to be an activity that functions as the means of accomplishing the root-meanings (action of offering etc.).

Further, he points out that suppose the relationship of being the qualifier and the qualificand is conceded between the action and also the activity, then the *kāraka* case endings such as the instrumental *'ena'* and also the accusative, *'am'*, (found after the verbal derivatives *'aśvamedhena'*, *'yajñaiḥ'* and *'yajñam'*) expressing the *kāraka* relationship of the instrumentality and the objecthood of the offerings would be come contradictory (since the qualifiers and the qualificand are expected to have the identical case endings).

Translation (P.128)

Refutation that *ekadeśa* has *kriyākārakabhāva*

XXXV.2. Now, it may be held as follows : The root-meanings such as sacrifice (i.e. offering) etc. are a collection of different actions, and the different constituents of such a collection function as different syntactico-semantical items viz. *kārakas* such as instrument, object etc. with respect to the activity. However, this position too is not tenable. For, in both cases, i.e. in finite verbs and *ghañantas* (or other derivations), only the collection of such actions is the meaning of the word. Further, it may be held as follows :

The verbal roots such as *'yaj'* (to offer) etc. in *'aśvamedhena yajeta'* etc. refer to the accomplishing activity. Also, the same roots such as *'yaj'* include, in their reference, the objecthood and also the instrumentality of the root-meanings (offerings etc.) in general. However, in such a reference, the syntactico-semantical relations of the root-meanings are perceived particularized as the objecthood of the offering and the instrumentality of the Aśvamedha offerings etc., through the use of the accusative and instrumental words such as *'yajñam'* ,*'aśvamedhena'* etc. For instance, consider the meanings referred to by the verbal roots *'muṇḍay'* and *'upaślokay'* in 'he shaves the boy' (*māṇḍayati māṇavakam*), and 'he praises with the Mālinī verse' (*malinyā upaślokayati*). Here, the verbal roots *'muṇḍay'* and *'upaślokay'* refer to the activity of shaving and also to that of praising which include (imply) in their reference, the syntactico-semantical relations of the object of shaving and also that of the instrument of praising in general; and then the words *'māṇavakam'* and *'mālinyā'* provide the particular object of shaving and the particular instrument of praising, i.e. the boy and Mālinī respectively. However, this position is also not tenable. For, since in the statements such as 'he offers his own sacrifices' *(svam yajñam yajati)*, 'he has offered by means of many sacrifices' (*bahubhir yajñaiḥ īje*) etc., the verbal root (*yaj*) (found in the derivatives *'yajñam'* and *'yajñaiḥ'*) would refer to the activity (conducive to the offering); and also, since the activity would be accepted as particularized as 'ones own' and 'many' due to the agreement of the verbal derivatives *'yajñam'* and *'yajñaiḥ'*, with *'svam'* and *'bahubhiḥ*, the activities, (referred to by the verbal derivatives and also by the finite verbs) would have an undesired contingency of possessing the syntactico-semantical relations of being both the qualifier and the qualificand.

Note : Pūrvapakṣin comes up with several alternative suggestions. He suggests that the verbal root *'yaj'* etc. in *'aśvamedhena yajeta'* etc. can denote the activity in general as implying the syntactico-semantical notion of the instrumentality of the root-meanings (action of offering etc.). However, the words such as *'aśvamedhena'* etc. particularize the same offering etc. as the *Aśvamedha* offering; and thereby, provide the particular instrument of the activity. This instance is similar to the instance of *'muṇḍayati māṇavakam'* and *'mālinyā upaślokayati'* etc. wherein the verbal roots, viz. *'muṇḍay'* and *'upaślokay'* refer to the activity as conditioning the objecthood and also the instrumentality of the boy and the verse in general. However, the word *'māṇavakam'* and *'mālinyā'* particularize the objecthood and also the instrumentality of the same; and thereby provide the particular object of shaving and also the particular instrument of praising, viz. boy and Mālinī.

However, Sidhhāntin refutes such a suggestion by stating that in statements such as *'svam yajñam yajate'* and *'bahubhir yajñaiḥ* īje', the syntactico-semantical relations such as the objecthood and the instrumentality of the offering (*yajña*) would become untenable with the activity. He states that since in such cases, the verbal root *'yaj'* found in the verbal derivatives, namely, *'yajñam'* and *'yajñaiḥ* would be required to denote the activity particularized as 'ones own' and also as 'many' due to their agreement with *'svam'* and *'bahubhiḥ'* respectively, the same activity would have to relate, as a particular qualifier, to the activity, referred to by the verbal roots in *'yajati'* and *'īje'*, in general. Now, when something relates, as a particular qualifier, to something else, the two entities, being particular and general notions, would never be accepted to have the syntactico-semantical relations of *kāraka* and *kriyā* respectively. Thus, the position that the verbal root itself refers to the activity in general which implies the syntactico-semantical notion of the instrumentality, the objecthood etc. of the action is untenable.

Translation (P.130-32)

Conclusion that the activity should be accepted as the meaning of the conjugational endings

XXXV.3. Also, suppose the verbal root (*'yaj'* in the verbal derivatives such as *'svam yajñam yajate'* etc.) is held as not denoting the activity (to overcome the problems of the relationship of the qualifier and that of the qualificand), then the same verbal root would become established as deviating from the reference to the activity. And, consequently, the verbal root (such as *'yaj'*) becomes unfit to refer to the same activity in the finite forms (*yajati* etc.) as well. By this, the statements such as 'he cooks,' i.e. 'he performs the cooking of rice' *(odanapākam pacati)* etc., become commented upon.

Thus, the elders confirm the sense of the verb *'karoti' (karotyartha)*, i.e. the activity, as the meaning referred to by the conjugational endings in the finite verbs. And such an activity is quite distinct from the root-meanings such as 'cooking', 'offering' etc. The root-meanings such as 'offering', in such cases, may be referred to by the nominal words such as *'aśvamedha'* (in *aśvamedhena yajate);* and the syntactico-semantical relation of the instrumentality etc. (*kārakabhāva*) is expressed by the (instrumental and other) case endings found after *'aśvamedha'* etc.

Also, it should be noted that, in participial constructions such as 'he has made offerings by means of sacrifices' *(iṣṭavān yajñaiḥ)* etc., the cognition of such a reference to the activity is not contradictory. This is so because, in such cases too, the activity is understood, since the same activity, being the chief qualificand of the substance, i.e. the agenthood, needs to be implied.

Note : Siddhāntin refutes the alternative position of the Pūrvapakṣin as follows :

The verbal roots, in verbal derivatives such as *'yajñam'* etc., cannot be held to refer to the activity. For, supposing the verbal roots in the verbal derivatives refer to the activity, then the relation of the qualifier and the that of qualificand (*viśeṣaṇa viśeṣyabhāva*) between the activity, referred to by the verbal roots in the verbal derivaties *'yajñam'* etc., and also the activity, referred to by the finite verbs *'yajate'* etc., would contradict the syntactico-semantical relation of the instrumentality etc. of the actions 'offering' etc. with the activity.

Also, suppose the verbal roots in *'yajñam'* etc. do not refer to the activity, then, owing to the deviation, the same verbal roots in the finite forms such as *'yajate'* etc. too could not refer to the activity; and thus, the whole theory collapses. Therefore, according to the Siddhāntin, it should be accepted that the activity, as distinct from the action, is referred to by only the conjugational and other affixes in finite verbs. Also, it should be accepted that the action, which is referred to by the verbal roots in the nominal words such as *'aśvamedhena'*, would have its *kārakabhāva* expressed by the instrumental and other case endings. In such a theory, since the activity, as distinct from the action, is referred to by theconjugational endings, *'ti'* etc., the same can be construed as the chief qualificand of all the *kāraka* relations. Also, in the case of *'iṣṭavān yajñaiḥ'* etc., wherein no conjugational ending is found, the activity can be understood as implied since the agenthood expressed, by the *'kṛdanta'* form, namely, *'iṣṭavān'* requires an activity to condition it, i.e. necessitates the implying of the activity to accomplish the action of offering. Thus, the instrumentality etc. of the action of offering etc. can be related to the 'implied activity'.

Translation (P.132)

Refutation of the objection that *'karaṇatva'* of the root-meanings becomes untenable

The objection stated, namely, that "there occures the loss of the instrumentality *'karaṇatva'* in the root-meanings (cooking etc.) due to the cognition of the objecthood in the same root-meanings with respect to the activity" can be ascribed to only those who have not been properly elaborated about the real nature of the instrumentality. This can be explained as follows :

Verse 36

The instrument (axe etc.) is verily the item directly pervaded by (i.e. involved in) the operation (i.e. the activity) of the agent everywhere. And therefore, the primary object, which is brought about by such an instrument, covers, i.e. conceals, the agent. Or that the instrument, pervaded by (i.e. involved in) the operation of the agent, covers, i.e. conceals, the agent due to the fact that the object (effect) is directly produced by the same.

Translation (P.133-134)

Explanation of the verse 36

XXXVI.1. Never, on account of the pervasion (i.e. controlling) of the root-meaings by the activity, could there arise the contingency of either the occurrence of only the objecthood or the loss of the instrumentality in the root-meanings (i.e. in the action of cooking etc.). For, in that case, the same contingency of the objecthood and also the loss of the instrumentality could occur in the case of the axe etc. For instance, the agent of the cutting etc. (i.e. the wood-cutter) does not directly pervade, i.e. is not engaged in (the production of), the effect 'separation'; rather, he directly pervades (i.e. is engaged in) (the operation of) only the instrument 'axe' etc. And, therefore, only the instruments 'axe' etc. directly produce the effect 'separation' etc. The operation of the agent, whcih can be characterized as the lifting or felling (dropping down) of the axe etc., has only the instrument 'axe' (and not the effect 'separation') as its immediate object. Since the operation of the instrument 'axe' is immediate (i.e. is intimate) in producing (the effect of) the action, the same (axe) attains the state of being the most efficient means. And also, since the instrument (i.e. axe) is of the nature of having its movement (i.e. the operation of going up and down) dependent on the operations of the agent, the same (agent) is considered to have independence. This is in spite of the fact that the agent contributes only indirectly (towards the accomplishment of the effect). Otherwise, suppose this position were not to be accepted, then the instrumentality in the axe etc. could never be established (since everywhere only the axe contributes directly towards the accomplishment of the effect.)

Note : Siddhāntin explains that finite verbs such as *'pacati'* have been analysed as *'pākam karoti'* (he performs cooking), wherein the root-meanings such as 'cooking' function as the object of the activity. However, such an analysis cannot be taken to mean that the root-meaning can function as only the object everywhere and its instrumentality is totally lost. He states that, in any operation involving an instrument, only the instrument functions as the immediate item with respect to the production of the effect; and therefore, the same is the most efficient means. The agent is engaged directly in the operations of only the instrument; and hence, he is connected with the primary object (effect) only indirectly through the isntrument. Thus, the agent is only mediate and not immediate to the production of the effect.

Also, he explains that the root-meanings (action of cooking etc.) cannot be considered to be merely the objects (i.e. the effects) of the activity by ignoring their instrumentality due to the fact that the same root-meanings are pervaded by the activity, i.e. the operation of the agent. If such were the case, then the axe etc., which are actually the instruments, could also be considered to be merely the objects and not the instruments with respect to the action of cutting. This is so because, even the instruments such as axe etc. are directly pervaded by the activity, i.e. operation of the agent, namely, lifting and felling (dropping down) of the axe; and hence, the pervasion by the activity of the agent is same. Thus, in spite of the fact that, in the analysis of finite verbs such as *'pacati'* as *'pākam karoti'*, the root-meanings *'pāka'* etc. are the objects of *karoti*, and are pervaded by the activity of the agent, the same (root-meanings 'cooking' etc.) need not be considered as merely the objects by loosing their instrumentality. Further, Siddhāntin makes an interesting observation here with respect to the independence of the agent. He states that the agent is always independent with respect to the operations since the operations of the instrument etc. such as going up and down of the axe etc. are totally dependent on him. This is despite the instrument being more immediate to the accomplishment of the effect compared to the agent. Thus, in spite of the fact that the instrument is immediate and so is directly contributing towards the effect, i.e., in spite of the fact that the agent is not immediate and so is only indirectly contributing towards the effect, the same agent is independent in all the operations.

Translation (P.135)

Statement that kartṛvyāpāravyāpti neither produces the objecthood nor destroys the instrumentality in the root-meanings

Verse 37

(Suppose the pervasion (i.e. controlling) by the agent's operation is meant to produce the objecthood and to promote the loss of the instrumentality in the root-meanings, then) there would occur the loss (lit. absence) of all the *kārakas* excepting the grammatical agent and the object. Since only the employment of the various *kārakas* is considered (lit. desired) to be the operation of the agent everywhere, all the *kārakas* would become only the objects of such an operation of the agent.

Translation (P.136)

Explanation of the verse 37 that *kartṛvyāpāravyāpti* is not conducive to the objecthood

XXXVII.1. Now, under such a circumstance, even the talk (i.e. the existence) of other *kārakas* (such as the instrument, the locus etc.), excepting the grammatical agent and the object, would be destroyed. Since only the employment (i.e. controlling) of the *kārakas* is the operation (i.e. the activity) of the agent, all the *kārakas* would have only the contingency of becoming the object of such an operation (controlling) of the agent; and therefore, the objecthood would occur everywhere in the *kārakas*.

Note : Siddhāntin explains that suppose the root-meanings (cooking etc.) are considered to be only the objects on account of the fact that they are pervaded, i.e. controlled, by the operation of the agent, then all the other *kārakas* too would become only the grammatical objects, since they too are pervaded, i.e. controlled, by the agent. Consequently, the other *kārakas,* excepting the grammatical object and the agent, would cease to exist. This is so because, the very function of the agent is to control or employ the *kārakas*. Thus, the controlling or employment is same with respect to both the root-meanings and the other *kārakas.*

Siddhāntin explains, further, that suppose the pervasion (i.e. employment or controlling) by the activity of the agent *kartṛvyāpāra vyāpti* is held to be conducive to the objecthood and also to the loss of the instrumentality of the *kārakas,* then the very existence of the other *kārakas,* namely, *apādāna, karaṇa* etc., excluding the grammatical agent and the object, becomes untenable; for, all the *kārakas* are invariably pervaded, i.e. controlled, by the activity of the agent; and therefore, become only the objects of the activity. Thus, the division of the *kārakas* that some are objects and some are instruments, etc. would become untenable.

Translation (P.136-138)

Refutation of the position that *karmetaravibhāga* is untenable

XXXVII.2. Now, in that case, what way is the distinction of the *kārakas,* (such as *sampradāna, apādāna, karaṇa* etc.) from the grammatical object (*karma*) and the agent (*kartṛ*) **is tenable ?**

Also, now, supposing the operation (activity) of the **agent culminates or ends up in to** mere promotion of the instrumentality (due to its pervasion of the instrument), then how can the object *kārakas* (i.e. the root-meanings) be stated to attain the objecthood since the same (object *kārakas)* are devoid of the pervasion by the operation of the agent.

Here we state (the answer to both the above objections as follows) :

Translation

Verse 38

In the case of the intention, i.e. expectation, of the agent to obtain, through his activity, some other *kārakas* (i.e. instrument etc.), the root-meanings etc. would be considered as 'non-objects'. This is so because, the root-meanings etc., which are intended to be some other *kārakas* (i.e. instrument etc.), are devoid of the state of being what are most sought after by the agent. Also, when the *kārakas* such as the root-meanings are considered to be only *phalas* (i.e. the objects to be accomplished), the same would become the objects due to the fact that the same are sought most to be obtained through the activities of the agent. Thus, the objecthood can be admitted in spite of the fact that the activity of the agent occurs in the *kārakas* which are other than the objects (i.e. instrument etc.).

Note : Pūrvapakṣin raises two important objections : i) suppose the pervasion by the operation (activity) of the agent is meant to produce the objecthood in the *kārakas* (i.e. the root-meanings etc.), then the division of the *kārakas* as the objects *(karma)* and also as the non-objects (*akarma*) (i.e. *sampradāna, apādāna, karaṇa* etc.) would become untenable. This is so because, all the *kārakas* are only pervaded (i.e. controlled) by the activity of the agent and hence are only the objects. Also, ii) suppose only the instrument is considered to be pervaded (controlled) directly by the activity, then, no *kāraka* (including the *karmakāraka)* can be considered to be the object *kāraka,* since nothing but instrument is pervaded by the activity.

However, Siddhāntin refutes both the above objections on the following grounds : In the case of the agents expectation to consider the other *kārakas* as the instrument etc., the *kārakas,* which are other than the objects, would not become the grammatical objects, since the same (other *kārakas*) would lack the 'most desired' state, the essential precondition for considering a *kāraka* as the object. Thus, despite the pervasion by the activity, the other *kārakas* would not become objects. And, consequently, the distinction between *karmakārakas* and non-*karmakārakas* could be maintained. Also, in the case of the agent's expectation to seek some *kāraka* as the most desired item to be obtained through his activity, the same *kāraka* attains the state of the objecthood despite the pervasion by the activity. Thus, mere pervasion by the activity is neither conducive to the state of the objecthood nor (is) a cause of the loss of the instrumentality.

Translation (P.138-139)

Explanation of the verse 38 that the instrumentality and also the objecthood are not contradictory to the root-meanings

XXXVIII. 1. The *kāraka, viz.* the instrument, which

becomes the object of (i.e. which becomes pervaded by) the activity, meant to produce some other entity, i.e. effect, due to the lack of any other alternative, i.e. due to its immediate nature, has been declared to be the non-object due to its lack of the excellence, i.e. the most desired status. Also, the *kāraka*, which is considered to be the goal of the activity, has been declared to be the grammatical object. For, only such a *kāraka* (i.e. goal) is being sought most to be obtained through the activity despite the same (activity) pervading, i.e. associating, itself with some other *kārakas* such as the instrument etc. Nevertheless, the activity, which is prompted (i.e. undertaken) with the intention of accomplishing such a goal (i.e. object), can be explained to have its relation with the other *kārakas* such as the instrument (*karaṇa)* due to the untenability of its relation directly with the grammatical object. Thus, the cognition (of the instrumentality) and also the illustration of the accomplishability (i.e. the objecthood) with respect to root-meanings (i.e. with respect to the action of cooking etc.) are not contradictory to each other. This is despite the said root-meanings functioning as the instruments with respect to the activity. This instance of the cognition of the instrumentality and the illustration of the objecthood with respect to the root-meanings is similar to the instance of the cognition of the instrumentality and the illustration of the objecthood with respect to the axe in the instrumental statement such as 'he cuts with an axe' (*paraśunā chinatti)* and in the accusative illustration such as 'he employs (i.e. uses) the axe' (*paraśuṃ prayuṅkte)*. In the instrumental statement, the instrumentality of the axe is cognized. However, in the accusative illustration, the instrumentality of the axe is not cognised, but rather, the objecthood of the same is illustrated, since the axe is to be lifted up and is to be felled (dropped) down, i.e. since agent lifts the axe and drops it down, for the cutting (the things) into t wo'.

Note : Now, Siddhāntin explains as to when a *kāraka* is to be considered as the instrument and also as to when the same is to be considered as the object. According to the Pāṇiniyan rule, *'kartur īpsitatamam karma'* (i.4.48), only the *kāraka*, which the agent seeks most to obtain through his activities, can be considered to be the object; whereas the instrument, since it is not desired most to be obtained through the activity of the agent, cannot be considered to be the object. Thus, despite the instrument being pervaded by the activity due to its immediacy, the same (instrument) cannot be considered to be the object. Also, the *kāraka*, which is desired most to be the goal (i.e. the effect to be accompanied) through the activity of the agent, can be considered to be the object regardless of whether or not such an object is pervaded by the activity. This is so because, the pervasion of the other *kārakas* by the activity too is meant only to produce the object.

Further, the Siddhāntin explains as to how the other *kārakas* too can be associated with the activity inspite of the fact that only the object is to be obtained. According to him, the *kārakas*, that are other than the instrument, cannot be directly associated with the activity, since the agent does not operate directly with the help of other *kārakas*. Nevertheless, the other *kārakas*, including the object, can be indirectly associated with the activity due to their state of being accomplished by such an activity. Thus, the other *kārakas* too can be considered as associated with the activity.

The root-meanings (the action of 'cooking' etc.), which are originally the instruments, can therefore, be cognized as the instruments and also illustrated as the objects without any contradiction. This instance is similar to the cognition of the instrumentality in the axe in *paraśunā chinatti* and also the illustration of the objecthood in the axe in *'paraśum udyacchati nipātayati'*. When one states that 'he cuts with an axe' (*paraśunā chinatti*), one cognizes the instrumentality in the axe as the same axe functions as the instrument of cutting in such statements, also when one states that 'he lifts up and drops down the axe' (*paraśum udyacchati nipātayati)*, one illustrates the objecthood in the axe as the same axe functions as the object of lifting up etc. Thus, the cognition of the instrumentality and also the illustration of the objecthood in one and the same axe is found in the language. Similarly, the cognition of the original state of the instrumentality and also the illustration of the objecthood in the root-meanings (cooking etc.) is not contradictory to each other.

Translation (P.140-141)

Objection that *kartṛvyāpāra*, which is identified with activity *(bhāvanā)*, is only *dhātvarthāntara*

Some may object here as follows :

The operation of the agent (*kartṛvyāpāra)* such as the putting the vessel on the fire, etc., which is identified with the accomplishing activity, constitutes the meaning (i.e. denotation) of different verbal roots, i.e. *adhiśri* (to put on the fire etc.) *dhātvarthāntara* which are totally different from conjugational endings; and therefore, the position that the operation of the agent is the activity expressed by the conjugational endings is untenable. However, the Siddhāntins state the reply with respect to such an objection as follows :

Verse 39

The root-meanings such as 'cooking' *(pāka)* and 'putting vessel on' *(adhiśryaṇa)* can be appropriately explained in two ways due to the distinction of forms to be established between the root-meanings as the object to be accomplished and also the activity as what accomplishes such an object. (In '*pākam karoti*,' the *pāka* has the form of the object to be accomplished, whereas the *adhiśrayaṇa* has the form of an accomplishing activity). Therefore, despite being the meaning elsewhere of a distinct root such as '*adhiśri*' (to put the vessel on thefire etc.), the operation cannot be denied its distinct nature of being the activity, since it is conducive to the production of another object, i.e. *pāka* etc.

Translation (P.141)

Explanation of the verse 39 that *kartṛvyāpāra* can be meaning of the conjugational endings

XXXIX. 1. Thus, it has been explained that, in no way, the activity can constitute the meaning of the 'verbal roots' such as '*pac*,' '*yaj*' etc., which are used before the conjugational endings such as '*ti*' in such expressions of finite verbs as '*pacati*' (he cooks), '*yajati*' (he sacrifices) etc. Also, it has been explained that the denotation of such an activity (in the form of the putting of the vessel on the fire etc.) by totally different verbal roots (such as *adhiśri*) etc. does not lead to the loss of our own theory (view); for, this instance of the denotation of the activity is similar to the denotatin of the activity by the verbal roots in *'karoti'* (he performs) and *'bhāvayati'* (he makes it accomplished).

Note : An objection is raised that the operation of the agent (*kartṛvyāpāra*), which is identified with the activity (*bhāvanā*), is actually the meaning of a totally different verbal root; and hence, the same cannot be held to be the meaning of the conjugational endings. For instance, the operation of the agent, in the case of the cooking, can be described to be the putting of the vessel on the fire etc. And such an operation is actually the meaning of a separate verbal root, namely, *'adhiśri'* (to put vessel on); and hence, the so called activity cannot be the part of the meaning of a finite verb such as*'pacati'* or *'yajati'* etc.

However, Siddhāntin refutes such an argument as follows:

The meanings of the verbal roots would be explained to have two – fold nature, i.e. that of being an object which is to be accomplished such as cooking (*pāka*) and also that of being a *kriyā* or *bhāvanā* which accomplishes such an object. For instance, *'pacati'* (he cooks) is explained as *'pākam karoti'* (he performs cooking) wherein the cooking is an object to be accomplished and also the performing is the *kriyā* which accomplishes such a cooking. Consequently, despite the operation of the agent being the meaning of some other verbal root such as *'adhiśri'* elsewhere, the same can be the meaning of the conjugational endings in finite verbs such as *'pacati'* (he cooks), *'yajati'* (he makes offerings) etc. Here, the activity (*bhāvanā*), which is nothing but the operation of the agent and which functions as the *kriyā* in accomplishing the action, is not unjustified in being assumed as the meaning of the conjugational endings that produces another thing, namely, the action of cooking etc. Also, Siddhāntin establishes that never the activity is the meaning of the verbal roots that are used as preceding the conjugational endings in finite forms of verbs such as *'pacati'*, *'yajati'* etc. He states that the reference to the activity elsewhere by other verbs such as *'adhiśrayati'* (puts the vessel on fire) does not contradict the theory that the same activity is the meaning of the conjugational endings in finite verbs, since such a reference to the activity is similar to the reference to the activity by other verbs such as *'karoti'* or *'bhāvayati'* in the explanation of the finite verbs such as 'pacati' = *'pākam karoti'*, 'yajati' = *'yāgam bhāvayati'* etc.

Translation (P.143)

Description of the nature of *'dhātvartha'*

Verse 40

The scholars declare (establish) the denoted meanings of the verbal roots *(dhātvartha)* to be the particular qualities (attributes), or actions that are already accomplished in nature, that have the form of non-activity and also that abide in either the agent or the object.

Explanation of the verse 40 that only qualities etc. are root-meanings

XL. 1. For instance, the meaning denoted by the verbal root *(adhi) 'śri'* (to place vessel on fire) is the particular type of contact between the vessel and also the fire place; and the meaning denoted by the verbal root *'āsiñc'* (to pour water) is the particular type of contact between what is to be poured in such as the water and also the container (substratum) such as the vessel. This way, everywhere, some kind of quality etc. are to be understood as the meanings of the verbal roots. The meanings of the verbal root *'pac'* (to cook), however, is either the separation, i.e. slackening of the parts of rice (grains) or the separation of the contacts that exist among the loose parts of the rice (grains).

Note : After describing the two – fold nature of the meanings of the finite verbs as that of the object *kāraka* which is to be accomplisdhed and also as that of the activity which accomplishes such an object *kāraka*, Siddhāntin explains the exact nature of the verbal root-meanings. According to him, the denoted meanings of the verbal roots are the particular qualities such as 'contact' (*'saṁyoga'*), 'separation' (*'vibhāga'*) etc. which are of accomplished nature (*labdhātman* or *siddhasvabhāva)* and non-activities (*akriyārūpa)*, i.e. which do not function as the cause of accomplishing an action. He further states that such root-meanings inher in either the agents or the objects of the action. For instance, consider (*adhi) 'śrayate'* (he puts the vessel on fire). Here the verbal root-meaning is the contact between the vessel and also the fire – place which inhers in the object, the vessel. Or for instance, consider the verb *'yajati'* (he offers). Here the root meaning is a particular resolve to perform a ritual which inhers in the agent, the *yajamāna*. In the same way, everywhere, the meanings of the verbal roots are qualities etc. that are already established and are of the nature of non-activity,

In the case of the verbal root *'pac'* (to cook), however, the root-meaning is either the separation, i.e. slackening of the contacts, of the parts of rice grains or the separation of the contacts that exist among the different parts of rice grains. Thus, Siddhāntin considers the root-meanings 'cooking' etc. to be identical with the effects, namely, contact, separation etc.

Translation (P.144)

Description of the nature of the activity

Verse 41

Scholars declare the meaning of the verb *'karoti'* (performing), i.e. the activity, as something characterized by the removal of the inactive or passive state (indifference) and also as the cause of the root-meanings (i.e. the action of cooking etc.). And such an activity is (considered to be) a synonym of the movement (*spanda*) and also of the operation or effort (*vyāpāra*).

Explanation of the verse 41 that the activity has the form of an operation

XLI. 1. This can be explained as follows :

The nature of the activity is distinctly perceived to have the form of an operation in cases such as 'he performs' (*karoti*), 'he moves' (*spandate*), 'he exerts' (*ceṣṭate*), 'he pervades' (*vyāpriyate*) etc. And such an activity is, therefore, distinct from the different kinds of contacts, i.e. root-meanings such as the contact between the vessel and the fire etc., which are perceived to have the form of qualities in cases such as 'he puts vessel on fire' (*adhiśrayati*), 'he pours water' (*udakam āsiñcati*), 'he cooks' (*pacati*) or 'he studies' (*paṭhati*) etc.

Note : Now, Siddhāntin explains that the activity, expressed by the verbal ending *'ti'* etc., is distinct from the root-meanings. He clarifies that the activity, which can be the meaning of the verb *'karoti'* (he does or performs), should be understood to be devoid of the inactive or passive (indifferent) state by disassociating itself from the inactivity (*niṣkriyatva*) or passitivity (indifference) (*audāsīnya)*, since the same is nothing but the absence of the activity.

The explanation of the activity as distinct from the root-meanings, i.e. qualities such as 'contact' etc., is based on the fact that the activity is experienced to have the nature of being an operation or effort in the expressions such as *'karoti'* (he performs), *'spandate'* (he moves), *'ceṣṭate'* (he exerts) etc; whereas the root-meanings such as 'cooking' etc., which can be identified with the effect such as contact, separation etc., are experienced to have the nature of being the qualities in the expressions such as *'adhiśrayati'* (he puts vessel on fire), *'udakam āsiñcati'* (he pours water in the vessel) etc. Also, Siddhāntin states that the activity is the cause of the root-meanings, since the same activity is conducive to the qualities such as 'contact', separation which are identical with the root-meanings. Thus, the activity, as the meaning of the conjugational endings, and also as characterised by the loss of the inactivity or passivity, has the nature of an operation or effort which produces the root-meanings.

Translation (P.145)

Refutation of the objection that *'calati pratyaya'* is based on particular qualities such as *'samyoga'* or *'vibhāga'*

Now, it should not be objected that the knowledge of movement *calatipratyaya* such as *'calati'* (he moves) (which is actually based on the operation) is based merely on the particular qualities such as 'contact' (*samyoga*), 'separation' (*vibhāga*) etc. which are actually intended to be the effects produced from it (activity). For, the reason can be explained as follows :

Vessel 42

Despite the presence of the particular qualities such as 'contact' and 'separation', the production (i.e. existence) of the knowledge of the operation (i.e. movement) such as 'he moves' (*calati)* is not experienced in the case of the people who have come to a halt after exerting (i.e. going, cooking etc.)

Translation (P.146)

Explanation of verse 41-42 that the knowledge of the operation is based on the operation

XLII. 1. The absence of contact (*samyoga*) with the next region and also that of the separation (*vibhāga*) from the region left behind, which are produced from the action of moving (going) etc., are not found to exist eve when some one has already stopped (from moving) after making a journey (i.e. only the presence of the qualities such as contact and separation are found to exist after the activity is over). Therefore, the knowledge of the operation, i.e. movement, such as 'he moves' (*calati)* would never cease to continue supposing such a knowledge is held to have been produced from (i.e. based on) the qualities such as 'contact' and 'separation'.

Note : Siddhāntin explains that suppose the knowledge of the operation (movement) such as 'he moves' (*'calati)*, which ascertains the nature of the activity as distinct from the root-meanings, is held to have been based on the qualities such as 'contact' and 'separation', which are produced from such an activity, then the same would become necessary to occur even in the case when someone has completed his journey and has stopped moving. This is so because even after the completion of the actual activity, i.e. after the cessation of the activity, the qualities produced from the activity would still remain to exist. Thus, the knowledge of the operation such as *'calati'* cannot be accepted to have been based on the qualities produced from the activity. On the contrary, the knowledge of the operation must be regarded as being based on, i.e. produced directly from, the operation (activity) only. Consequently, it becomes necessary that in order to explain such a knowledge as *'calati'*, the activity, must be conceded as distinct from the root-meanings (action or quality).

Translation (P.147)

Refutation of the view that the knowledge of the operation is based on the collection of qualities

Verse 43

How can there be the collection of the qualities such

as contact between the region left behind and the region coming next, since the same is interrupted due to the loss of continuity between them by separation. Thus, the collection of the qualities such as contact etc. cannot be the basis of the knowledge of the operation such as *'calati'* (he moves). Also, how could there be the perception of the qualities such as contact and separation which occur in the future time (since perception can be the means of the knowledge of only the qualities of the present time). Thus, the future qualities such as contact and separation etc. too cannot be regarded as the basis of the knowledge of the operation such as *'calati'*.

Translation (P.148-9)

Explanation of the verse 43 that the knowledge of the operation cannot be based on any kind of quality

XLIII. 1. Also, the position that "the knowledge of the operation (movement) such as *'calati'* (he moves) is based on the collection of the qualities such as the separation and the contact which are produced without any loss of continuity between the region left behind and the region coming next" is also not correct. For, the contact with the next or subsequent region is not produced unless and until there occurs a separation from the region left behind. Also, the separation (which functions as the cause of the contact with the next or subsequent relgion) does not occur along with the contact with the region left behind in one substratum at one and the same time. Now, since the contact with the region left behind is completely destroyed due to the separation (which functions as the cause of the contact with the next or subsequent region), how can there exist the collection of such qualities as separation and contact in one and the same substratum at the same time.

Now, it should be noted as follows : The contacts are produced without any loss of continuity between them, i.e. uninterruptedly in one and the same substratum, means the qualities like contacts, which occur at the present time, have the state of being related through inherence to the contacts which would be defintely occurring in the future time in the same substratum. Now, since the qualities occur at both present as well as future times, how can the sense organ (perception), which cannot have future things as its objects, produce the cognition regarding the qualities, which occur both at the present as well as the future times.

Also, the mind of a person, who is not skilled in the practice of natural concentration (*yoga*), cannot perceive such objects as contacts etc. which occur at the future time. Moreover, in that case (suppose the qualities such as the contact and the separation, which would occur in a place at two different times (i.e. present and future), are held to be the basis of the knowledge of operation, then) the knowledge of the operation such as 'he moves' would become necessary from the qualities such as contact as well as the separation which are produced from the two different *śyena* birds at the post. (Thus, the knowledge of the operations cannot be held to have been based on, i.e. caused from, the qualities such as contact and separation).

Note : Siddhāntin rejects the Pūrvapakṣin's view that the knowledge of the operation such as 'he moves' (*calati*) can be based on the collection of the qualities such as contacts or separations. According to him, the collection of the qualities such as contacts is not tenable since different contacts (i.e. the contact with the region left behind and also the contact with the region coming next) are never found together in continuity due to the separation that occurs in between. Contact with the region left behind is terminated by the separation before the contact with the region coming next is produced. Thus, the knowledge of the operation such as 'he moves' (*calati*) can never be based on the collection of the qualities such as contacts, since the two contacts can never come together with each other in one locus. Also, he holds that, since sense orgas can perceive only present things, past and future contacts can never be perceived together in any locus. Therefore, the knowledge of the operation such as '*calati*' cannot be based on past and future contacts either.

It should be noted, therefore, that the Pūrvapakṣin's view that such a knowledge of operation can be based on the collection of the qualities which are produced continuously in one place such as a tree with a bird is untenable. The contact with the next region is never produced without the separation from the region left behind. And, also, the separation, which functions as the cause of the contact with the region coming next, can never be found to occur along with the contact with the region left behind since such a contact is always terminated by the same separation. Thus, the theory that 'the collection of the qualities such as the contact and also the separation is possible, and hence the knowledge of operation such as '*calati*' can be based on such collection' is also untenable.

Further, it should be noted here that, since the occurrence of the qualities such as the two continuous contacts in the present time is ruled out in one place, the collection of the qualities must be understood as the occurrence of a contact in the present time with the contact in the future time. However, such a position too is untenable, since the sense organs, capable of perceiving only the present things, can never perceive the qualities of the future time. Also, the mind of a person not used to *yogābhyāsa* can never perceive such future qualities. Moreover, suppose the knowledge of the operation such as 'he moves' (*calati*) is held to have been based on the qualities, which would occur in a place at two different times, then the same knowledge of the operation becomes necessary even in the case when the qualities 'contact' and 'separation', which belong to two different *śyena* birds, are found to occur in a tree. Thus, the theory, that the knowledge of the operation such as 'he moves' (*calati*) is based on the collection of the qualities is totally untenable.

Translation (P.151-52)

Refutation of the position that knowledge of operation is due to ādhāradeśa saṁyogavibhāga

It may be stated now as follows :

Such a knowledge of the operation is due to only the (qualities such as) the contact with and the separation from one's bodily parts occurring in the points of location.

However, this position too is not justified. This can be explained as follows :

Verse 44

The qualities such as the contact with and also the separation from the bodily parts (of fish), in the points of water (the locus), are found to occur without (causing) such a knowledge of the operation, such as 'fish moves' (*matsyaḥ calati)* with respect to the fishes, which have water as their space, i.e. locus, provided that the same (fishes) have a still (steady) body at such a time. Thus, the knowledge of the operation is not based on the qualities.

Translation (P.151-54)

Explanation

XLIV. 1. Unlike the post, which is not the points of locus of the *śyena* bird, the water is perceived to be the point of locus of fish(es).

However, despite the presence (occurrence) of the contact with and the separation from the parts of the fish(es) (in the points of the water, the locus), the fishes cannot be accepted as moving (i.e. as possessing the movement) when the same fishes are either not to be shaken due to the heaviness of their body or are still-bodied due to the forceful restraining current of water. Thus, the knowledge of the operation is not caused by the qualities of the parts of the body in the space, i.e. locus.

Also, it should be noted that since the sky is imperseptible, the perceptibility of the contact and also the separation, which occur in such an imperceptible sky, could not be obtained (ascertained). It cannot be argued, therefore, that such a knowledge of the operation (as *'calati'*) is based on the qualities such as the contact and also the separation of the parts of the collection (multitude) of the flashes of lightnings which pervade the sky. For, the knolwedge of the operation such as *'calati'* is produced in the sky pervaded by the darkness provided that there is suddenly a flash of lightning.

Therefore, an operation, which is synonymous with the activity (*bhāvanā*) and which is the meaning of the finite verbs such as *'karoti'*, *'calati'* etc., must be accepted. Such an activity has the nature of an entity distinct from the root-meanings, i.e. actions such as 'cooking', 'going' etc. and also from the qualities such as contact, separation etc. which are produced by means of the actions.

Note : Siddhāntin refutes the alternative position of the Pūrvapakṣin that "the knowledge of the operation such as *'calati'* is produced by the qualities 'contact' and also 'separation' of the bodily parts of an entity in its points of space (locus); and since the contact and the separation of the parts of the *śyena* bird in the post cannot be termed as the qualities of the moving entity in its locus, the absence of such a knowledge of operation can be explained during the sitting and also flying of *śyena* bird on and from the post respectively".

He states that even during the presence of the contact of the parts of the fishes in the water, the knowledge of the operation that 'fishes move' (*matsyāḥ calanti)* is never made provided that the fishes are too heavy or big to move and therefore, cannot be dragged away. On the other hand unlike the post, which can be claimed to be the non-point of space, i.e. the non-locus of the *śyena* bird, the water cannot be claimed to be the non-point of space, i.e. the non-locus of the fishes. Water is indeed the locus of the fishes. Thus, the qualities such as the contact and also the separation of the bodily parts in the point of the space (loucs) cannot be claimed to be the basis from which such a knowledge of operation is produced.

Also, Siddhāntin refutes the Pūrvapakṣin's argument that the sky (*ākāśa*) alone is the locus of things such as birds since the same provides the space for all things. According to him, since the sky is imperceptible, even the contact and the separation etc., when they occur in the sky, become imperceptible. Therefore, such imperceptible qualities like contact and separation in the sky cannot be claimed to be the basis on which the knowledge of the operation with respect to the birds such as 'birds move' *śyenāḥ calanti'* is established.

Lastly, Siddhāntin refutes the argument that the contact and also the separation of the bodily parts of the multitude of the flashes of lightning in the sky are the basis of the knowledge of the operations such as 'bird is moving, (*śyenaḥ calati).* According to him, the knowledge of the operation such as 'bird is moving' is produced from even a flash of lightning when the whole of sky is full of darkness. And, in such cases, the contact and also the separation of the parts of the flashes of lightning cannot be claimed to be the cause of the production of such a knowledge as such flashes are momentary. Now, since the view that the knowledge of the operation such as *'calati'* is based on the qualities such as contact and separation is untenable, an operation (*vyāpāra*), which is synonymous with the activity (*bhāvanā*) and which is the meaning of the conjugational endings (*tiṅ* etc.), must be accepted as distinct from both the actions such as cooking and also the qualities such as swelling etc. which are produced by means of the actions.

Translation (P.155)

Objection that *'dhātvartha'* cannot be *'bhāvanākaraṇa'*

XLIV. 2. Now, it may be objected as follows :

As stated above, the root-meanings (*dhātvartha*) such as the action of cooking or moving etc. are produced from the activity (*bhāvanā*). And the effects (such as 'heaven' etc.) are produced from such root-meanings. Therefore, how can the same root-meanings, which are produced from the activity, be functioning as the most efficient means (*karaṇa*) with respect to the same activity. Also, therefore, how can the effects heaven etc., which are not accomplished through the activity, be functioning as the objects of the same activity. Thus, the same root-meanings (which produce the effects) must be considered as the activity (*bhāvanā*) due to their efficiency in producing the effects. Also, since there cannot be any separate activity avaiable in between the effects 'heaven' (etc.) and also the root-meanings 'action of offering etc.', no distinct activity, which has the root-meanings as its most efficient means, can be established.

Note : Another objection raised against the activity (*bhāvanā*) is as follows : Since the root-meanings such as the action of cooking or offering etc. have been produced from the activity (*bhāvanā*), the same root-meanings cannot be held to be the most efficient means with respect to such an activity. To consider the root-meanings as the means with respect to the activity, the same activity must be produced through the root-meanings. Also, since the effects such as heaven etc. are produced from the root-meanings (action of offering etc.), the same effects cannot be the objects of the activity. (They can be the objects of only the root-meanings). On the contrary, the activity itself is supposed to be producing the effect. Therefore, in no way, can the activity be assumed to be distinct from the root-meanings that have the effects (heaven etc.) as their objects. Thus, the root-meanings themselves, producing the effects, can be considered to be the activity, since no activity, that is distinct from both the effects and the root-meanings, can be established.

Translation (P.156)

Refutation of the objection that *dhātvartha* cannot be *bhāvanākaraṇa*

No, this objection has already been answered. Our position can be stated as follows :

Verse 45

The agent, who is desirous of some fruit (effect), is found making an effort, i.e. is exerting one's own self directly towards the instrument (*karaṇa*) and not towards the effect. Therefore, the root meanings, which are the instruments with respect to the effects, become the objects of the activity. Nevertheless, since the same root-meanings assume the instrumentality with respect to the production of the prominent aspect (i.e. the effect), the same can be considered to be the instruments with respect to the activity as well. (Thus, the root-meanings can be both the instruments with respect to the effects and the objects with respect to the activity). Also, since the operation has the sameness of form, i.e. identity, with the activity due to the production of the effects by means of the root-meanings, the same root-meanings can be considered to be the instruments with respect to the activity directly as well.

Translation (P.158)

Explanation of the verse 45 that *dhātvartha* can be *bhāvanākaraṇa*

XLV. 1. The objecthood of the effects (such as heaven) and also the instrumentality of the root-meanings (such as offering) are not essentially different in characteristics from the objecthood of other effects (such as becoming two etc.) and also from the instrumentality of other instruments (such as axe etc.). It has already been demonstrated that the (operation of the) agent does not pervade directly the effect such as the 'becoming two' (*dvidhābhavana)* in cases like 'he cuts with an axe' (*paraśunā chinatti*) etc. On the contrary, the same (operation) pervades the instrument such as axe (*paraśu*) directly, since the agent has the characteristics of one who employs (controls) the means of the operation etc.

Nevertheless, such an operation can be taken to culminate into (the accomplishment of) the effect as well, since the same (operation) is undertaken with the intention (purpose) of accomplishing the effect alone. Also, since there exists no other way of accomplishing the effect (except indirectly through the instrument), the effect itslef is considered as the object. However, the difference between the root-meanings (offering etc.) and the regular instruments such as axe etc. is as follows : While the root meanings (action of offering etc.), since they are unaccomplished (*asiddha)*, are to be used in accomplishing the effects by accomplishing the same, the axe etc., since they are already accomplished (*siddha)*, are to be used in accomplishing the effects by the operation of lifting up and dropping down etc.

Now, the difference between the effects such as heaven and the regular effects such as becoming two is as follows : Since 'the becoming two' (*dvihābhavana)* is the effect of cutting tree, the objecthood of the tree (which is being cut) etc. can be explained only due to their agenthood with respect to the effect of becoming two etc. The objecthood of the tree is indicated, further, by lifting up and dropping down of the axe (meant exclusively for the sake of the accomplishment of the becoming two of the same tree).

Also, in the case of 'he cuts' (*chinatti)*, the instrumentality of the axe with respect to the becoming two of the tree is dependant on the prominent, i.e. the effect of becoming two. This is so because, the sameness of form of operation i.e. identity with the activity is dependant on the operation of lifting and dropping of the axe, the instrument. The statement such as '*chinatti*' (he cuts) does not denote mere operation of lifting and dropping of the axe, when the effect such as the becoming two of the tree is impossible to accomplish (due to the hardness etc.). Similarly, in the context of '*yajeta svargakāmaḥ*' too, the operation of the agent (sacrificer), which produces the root-meaning (offering) and facilitates the effect (heaven) to be accomplished by way of the performance of the offering, acquires the designation of the accomplishing activity (*bhāvanā*) due to the fact that the same is meant for the accomplishment of the effect (heaven). And the same operation, has acquired the sameness of form, i.e. identity, with the activity due to its efficiency in producing the effect, such as the same prominent aspect 'heaven', by means of the root-meanings, the actions. Therefore, the operation has the root-meanings (offering etc.) as its instruments in producing the effect 'heaven' etc., and also has the effects 'heaven' etc., identical with the objects, as its objects. Thus, no difficulty can be envisaged in assuming an activity in addition to the root-meanings and also the effects.

Note : Siddhāntin refutes, the objection of Pūrvapakṣin that no activity can be envisaged in addition to the root-meanings 'offering' etc. and also in addition to the effects 'heaven' etc. According to the Siddhāntin, as stated already, the person desirous of an effect, always undertakes an activity which pervades the instrument (means of accomplishing the effect); he never undertakes an activity which directly pervades the effect as such. Nevertheless, since the agent undertakes the activity with the intention of accomplishing the effect, the same activity can be considered to have the effects (heaven) etc. as its goal, i.e. objects. Further, despite the root-meanings (offering etc.) being the objects of the activity, the same do not cease to be the instruments as well. This is so because, the root-meanings, by being the instruments with respect to the accomplishment of the effects (the prominent), can be viewed to be functioning as the instruments with respect to the activity as well. Moreover, since the operation of the agent is identical with the activity (i.e. *bhāvanā*) due to its efficiency in producing the effects by means of the root-meanings, the same root-meanings can be considered to be the instruments directly with respect to the activity as well.

Siddhāntin points out, further, that the objecthood of the effects (heaven etc.) and also the instrumentality of the root-meanings (offering etc.) with respect to the activity are not really different from the regular objecthood of the effect (of becoming two etc.) (*dvidhābhavana*) and also the instrumentality of the axe etc. with respect to the cutting etc. This is so because, in such cases too, (the operation of) the agent does not directly pervade the effect 'the becoming two'; but rather, it pervades only the instrument 'axe' directly. For, the agent is one who employs the instrument 'axe' etc. through his operation.

Nevertheless, it should be noted that despite the operation of the agent pervading only the instrument (and not the effect), the effect need not be excluded from becoming the object (i.e. only the instrument need not become the object) of the operation. For, the operation pervades, indirectly (through the instrument) the effect as well. Also, since ultimately what is accomplished is the effect, and not the instrument, only the effect deserves to be the object of the activity. However, the difference between the conventional instruments such as the axe etc. and the root-meanings such as the action of offering etc. is that while the conventional instruments (axe etc.), being what are already accomplished, are undertaken to accomplish the effects through the operation such as lifting up and dropping down, the root-meanings, not being what are already accomplished, are undertaken to accomplish themselves so that one can accomplish the effects as well.

The conventional objecthood of the tree is explained on the ground that the same (tree) is the agent of becoming two; and therefore, it functions as the object with respect to the action of cutting. And, the tree is the most desired thing to be obtained through the action of cutting for the sake of becoming two. Thus, the tree becomes the object of cutting by becoming the object most desired to be obtained through the action of cutting which can be characterized as the lifting up and dropping down of the axe.

In the case of *'paraśunā chinatti'*, the axe functions as the instrument with respect to the accomplishment of the effect 'becoming two', since the very accomplishment of the prominent, i.e. the effect, depends upon the lifting and dropping of the axe. Nevertheless, the same axe functions as the instrument with respect to the operation of cutting as well, since the identity of the operation with the activity leading to the accomplishment of the effect (becoming two) is itself dependent on the lifting and also the dropping of the axe. Never does the statement such as *'paraśunā chinatti'* (he cuts with an axe) express the mere operation such as lifting and dropping (wherein the axe is the object *kāraka* of lifting and dropping) suggesting the fact that the effect of becoming two is impossible to accomplish due to the hardness etc. Thus, axe is the instrument both ways with respect to the accomplishment of the effect as well as with respect to the activity of accomplishing the effect.

Now, on the analogy of the operation of the wood-cutter, the operation of the agent (sacrificer) in the case of '*svargakāmo yajeta*' etc. too can be accepted as obtaining the status of 'accomplishing activity' (*bhāvanā*) in view of the fact that the same is intended to accomplish the effects (heaven etc.) either directly or indirectly through the root-meanings (offering etc.). Also, since the operation accomplishes the effects (heaven etc.) through the instrumentality of the root-meanings (offering etc.), the same operation can be accepted as having the effects 'heaven' etc. as its objects and the root-meanings (action of offering etc.) as its instruments. Thus, an activity which is totally different from both the effects as well as the root-meanings, must be recognised as the meaning of the conjugational endings.

Translation (P.164-65)

Explanation that *vyāpārāntarānupāalambha* is not a fault

XLV. 2. In the instance such as 'the tree becomes divided into two parts' (*dvidhā bhavati)* or 'he makes the tree into two parts by an axe' (*dvidhābhāvayati purvaśunā)*, no distinct operation of the agent apart from that of the instrument either in the form of an operation that is accomplished by the other (i.e. the instrument 'axe') or in the form of an operation that accomplishes the other (i.e. the effect of becoming two) is found in between the effect, namely, the becoming two of the tree, and also the instrument, namely, the axe. Nevertheless, the instrumentality of the axe is not contradictory; for, the accomplishment of the prominent item (i.e. the effect of becoming two) is dependant on the (lifting and also dropping of the) axe.

Similarly, in the instance of '*yajeta svargakāmaḥ*' also, (despite the absence of a distinct operation of an agent in between the effect, namely, heaven and also the instrument, namely, the, root-meaning), the instrumentality of the root-meaning 'offering' is not contradictory. This is so because, the establishment of the distinction between the *kāraka* cases (such as the instrumental, accusative etc.) is dependent on the contribution of the *kāraka* items to the accomplishment of the effect, which assumes the prominent status with respect to the action (and not dependent merely on the operation as such).

For instance; it is said as follows :

Verse 46

Kārakas (such as the instrument, the object etc.) attain the unity of sentence (i.e. come together as semantically related to an operation in a single sentence) taking into consideration the fact that the prominent item (i.e. effect) is to be produced. Nevertheless, the *kārakas* do not attain the unity of sentence taking into consideration the nature of the operation, since the same operation, which leads to the accomplishment of other things, cannot be considered by nature, to be what is accomplished by means of other *kārakas*.

Translation

Explanation

XLVI. 1. Thus, the non-perception (non-obtainment) of a distinct operation in between the effect and also the root-meaning 'action' is not a fault (in establishing the existence of a distinct activity).

Note : In the case of the accomplishment of an effect, involving an operation, no separate or distinct operation of the agent (apart from that of the instrument) is found to occur either as an operation that is produced out of another instrument or as an operation that produces another effect. For instance, in the case of the accomplishment of the effect such as 'becoming into two parts', no distinct operation of the wood-cutter (apart from that of the instrument 'axe') can be found to occur between the axe and also the becoming into two parts either as an operation produced out of the instrument 'axe', or as an operation that produces the effect of becoming into two parts. However, in spite of such an absence of a distinct operation of the agent, the axe is indeed considered to be the instrument in accomplishing the effect 'becoming two'. This is so because, the instrumentality of the axe depends upon the capacity of the axe to produce the effect 'becoming two'. The *kāraka*-hoods such as the instrumentality etc. are actually dependent on the production of the effect and not on their capacity to produce another operation which may accomplish indirectly the effect. Thus, in spite of the fact that no distinct operation of the agent 'wood-cutter' is found to exist, the instrumentality of the axe can be established.

Now, since the instrumentality of a *kāraka* item is not dependent on its capacity to produce another operation, but rather is dependent on its capacity to produce an effect such as the becoming into two parts etc., the instrumentality of the root-meaning (offering) in '*yajeta svargakāmaḥ*' too can be explained on the basis of its (root-meaning's) capacity to produce the effect (heaven). And hence, the absence of the perception of another operation in between the root-meaning (offering), i.e. the instrument, and also the effect (heaven) does not impede the establishment of a distinct operation of the agent (sacrificer) which is identical with the activity. Actually, the operations do not determine the function of *kārakas* in a sentence; rather, the effects, which are produced out of the root-meanings (*kriyā*), determine the function of different *kārakas* in a sentence. This is so because, the operation of an agent, which indirectly contributes towards the accomplishment of the effect, is not itself accomplished through any other operation of the instrument etc. Thus, the absence of another operation, produced by the root-meanings, does not hinder the establishment of a distinct operation apart from the root-meanings and also the effects.

Translation (P.166)

Objection that the activity cannot be explained with respect to ātmakartṛka verbs

Now, it may be objected that the activity, as a form of movement, cannot be explained with respect to the finite usages such as 'he offers' *(yajati)*, 'he knows' (*jānāti*) etc., which have non-moving selves as their agents (*ātmakartṛka*). However, some scholars, i.e. followers of Patañjali, provide the explanation for such an objection as follows :

Explanation of the activity by the followers of Pathañjali

Verse 47

People understand (cognize) only a volitional or

conscious effort (*prayatna*) to be the activity by the word '*yateta*' (one should exert), which is an explanation of the conjugational endings of finite verbs in the Mahābhāṣya. Therefore, the conjugational endings express only a volitional or conscious effort in the case of 'he offers' (*yajati*), 'he knows' (*jānāti*) etc. which have non-moving selves as their agents (*ātmakartṛka*). Also, the use of the conjugational endings such as 'ti' in '*ratho gacchati*', which have non-sentient beings as the agents, should be explained as only the metaphorical (figurative) or secondary usages. However, due to the abundance of such usages, the notion or knowledge of metaphorical (figurative) or secondary usage is not prevalent.

Translation (P.167)

Explanation of the verse 47 that the conjugational endings express only volitional effort

XLVII. 1. The Mahābhāṣya passage such as "one should exert in such a way that something comes into being", which is an explanation of the conjugational endings in finite verbs, has demonstrated only a volitional effort, that is conducive to the production of the effect, to be the meaning of the conjugational endings. Thus, the conjugational endings can be held to be expressing only the volitional effort in the case of intransitive usages such as 'he offers' (*yajati*), 'he knows' (*jānāti*) etc. which have non-moving selves as the agents. The use of the conjugational endings such as '*ti*' in '*ratho gacchati*' (chariot moves) etc., the statements which have non-sentient beings as agents, is due to the metaphorical or secondary usage. Nevertheless, ,the knowledge of the metaphorical or secondary usages is not prevalent on account of the abundance of such usages.

Note : Pūrvapakṣin's objection is that the activity, when considered as having the form of movement, cannot be explained with respect to the usages which have non-moving selves as their agents (*ātmakartṛka*) since they do not involve any movement (*parispanda*) as such. In the cases such as 'he offers' (*yajati*), 'he knows' (*jānāti*) etc., no physical movement (*parispanda*) can be found since the agent has merely volition (*icchā*) or knowledge (*jñāna*) as his activity. Siddhāntin, however, at first gives an account of the explanation of some scholars following Patañjali.

According to these scholars, tne activity must be held

to be mere volitional effort (*prayatna*); and the use of the conjugational endings referring to the activity, can be explained as being figurative (metaphorical) or secondary in the case of the statements which have non-sentient (inanimate) beings as agents. They hold so on the ground that Mahābhāṣya, while explaining the meaning of the conjugational endings as "one should exert in such a way that something comes into being", has clearly demonstrated that only a volitional effort, that is conducive to the origination of an effect, can be the meaning of the conjugational endings. Also, according to them, the activity, as volitional effect, can be explained in the case of finite usages such as '*yajate*' (he offers), '*jānāti*' (he knows), which have the non-moving self as the agents, since volitional effort, accomplishing the making of oblations (in '*yajati*') and the awareness (knowledge) in (*jānāti*) is tenable for the non-moving agents.

Translation (P.167-170)

Refutation of the explanation of the followers of Patañjali

XLVII. 2. The explanation "that such usages as '*ratho gacchati*' are figurative; but due to the abundance of such usages, the same are not cognized to be so" can be a tenable answer provided that the figurativeness of the usages is already established (i.e. that only volitional effort (*prayatna*), and not simply movement (*parispanda*), is established as the activity). However, when the perception (of figurative as well as non-figurative usages) is equally strong, and also when no other person (who can prove the figurativeness of such usages) can be present, the establishment of such a figurativeness is impossible. Moreover, the assumption of the contrary position (that only the movement (*parispanda*), and not the volitional effort (*prayatna*), is the activity) cannot be avoided; and hence such a position that usages such as '*ratho gacchati*' are figurative cannot be established.

Explanation that the activity is common to both the effort and movement

Verse 48

Since the activity (*karotyartha*) cannot be restricted to the volitional effort (*prayatna*), the meaning of the verb 'karoti' (i.e. the activity) should be considered to have a general nature which would be common to both the volitional effort (*prayatna*) as well as to the movement (*parispanda);* and the generality of the activity is the loss of the inoperativeness, (i.e. cessation of the passivity). This is so because, the origination of the loss of the inoperativeness, i.e. cessation of the passivity, is seen with respect to both the volitional effort and the movement.

Translation (P.169-70)

Explanation of the verse 48 that

XLVIII. 1. Meaning of the verb *'karoti'*, i.e. the activity, is really the loss of the inoperativeness (the cessation of passivity); for, the perception of the activity is absent (i.e., is not produced) with respect to an item whih is inoperative (passive). Now, the two-fold nature of the cognition of the loss of the inoperativeness (the cessation of passivity) can be explained as follows : It arises due to the volitional effort in the self, i.e. the sentient beings, and also it arises due to the movement in the other (than self), i.e. the non-sentient beings. This fact is further explained as follows :

The people recognize the self (i.e. the sentient being) as having the volitional effort, non-passive, engaged in the activity and also as full of operation; whereas they recognize the other viz., the non-self (the non-sentient being) as having only the movement, or vibration. Now, since the volitional effort as well as the movement, have the general nature of the loss of inoperativeness (the cessation of passivity) by being the objects of the cognitions involving the activity, the same can be considered to be the meanings of the term 'activity' (*kriyā*). Thus, in the instance of verbs such as *'yajate'*, *'jānāti'* etc., which have the sentient beings as their subjects, the volitional effort and also the movement need not be absent. Also, in justification of the fact that the volitional effort too is the activity, Bhāṭṭas have stated as follows:

"The movement alone (excluding the volitional effort) is not the activity for us (the ritualists) like for the Kaṇabhojins."

Note : According to the Siddhāntin, the position "that the usages such as *'ratho gacchati'* etc. are merely figurative, but not recognized to be so due to the abundance of such usages" is not acceptable. For, the conjugational endings cannot be established to refer to only the volitional effort (excluding the movement) on account of the fact that the conjugational endings are used in the case of both the sentient and the non-sentient beings. Since our understanding regarding the different usages, involving the sentient as well as the non-sentient beings as the subjects, is alike, and also since there is no criterion as to why should only the volitional effort, and not the movement, be regarded as the meaning of the conjugational endings, even the contrary (i.e. the movement) cannot be avoided from being established as the meaning of the conjugational endings. Thus, according to Siddhāntin, the usages such as '*ratho gacchati*' cannot be explained in the theory that the volitional effort alone is the activity, and therefore, the same (activity) must be accepted to have a general nature which is common to both the volitional effort as well as to the movement by distinguishing it from the non-operativeness (the passivity). Also, according to him, the volitional effort and also the movement have been cognized to be distinct from the passivity, since the activity is not perceived in the case of a person or a thing that is passive or still.

Now, the two-foldness (of the knowledge) of the cessation of the passivity can be explained as follows : The cessation of the passivity is obtained in the case of the sentient beings, who have the volitional effort, due to their volitional effort, i.e. activity; whereas the same cessation of the passivity is obtained in the case of the non-sentient beings, who do not have volitional effort, due to their movement, i.e. activity. For instance, the sentient being such as Devadatta, who has volitional effort to undertake an action such as cooking etc. obtaines the cessaion of the passivity, i.e. the activity, due to his effort in cooking etc; whereas the non-sentient being such as the chariot, which does not have the volitional effort, obtains the cessation of the, assivity i.e. the activity, due to its movement in going etc. Thus, the activity, which has a general nature common to both the volitional effort and also to the movement, should be considered as a property of both the sentient as well as the non-setient beings.

Translation (P.171-172)

Objection that the movement (*parispanda*) occurs in the sentient being as well

Now, it may be held that, the movement (*parispanda*) serves a useful purpose in being considered as occurring in the sentient beings as well, since the same movement is better known as the activity.

Refutation of the objection 'that movement occurs in the sentient beings'

Verse 49

This, i.e. the movement of the sense organs such as the mind and also that of the gross elements such as the body, is considered to belong to the self, i.e. the 'sentient being such as Devadatta' due to the fact that the same movement is produced by the volitional effort of the sentient beings, just as the operation of becoming soft of the rice grains is considered to belong to the sentient being (Devadatta etc.) due to his ability in controlling of the syntactico-semancical items (*kārakas*) in the case of such operations of becoming soft etc.

Translation (P.172)

Explanation of the verse 49 that the movement of the mind and body are held to belong to self

LIX. 1. (The movement of the sense organs such as the mind and also that of the gross elements such as the body is produced due to the volitional effort of the sentient beings; and therefore, the same are held to belong to the sentient beings; and this can be explained as follows): The awareness (regarding an entity) and also the volition (mental resolve) (for offering the *dravya* to the gods etc.) are produced in the self (sentient being) due to a peculiar contract between the self (i.e. sentient being) and also the mind. And, to facilitate such a peculiar contact between the self and also the mind, action (*karma*) in the mind is accepted as the cause. Now, the action in the mind, which has the form of movement (*parispanda*), is caused from the volitional effort and the unseen merit, which are inherent in the self (sentient beings). Further, the movement, characterized by the production of the materials etc., is produced in the gross elements (i.e. the body etc.) on the basis of the volitional effort of the self (sentient being). Thus, both types of the movements (occurrig in the mind as well as to the body) can be stated to belong to the self since the same movements are due to the volitional effort of the self.

This instance is similar to the instance of the operation of becoming soft (*viklitti*) etc. The operations such as the becoming soft (*viklitti*), the splitting, i.e. the becoming two (*chidā*), the destruction (*bhidā*) etc., are actually inherent, i.e. occurrent in the objects such as the rice grains (the tree and the pot) etc; and therefore, do not inher in the agents such as Devadatta etc. However, they are considered as the operations of the agent 'Devadata' etc. on the ground that the sentient beings such as 'Devadatta' etc. have the agenthood with respect to such operations. This is explained by the fact that all the *kārakas*, including the agentive *kāraka*, are construed as the instruments with respect to the accomplishing operation bringing about the prominent (object); and thus, form a singularity of sentence (i.e. syntactico-semantical unity). It cannot be accepted, however, that the *kārakas* (syntactico-semantical items) acquire the instrumentality etc. (with respect to the accomplishing operation) due to being the instruments with respect to their own operations; since the individual operations are distinct with respect to different *kārakas*, the syntactico-semantical unity (i.e. the singularity of sentence) would become untenable. Therefore, since all the *kārakas* are to be controlled by the agentive *kāraka* alone, all the operations of the different *kārakas* would become the operation of the agent *kāraka*. Consequently, the operations of all the *kārakas* become included or merged in accomplishing activity of the agent itself; and due to such a nature of the operation, i.e. activity, other *kārakas* would also acquire the instrumentality with respect to the accomplishment of action. Since, the operations of all the individual *kārakas* become the operation, i.e. the accomplishing activity, of the agent due to their inclusion into the same activity, the agentship also is justified for the agentive *kāraka* through the operations of the other *kārakas*.

Note : Siddhāntin refutes the position of the followers of Patañjali that the movement (*parispanda*) must be admitted in the case of the sentient being as well. According to him, the position that the movement, compared to the volitional effort, is better qualified to be considered as the activity (*kriyā*) since the people regard only the movement as the activity is not tenable.

Siddhāntin states that the self, although not possessing any movement in reality, is considered to possess the movement by convention. Siddhāntin explains that the movement, which inheres in the mind and the body, is regarded as belonging to the self, since the same movement is accomplished through the volitional effort of the self. And this instance is similar to the instance of considering the operation of becoming soft (*viklitti*), which inheres in the rice grains, as belonging to the sentient agent 'Devadatta' etc. The operation of becoming soft etc., despite being inherent in the object such as 'rice grains', is considered to belong to the agent 'Devadatta' etc. due to the fact that the agents 'Devadatta' etc. employ the *kārakas* i accomplishing the operation, i.e. due to the fact that the same operation of becoming soft i produced by the effort (operation) of the agent.

Now, the process of accomplishing the movement in the mind and the gross elements such as body can be explained as follows: First, there arises, the awareness (*vijñāna*), volition (*saṅkalpa*) and desire (*icchā*) in the self due to a peculiar contact between the self and also the mind. And the peculiar contact between the self and the mind, which produces such a volition, awareness etc., is accepted as produced by the movement. Now, the movement, which is accepted as the cause of volition etc. is of two types : That occurring in the mind and also that occurring in the gross elements. Here, the movement in the mind, which has the form of activity is produced by the merits such as *dharma* etc. and also the volitional efforts such as an operation inherent in the self, the sentient being. On the other hand, the movement in the gross element, i.e. body etc., which can be described as lifting the objects etc., is produced simply by the volitional effort of the self. Now, since the movement inherent in the mind as well as that inherent in the body are produced by the volitional effort, i.e. operation of the self, the same are viewed as belonging to the self (sentient being).

In this connection, the following points must be noted :

Since all the *kārakas* (including *'kartṛ'*, *karaṇa* etc.) form a syntactico-semantical unity or singularity of sentence with the verb, the same are construed with the activity of the agent accomplishing the prominent object'. Suppose the *kārakas* are held to assume the *kārakahood* such as the agenthood, instrumentality etc. due to their own operations, then there would be no syntactico-semantical unity due to the difference between the individual *kāraka* relations.

Now, Siddhāntin concludes that, since the *kārakas* such as the object, instrument etc. are to be controlled by the agent (sentient) *kāraka*, the operations of all the *kārakas* would also belong to the agent *kāraka*. This way, the operations of all the *kārakas* can be included in the activity of the agent; and through such operations, agent could be considered to assume the agenthood in accomplishing the effect.

Translation (P.176-77)

Answer to the objections that i) there are no two separate *kriyās*, that ii) there is no relation betweeen the root-meanings and the activity; and that iii) there cannot be instrumentality for the root-meanings can be stated as follows :

Verse 50

Since the form of the activity (*kriyā*) of the root-meanings (*dhātvartha*) is conditioned by their association with the activity expressed by the other, i.e. conjugational endings, no separate activity need be recognized. Also, since the root-meanings are considered to be what are accomplished (i.e. objects) due to their association with the activity, the meaning of the conjugational endings, the same are established to have the syntactico-semantical relation with the meaning of the conjugational endings, i.e. the activity. Also, (since the root-meanings are to be accomplished due to their association with the activity), the instrumentality of the woods etc. is established in accomplishing the root-meanings.

Translation (P.177-179)

Explanation of the verse 50 that *Kriyātva* of root-meanings is not coutradictory

L.1. The root-meanings (i.e. the actions or qualities

such as the becoming soft etc.) are perceived to have the form of the activity (*kriyā)* due to their association with, i.e. qualification of, the accomplishing activity. Consequently, the state of being an activity (*kriyātva*) of such root-meanings, which are included in the accomplishing activity itself, is due to their mere association with the activity. Thus, how can there be the perception of two distinct activities, (namely, an activity in the form of the root-meanings and also an activity in the form of the meaning of the conjugational endings). For instance, the distinction between the forms is not perceived in the case of the substances such as the cows that are associated with the generic property (of the cowness) and with the quality (of white colour).

The root-meanings have the accomplishability (objecthood) (*sādhyatā*) due to their association with the activity. Therefore, such an accomplishability of the root-meanings does not destroy their (root-meanings') own association with the activity; for, in the case of the absence (i.e. destruction) of such an association, there would arise an occasion for the contingency of their own absence, i.e. destruction. Thus, even the association of the root-meanings becomes tenable with the *kārakas* such as the instrument (*kāṣṭhaiḥ*) etc. The root-meanings, which do not acquire (i.e. obtain) the state of being what are to be accomplished (i.e. the objecthood) due to their association with the activity, cannot be justified in having an association with the instrument either. Therefore, the root-meanings must be admitted as acquiring the accomplishability (i.e. the objecthood) due to their association with the activity only. And this is so because, only that which obtains the state of being (what is) accomplished due to its association with the activity, becomes tenable for being considered as having the form of the activity (*kriyā),* and therefore, becomes eligible for having an instrument.

Note : The verse 50, answers the objections raised earlier that i) no two separate activities (*kriyās)* (one in the form root-meanings and the other in the form of the accomplishing activity) are perceived to have been denoted by the verbal roots and the conjugational endings in finite verbs; that ii) no utterance of the verbal roots and the conjugational endings together is possible because both of them refer to the same entities, i.e. entities that are to be accomplished *(sādhya)*; iii) and that syntactico-semantical relation of the instrumentality of *'kāṣṭhaih'* is not possible with either the root-meanings or the activity (because while the former are non-*kriyās*, the latter is interrupted by other *kārakas)*. The first objection is answered by stating that the root-meanings (cooking etc.) obtain the state of the activity (*kriyātva*) due to their association with the activity and not due to their own nature; and therefore, a distinct activity need not be perceived in the form of root-meanings apart from the activity. The second objection is answered by stating that the root-meanings obtain the state being of what are to be accomplished due to their association with the activity (and consequently, both the root-meanings and the activity are not to be accomplished); and therefore, utterance of the verbal roots and the conjugational endings together is tenable. The third objection is answered by stating that the root-meanings (cooking etc.) are accomplished (due to their association with the activity); and therefore, the same can have an instrument such as wood (*kāṣṭhaiḥ)* in (*kāṣṭhaiḥ pākaḥ*) etc. Now, the refutation of the objections can be further elaborated as follows :

Firstly, as regards the non-perception of the two activities : Acceptance of the two distinct activities (one in the form of the root-meanings and the other in the form of the activity), is not contradictory despite the non-perception of the two distinct activities. For, an entity, which has distinct forms due to the difference between its associations, need not be perceived so as having two distinct forms. For instance, the substance such as the cow, which differs between its forms of the cow individual and the white animal due to its associations with the general property of the cowness and the white colour, need not be perceived to have two distinct forms.

Similarly, the root-meanings, being of the type of actions or qualities such as the becoming soft, which differ between their forms due to their associations with the activity, need not be perceived to have the two distinct forms, i.e. the form of the object which is accomplished and the form of the activity which is accomplishing. Thus, despite the non-perception of the two activities, the position that 'there are two activities (one in the form of the root-meanings and the other in the form of the activity) is not contradictory.

Secondly, as regards the utterance of the verbal roots and the conjugational endings together. The root-meanings such as the becoming soft (i.e. cooking) etc. become the objects to be accomplished due to their associations with the accomplishing activity of the agent; nevertheless, such a status of the accomplishability of the root meanings does not destroy their syntactico-semantical relations, i.e. associations, with the activity. For, when their associations with the activity is destroyed, the very state of the accomplishability of the root-meanings also gets destroyed. Now, since the associations of the root-meanings with the activity is established, the objection that "the utterance together of the verbal roots and the conjugational endings, which refer to the root-meanings and the activity respectively, does not become tenable" also becomes answered.

Lastly, as regards the instrumentality of the woods : Since the root-meanings are to be accomplished due to their associations with the activity, the same become eligible for having an instrument such as woods. Thus, the objection that "the statements such as *'kāṣṭhaiḥ pākaḥ'* (the cooking is by means of woods), wherein the root-meaning 'cooking' has the woods as its instrument, cannot be explained since the root-meanings cannot have an instrument" also becomes answered.

Translation (P.179)

Answer to the objection that the distinction between *'viklidyanti'* and *'pacanti'* etc. is not tenable

The objection that "since the verbal roots *'viklid'* (to become soft) and *'pac'* (to cook) have the same meaning, the distinction between the statements such as *'viklidyanti'* (rice grains become soft) and *'pacanti'* (they cook rice grains) would become untenable" can be answered as follows:

Verse 51

The grammatical agent is desired to be the one who has his operations referred to by the conjugational endings as the chief qualificand of the root-meanings, (and not the one who has his operations referred to by the roots).

Therefore, the statements such as *'viklidyanti'* (rice grains become soft) and *'pacanti'* (they cook rice grains) can differ in their references.

Translation (P.179-181)

Explanation of the verse 51 that the distinction between *'viklidyanti'* and *'pacanti'* can be explained due to the distinction between the operations

Ll. 1. The grammatical agent is certainly not the one who has his operations referred to as the non-qualifier, i.e. as the prominent, by the verbal roots so that the meanings of the conjugational endings would become contracted, i.e. would become identical. However, the grammatical agent is the one who is intended to have his operations, referred to as the chief qualificand with respect to the meanings referred to by the verbal root. So, everywhere, the meaning, referred to by the verbal root, functions as only the qualifier of the operation of the agent which (i.e. the operation) is either the meaning to be referred to by the conjugational ending (in *kim karoti, pacati* etc.) or the meaning to be implied even without the conjugational ending (in *kā kriyā pākaḥ*, etc.). Therefore, in the statements such as *'viklidyanti'* (rice grains become soft), the conjugational endings refer to the operation of the rice grains which functions as the prominent, i.e. the chief qualificand, with respect to the root-meaning, i.e. the becoming soft. And such an operation is produced by the intense contact with the parts of the burning fire; and is located in the parts of the rice grains; and thereby has the nature conducive to boiling of the water in the vessel. On the other hand, in the case of the statements such as *'pacanti'* (They cook rice grains) etc., the conjugational endings refer to the operation of the sentient beings, namely, 'Devdatta' etc. (which functions as the chief qualificand with respect to the root-meaning). Such an operation is characterized by the placing or putting of the vessel (pouring the water) etc., and is referred to by the conjugational ending (*ti*), occurring after the verbal root *'pac'* etc. Therefore, since the distinction between the senses (operatio of rice grais ad Devadatta) and also the distinction between the form (s) of the agents (such as the 'rice grains' and 'Devadatta) are established, there occurs no undesired contingency of contraction, i.e. identity of the meanings of the conjugational endings with that of the roots in *'viklidyanti'* and *'pacanti'*.

An objection can be raised now as follows : Since the verbal root *'viklid'* (to become soft) has synonymity (i.e. has the nature of being the root of the same meaning) with the verbal root *'pac'* (to cook), how can the speakers of the language intend only the operation (leading to the becoming soft) of the rice grains by the conjugational ending *'ti'* occurring after the verbal root *'viklid'* and not the operation (leading to the cooking) of Devadatta as well like they intend by the conjugational ending *'ti'* occurring after the verbal root *'pac'*. However, the answer to such an objection is as follows : In spite of the fact that both the roots *'viklid'* and *'pac'* have the synonymity in meaning, the same verbal roots *'viklid'* and *'pac'* have distinction between their forms (i.e. their syllables); and therefore, the conjugational endings *'ti'*, occurring after the verbal roots *'viklid'*, and *'pac'*, have distinct powers of denotation in the sense of their meanings (i.e. operations).

Note : The verse 51 answers the objection that "the statements *'viklidyanti'* (rice grains become soft) and *'pacanti'* (They cook rice grains) cannot differ in their senses due to the fact that both the verbal roots, i.e. *'viklid'* (to become soft) and *'pac'* (to cook) essentially refer to one and the same action". The point to be noted here is that, according to the Siddhāntin, the agent (*kartṛ)* should be defined as the one who has his operation (activity) referred to as the chief qualificand (i.e. nucleus) of the root-meanings (such as the cooking etc.) by the conjugational endings; and not as the one who has his operation referred to as the chief qualificand by the verbal roots. And therefore, while the conjugational ending 'ti', occurring after the verbal root *'viklid'* (to become soft), refers to the operation of the rice grains (i.e. the operation leading to the becoming soft of the rice grains), the conjugational ending 'ti', occurring after the verbal root *'pac'* (to cook), refers to the operation of cooking belonging to the sentient being 'Devadatta'. Thus, the statements *'viklidyanti'* and *'pacanti'* can be stated to in between their references, since the conjugational endings occurring after the verbal roots *'viklid'* and *'pac'* refer to the operation leading to the becoming soft of the non-sentient rice grains and also to the operation leading to the cooking belonging to the sentient 'Devadatta' respectively. Maṇḍana firmly believes that the agent is not the one who has his operation (activity) referred to by the verbal roots. In such a theory, he states, since both the verbal boots (i.e. *'viklid'* and *'pac'*) refer to one and the same action, the conjugational endings 'ti' etc., occurring after such roots, would also need to refer to the operation that leads to the same action; and thus, due to the sameness of the meanings of the verbal roots *'viklid'* and *'pac'* and also that of the meanings of the conjugational endings following them, the statements such as *'viklidyanti'* and *'pacanti'* would not differ in their senses. Therefore, the agent must be admitted to be the one who has his operations referred to by the conjugational endings which (operations) always function as the chief qualificands of the meanings referred to by the verbal roots. And this is explained by the fact that the meanings of the verbal roots are always found to be the qualifiers of the operations which are either directly expressed by the conjugational endings in instances like *'kim karoti - pacati'* or indirectly implied by the *ghañantas* in instances *like 'kā kriyā* pākaḥ' wherein no cinjugatuinal ending is found to occur. Thus, by accepting that the agent is the one who has his operations referred to by the conjugational endings, Maṇḍana can explain the distinction between the sense (s) of the statements *'viklidyanti'* and *'pacanti'* as follows :

The statement *'viklidyanti'* refers to the operation of the rice grains, which (operation) is produced from the contact with the parts, of fire, and is located in the parts of the rice grains themselves. Further, such an operation is the prominent, i.e. chief qualificand of the 'becoming soft', the meaning of the verbal root *'viklid'*. On the other hand, the statement *'pacanti'* refers to the operation of the sentient being 'Devadatta' etc., which (operation) can be characterised as placing the vessel on fire etc. and producing the cooking. Further, such an operation of the sentient being 'Devadatta' is the chief qualificand of the cooking, the meaning of the root *'pac'*.

Also , it should be noted here that despite the synoymity of the verbal roots *'viklid'* and *'pac'*, the conjugational endings, *'ti'* etc., that occur after such verbal roots, can be accepted to have distinct denotations in the sense of the operations of rice grains and in the sense of the operation of Devadatta respectively. This is explained by the fact that the verbal roots differ between their forms; and therefore, can influence the conjugational endings to express their own meanings. Thus, scholars use *'viklidyanti'* and *'pacanti'*, with the intention of expressing the operation of the rice grains and also that of Devadatta respectively.

Translation (P.182-183)

Distinction between the senses of *pratyayas* is due to the distinction between the bases

Verse 52

The declensional endings (*pratyaya*) such as *'as'* or *'āni'*, although identical, are perceived to have distinct denotations due to the distinction between their base-forms; and this is in spite of the fact that the bases in usages such as *'bhāryāḥ'* (wives), *'dārāḥ'* (*wife(s)*) and *'jalāni'* (waters), *'āpaḥ'* (waters) have synonymity in their meanings.

Explanation of the verse 52 that the endings can denote the distinct operations

LII. 1. In the case of *'jālāni'* (which has a plural ending 'āni' after the base *'jala'*), the plural ending (*āni*) expresses the sense of the plurality which is either inherent in the base meaning, i.e. individual instances of water, or inherent in the individual ities of water which function as the locus of the generality of water (*jalatva*), the alternative base-meaning as well. Similarly, in the case of *'bhāryāḥ'* (wives) (which too has a plural (*as*) ending after the base *'bharyā*), the plural ending (*as*) expresses the sense of the plurality which is either inherent in the base meanings, i.e. individual instances of wives, or inherent in the individual ities of wife which function as the locus of the generic property of *bhāryātva*, the alternative base-meaning.

On the other hand, in the case of *'āpaḥ'* or *'dārāḥ'* (which have the ever-plural ending 'as' occurring after the base *'ap'* (*āp*) and *'dārā'*), the plural ending *'as'* refers to the plurality which is either inherent in the many individual parts of the base-meaning, i.e. the waters (or wives) or inherent in the parts of the waters (or wives) which function as the locus of the waters (or wives), the abode of the generic property of the waters (or the generic property of the wives), the alternative base-meaning. Thus, (despite the non-difference between the forms of the conjugational endings), the denotation(s) of the conjugational endings can differ due to the difference between their base forms; and this is in accordance with the fact that the denotative powers of the conjugational endings are dependent on the (different) forms of the bases.

Similarly, in the case of the quasi passive *karmakartari* usage such as *'pacyante taṇḍulāḥ svayameva'* (rice grains, are cooked by themselves), the quasi passive conjugational ending *'te'*, occurring after the root *'pac'*, refers to the operation (of the rice grains), which is inherent in the rice grains wherein inhers the verbal root-meaning, i.e. the becoming soft as well. However, in the case of the active transitive usage such as *'devadattaḥ pacati taṇḍulam'* (Devadatta cooks rice grains), the conjugational ending 'ti', occurring after the verbal base 'pac', refers to the operation (of Devadatta), which inhers in Devadatta who is quite different from the locus of the verbal base-meaning, i.e. the becoming soft. On the other hand, in the case of *'viklidyanti'*, (rice grains become soft), the conjugational ending 'ti', occurring after the verbal root *'viklid;* refers to the operation (of the rice grains), which inhers in the rice grains wherein inhers the verbal base-meaning (i.e. the becoming soft) as well. Thus, everything is perfect.

Note : Verse 52 illustrates the theory that despite the identity of the endings, the same can denote different senses in different contexts. It shows that supposing the individual(s) *(vyakti)* etc. are the word-meanings, then the plural ending *'āni'* and *'as'*, occurring in *'jalāni'* and *'bhāryāḥ'* etc., can refer to the plurality of individual instances of waters and wives; and supposing the generic property (*jāti*) is the 'word-meaning', then the same plural endings can refer to the plurality of the individual ities of waters or wives wherein inhers the generic property of *jalatva* (or *bhāryātva*) as well. Also, it illustrates that supposing the individuals are the word-meanings, then, in the case of the 'ever-plural words' such as *'āpaḥ'*, *'dārāḥ'*, the plural endings *'as'* etc. occurring in *'āpaḥ'* and *'dārāḥ'* refer to the individual instances of the parts of the waters and also to that of the wives, since the everplural endings are used with the intention of denoting the plurality of the parts of an individual. Suppose, the generic property is word-meaning, then the plural endings refer to the plurality of the individual instances of parts which function as the abode of the whole *'avayavin'* possessing the generic property of *āpastva* and *dārātva*, the alternative base-meanings, since the ever-plural endings, after the ever-plural words, are used with the intention of denoting the plurality of parts. Thus, despite the identity of endings, the same endings, occurring after the regular nominal bases such as *'jala'* and *'bhāryā'* and also occurring after the everplural nominal bases such as *'āpas'* and *'dārāḥ'*, refer to the two distinct meanings, i.e. the plurality of individual instances of base-meanings and the plurality of the parts of the base-meanings, due to the fact that the nominal bases themselves differ between their forms, i.e. their natures, by taking ordinary endings and also the ever-plural endings.

Similarly, the conjugational ending, *'te'*, occurring after the verbal root *'pac'* in the quasi passive *'karmakartari'* usage such as *'pacyante svayam eva taṇḍulāḥ'* (the rice grains are cooked by themselves), refers to the operation of the rice grains (the object(s) functioning as the agents); and such an operation inhers in the rice grains which are also the abodes of the root-meaning, i.e the becoming soft. However, the conjugational ending 'ti', occurring after the verbal root *'pac'*, in the regular transitive usage such as *'devadattaḥ pacati taṇḍulam'* (Devadatta cooks rice grains), refers to the operation of Devadatta; and such an operation inhers in Devadatta, who is different from the abode of the root-meaning 'cooking', i.e. the rice grains. Also, on the other hand, the conjugational endings 'ti', occurring after the verbal root *'viklid'* in *'taṇḍulāḥ viklidyanti'*, refers to the operation of the rice grains; and such an operation inhers again in the rice grains, the abode of the root-meaning, i.e. becoming soft. Thus, the distinction between the denotations of the conjugational endings, occurring after the different verbal bases, becomes tenable due to the distinction between the forms of the verbal roots or bases.

Translation (P.184)

Refutation of the argument that since the *kārakas* are absent, the *karotyartha* or *bhāvanā* is absent in '*yajati*' etc.

Verse 53

Since the relation, i.e. concomitance, (of the activity) with the *kārakas* (syntactico-semantical items) such as the object is perceived to exist in the cases such as '*agnim cinute*' (he piles up the fire) and '*svam yajñam yajati*' (he offers his own oblation, i.e. sacrifice), the absence of the activity (*karotyartha)* cannot be posited by supposing the absence of the (relations with the) *kārakas*.

Translation (P.184-85)

Explanation of verse (53) that the activity is associated with distinct objects in *yajati* etc.

LII. 1. In the case of '*agnim cinute*', (he piles up the fire), the bricks or the sacrificial alter are the objects of the action of piling up (*cayana*), which is the meaning of the verbal root '*ci*', due to the non-intervention by any other operation. On the other hand, fire, which is being intervened by another operation, i.e. the activity, is a deviating factor; and hence, is not the object of the action of piling up. Such a fire, in reality, is the object of the activity expressed by the conjugational ending. (Thus, in the case of '*agnim cinute*', the activity is tenable since the same can be explained to have an object *kāraka* in the form of fire). It should be observed here that the word 'fire' (*agni*), in such statements, is not expressive of the sacrificial alter; but rather, is expressive of only the flaming. In this respect, it has been stated (in the Bhāṣya) as follows :

"The word fire '*agni*' is well established only in the sense of flaming". (Thus, '*agnim cinute*' is to be analysed as "while piling up the alter, he accomplishes the fire through piling").

However, it has been explained that, in the statements such as '*svam yajñam yajati*' 'he offers his own oblations (sacrifice)', the sacrifice is not the object with respect to any thing (i.e. the verbal root-meaning 'offering') except the activity, expressed by the conjugational ending, since the same sacrifice cannot function as both the action (*kriyā*) and the object (*karmakāraka*) with respect to one and the same root-meaning, i.e. offering. (Thus, in the statements such as *'agnim cinute'* and *'svam yajñam yajati'*, the activity is associated with a separate object, namely, fire, etc., apart from the object of the verbal root-meaning, and hence the argument that the activity is absent due to the absence of the grammatical object for such an activity in untenable).

Moreover, it should be observewd here that, in Mahābhāṣya (on P. i.4.49) also, the verb *'pacati'* is demonstrated to have relations with two distinct objects (i.e. rice grains and boiled rice) due to the distinction between the activity and also the verbal root-meaning (action of cooking or the effect of becoming soft). For instance, Mahābhāṣya states as follows : "Here, in the statement such as 'he cooks the rice grains into cooked rice" (*taṇḍulān odanam pacati*), the verb *'pacati'* (to cook) has a double meaning, since the statement is to be explained as "by cooking the rice grains, he accomplishes the boiled rice" (*taṇḍulān vikledayan odanam nirvartayati*).

Note : Verse 53 answers the objection raised by the verse 12; namely, that "the activity (*karotyartha* or *bhāvanā*) is held to be pervading the object (*kāraka*); however, since the object is impossible to explain with respect to the activity, in the case of *yajati* etc., the existence of a separate activity, apart from the root-meanings, as expressed by conjugational ending, is untenable".

Verse 53 states that the activity, in *'agnim cinute'* and *'svam yajñam yajati'*, can be explained to be pervading the object such as the fire etc; and therefore, the objection that due to the absence of *kārakas* such as the object, the distinct activity is not tenable to explain is incorrect.

Siddhāntin explains the existence of the object in *'agnim cinute'* as follows : In *'agnim cinute'*, the fire, expressed by *'agnim'*, functions as the grammatical object of only the activity and not that of the verbal root-meaning, i.e. 'piling up' (*cayana*). For, the same fire is intervened by the activity, and therefore, cannot be immediate to the action of piling up. On the other hand, the bricks (*iṣṭaka*) or the sacrificial alter (*sthala*), which are not intervened by anything, and therefore, are immediate to piling up, should be considered

— —

as the objects of the verbal root-meaning, i.e. piling up. Thus, the activity in *'agnim cinute'* does have *agni* (fire) as its object; and therefore, the supposition that the activity is absent due to the absence of the grammatical object is untenable. Also, it should be noted that the word *'agni'* does not express here the sacrificial alter so that the same could have been construed as the object of the verbal root-meaning, i.e. 'piling up'. For, it has been established in Bhāṣya that *'agni'* means only the flaming (fire), which can function as only the object of the activity.

In *'svam yajñam yajati'* too, the activity can be explained to have an object as follows : Here, the 'sacrifice', expressed by the accusative word *'yajñam'*, functions as the grammatical object of only the activity expressed by the conjugational ending; and not as the object of the action of offering expressed by the verbal root *'yaj'*. For, since no single entity can function as both the action and its own object, the sacrifice, expressed by the accusative *'yajñam'*, which is same as the action of sacrificing (offering), cannot function as its own object. On the other hand, the same (sacrifice) can function as the object with respect to the activity expressed by the conjugational ending. Thus, the Pūrvapakṣin's position that "the activity in *'yajñam yajati'* does not have a grammatical object; and therefore, the activity is absent due to the absence of the subject" is untenable.

Also, it should be observed that, the Siddhāntin views the activity as distinct from the root-meanings. For, according to him, Mahābhāṣya has stated that the verb *'pacati'* is associated with two distinct objects, namely, the rice grains (*taṇḍula*) and also the cooked rice (*odana*) in *'taṇḍulānodanam pacati'* (he cooks rice grains into cooked rice). And such a statement is to be explained on the ground that the activity is distinct from the root-meaning 'cooking'; and while the cooking has rice grains as its object, the activity has the cooked rice as its object. That is why such a statement is explained as *'taṇḍulān vikledayan odanam nirvartayati'* (he accomplishes the boiled rice by cooking the rice grains).

Translation (P.186)

Answer to the objection that *'bhāvayati'* and *'bhavati'* would

become synoymous if *'bhāvanā'*, which has the nature of *'kartṛvyāpāra;* is *pratyayārtha*

Verse 54

In the case of the causative usages such as *'bhāvayati'* (he makes it accomplished), scholars hold that the conjugational ending *'ti'* (occurring after the causative verbal base *'bhāvaya'*) refers to the causative activity of the causative agent (*prayojaka kartṛ vyāpāra*), which has the primitive activity of the primitive agent (*prayojya kartṛ vyāpāra*) as its object. On the other hand, in the case of the primitive usages such as *'bhavati'* (he or it becomes), the scholars intend that the conjugational ending 'ti' (occurring after the primitive verbal base *'bhava'*), refers to the primitive activity (of the primitive agent *prayojya kartṛ* vyāpāra), which has the 'becoming', the primitive verbal root-meaning, as its object.

Translation (P.186-87)

Explanation of verse (54) that causative and primitive expressions can be distinguished

LIV. 1. Since all the syntactico-semantical items (*kārakas*) like *'kartṛ'*, *'karaṇa'* etc. function as the agent with respect to their own activities, (otherwise, the same *'kartṛ'* etc. would become ineligible (unfit) for being considered as the *kārakas* in bringing about the action), and also since all the *kārakas* are enjoined with respect to their own activities, the conjugational endings, occurring after the causative verbal bases, refer to the activity of the causative agent (*prayojaka kartṛ vyāpāra)* such as impelling or motivating others, which (activity) has the activity of the primitive agent (*prayojyakartṛ vyāpāra)* as its object. On the other hand, the conjugational endings, occurring after the primitive verbal bases, refer to the activity of the primitive agent (*prayojya kartṛ vyāpāra)* which has the primitive verbal base-meaning as its object. Thus, there occurs no synonymity between the causative *'bhāvayati'* (he causes it to be accomplished) and primitive *'bhavati'* (he or it becomes).

Note : Verse 54 answers the objection raised by the verse 13. The objection raised was that "when the conjugational endings are accepted to refer to the activity, analysable into the operation of the agent, the causative and also the primitive expressions such as *'bhāvayati'* (he causes something accomplished) and *'bhavati'* (it becomes) respectively, would have no distinction between their meanings, i.e. would become synonymous". However, according to the Siddhāntin, such an objection is baseless. For, while the conjugational ending *'ti'*, in the causative expression *'bhāvayati'*, refers to the causative activity such as impelling, belonging to the causative agent, the conjugational ending *'ti'*, in the primitive expression *'bhavati'*, refers to the activity of the primitive agent. Also, while the causative activity has the operation of the primitive agent as its object, i.e. accomplishes the operation of the primitive agent, the activity of the primitive agent has the primitive verbal base-meaning as its object, i.e. accomplishes the verbal base-meaning. Therefore, since the causative activity of the causative agent and the primitive activity of the primitive agent differ mutually, the causative and also the primitive expressions *'bhāvayati'* and *'bhavati'*, wherein the conjugational endings refer to such mutually different activities, would also differ in their meanings; and so, the objection that 'such expressions would have no distinction in their meanings' is answered.

Translation (P.187)

The purpose of accepting the activity as the distinct sense expressed by the conjugational endings

Verse 55

Since the conjugational ending, such as *'ti'* in general, is accepted to have a reference to the activity, as distinct from the verbal root-meanings, the sense that "one should accomplish, i.e. attain, heaven by means of offering through the activity" (*yāgena svargam bhāvayet*) is arrived at by the analysis of the statement 'he who desires heaven should offer sacrifice' (*svargakāmo yajeta).*

Note : Now, the Siddhāntin explains the ultimate purpose of accepting the activity as a distinct meaning referred to by the conjugational endings. According to him, the real purpose of accepting the activity as a distinct meaning is the establishment of the sense such as one should accomplish the effect 'heaven' etc. by means of the offering through the activity in the statements such as *'svargakāmo yajeta'* etc. Also, by establishing such a snese as produced from the statements *'svargakāmo yajeta'*, Siddhāntin refutes the objection of the Pūrvapakṣin that the analysis of the sense such as 'one should accomplish the heaven by means of the offering through the activity' is mere assumption of unreality.

Translation (P.188)

Objection

LV. 1. How is it ?

Note : It is objected that such a sense need not be cognized since the heaven etc. are not perceived to be the effects accomplished through any activity. According to the Pūrvapakṣin, therefore, the activity need not be established as a distinct meaning referred to by the conjugational endings.

Translation (P.188)

Answer

Verse 56

Since the activity expects an effect to be accomplished, the phrases such as 'one who desires heaven' (*svargakāmaḥ*) should be accepted as intended to express the effects such as heaven to be accomplished. Thus, the cognition of the sense such as "one should accomplish the effect of heaven by means of offering through the activity" is produced from the words *'svargakāmo yajeta'*. And in spite of the fact that the phrase 'one who desires heaven' (*svargakāmaḥ*) is a qualifier (*viśeṣaṇa)* of the person, the same phrase can be accepted to express the prominent, i.e. the effect, 'heaven', since the theory that the qualifying phrases can express the prominent items (i.e. the effects or the objects to be accomplished) has been established by the fact that the qualifying words express the prominent in 'staff-bearer pronounces the orders' (*daṇḍī praiṣān anvāha)* etc.

Translation (P.188-92)

Explanation of verse (56) that the phrase *'svargakāmaḥ'* must be accepted to express the 'heaven' as the prominent, i.e. object

LVI. 1. In fact, the heaven etc. in the scriptural statements such as 'one who desires heaven should offer offerings (make oblations), (*'svargakāmo yajeta'*), are heard, (i.e. are construed), as the qualifiers of the person; nevertheless, the qualifying phrases such as *'svargakāmaḥ'* etc. (one who desires heaven), which are found enjoining the desirability of the heaven etc., must be understood as expressing the fact that the same heaven etc. are the prominent items (i.e. the objects). The theory that the qualifying phrases can express the prominent items is based on the fact that the scriptural statements such as 'the staff-bearer pronounces the orders' *'daṇḍī praiṣān anvāha'* and 'the red-turbaned ṛitviks are wandering' *'lohitoṣṇīṣā' ṛtvijāḥ pracaranti'* are perceived to have their qualifying words, namely, *'daṇḍin'* and *'lohitoṣṇiṣāḥ'* expressing the qualifiers such as the 'staff-bearer' and 'red-turbaned' as the prominent items.

The question may be asked now as to why such a theory is necessary ? However, the answer is as follows : An accomplishing activity (*bhāvanā*) expects that there should be an effect (i.e. object) that could be accomplished by it. And, since the heaven etc. too are perceived to be the effects (to be accomplished) due to their being desired, the same expects an activity that could accomplish it (heaven). Now, the instance of the word *'kāmaḥ'* in *'svargakāmaḥ'* expressing the fact that the base meaning 'heaven' is the object to be accomplished is similar to the instance of the usages consisting of a word ending in the accusative. In such cases as *'svargam yajati'* (he offers for accomplishing heaven), the accusative indicates the fact that the basemeaning such as heaven is the object to be desired, i.e. accomplished. Thus, it should be accepted that the cognition of (i.e. reference to) the person (who desires the heaven), is merely a repetition (*anuvāda)* (of the idea already implied otherwise through the activity) in the case of the compound phrase 'one who desires heaven' (*svargakāmaḥ).* This is so because, what is intended to be enjoined by such a phrase (of *svargakāmaḥ)* is merely the (accomplishability of the) heaven, since what is to be indicated by such a phrase is the particular item to be accomplished, i.e. the effect, heaven.

It should be noted here that in spite of the fact that the verbal root-meaning, i.e. the offering (sacrifice), is scriptural (i.e. immediate), the same cannot be considered to be the object to be accomplished; for, the knowledge of the injunction (such as 'one who desires heaven should offer sacrifice' which has a reference to the accomplishability of the heaven) is contradictory to the accomplishability of the root-meaning, i.e. the offering (sacrifice). On the other hand, since, in the viw that the verbal root-meaning, i.e. the offering (sacrifice), has the instrumentality towards the accomplishment of heaven, the scriptural statement can be construed, the root-meaning too is possible to be construed as non-object with respect to the activity without any contradiction to the scriptural statement assigning the instrumentality of the root-meaning, i.e. offering (sacrifice).

(Also, it may be objected that the verbal root-meaning, i.e. offering (the sacrifice), has no semantical competency for being related to the accomplishing activity as the means of accomplishing the heaven). However, such an objection is not valid; for, the knowledge of the semantical competency and also the lack of it (semantical competency) is dependent on the scriptural science; and hence, the same (semantical competency and lack of it) cannot be obtained otherwise through any other means. (The knowledge of the semantical competency is due to the absence of the contradictory knowledge of the lack of the semantical competency). The accomplishment of all the effects in geneal is also due to the instrumentality of the particular instances of individual verbal root-meanings (i.e. due to the instrumentality of particular actions such as the offerings (sacrifice)).

An alternative theory (i.e. objection) may be as follows : Since the phrase '*svargakāmaḥ*' is intended to express the idea of the qualifier, i.e. the heaven (here the qualificand is the person who desires heaven), the same qualificer, i.e. the heaven, can have only the secondary nature, i.e. attributive nature (as opposed to the prominent nature). And, since the heaven lacks the prominent nature, the same cannot be construed as the object, i.e. prominent, with respect to the activity.

However, such an alternative theory is also not correct. An activity expects first only an object to be accomplished (so that it can demonstrate its accomplishing nature); and, therefore, despite the heaven being the qualifier to the person, the same must be construed as the prominent with respect to the activity. Moreover, this is so because, the desire to accomplish something has only a secondary (indirect) reference to the sense of the means (instruments) such as the offering (sacrifice), and hence has a primary reference to only the objects to be accomplished.

Note : Verse 56 answers the objection that since the heaven is not perceived to be the object to be accomplished in the statement *'svargakāmo yajota'*, the cognition that 'one should accomplish the heaven by means of the offering through the activity', cannot be derived from the statement as such. The verse clarifies that the activities expressed by the conjugational endings, such as 'ta' in *'svargakāmo yajeta'*, expects an object to be accomplished (such as heaven) so that it can demonstrate its accomplishing nature. And, in order to fulfil such an expectation, the word 'one who desires' (*kāmaḥ)* in the phrase 'one who desires heaven' (*svargakāmaḥ)* must be held to express the fact that the heaven is the object (desired) to be accomplished; and therefore, the verbal cognition that 'one should accomplish the heaven by means of the offering through the activity' is derived from the words only.

Nevertheless, a problem may arise in the theory that the qualifying phrase, 'heaven' (*svarga)* in the compound 'one who desires heaven' (*svargakāmaḥ*), expresses the heaven, the qualifier, as the prominent one, i.e. as the object to be accomplished. (In the compound, heaven (*svarga*) functions as the qualifier of the person; and therefore, cannot be the prominent). However, this problem is answered by stating that the qualifying phrases, which repeat the ideas that have already been expressed, i.e. obtained otherwise, should be taken to express a new idea, namely, the qualifier as the prominent which is not obtained already. For instance, the phrase such as *'daṇḍī praiṣān anvāha'* expresses the qualifier, namely, 'staff-bearer' as the prominent, since the idea of pronouncing the order (*praiṣānvāha*) has already been obtained otherwise by *maitrāvaruṇaḥ praiṣānanvāha*; and therefore, does not need to be repeated again; whereas, the idea of 'the staff bearer' *'daṇḍin'* as the prominent one is not already obtained, and therefore needs to be expressed afresh. Also, the phrase *'lohitoṣṇīṣā ṛtvijaḥ pracaranti'* expresses the qualifier, namely, the red-turban as the prominent, since the idea of *ṛitviks*, wandering (*ṛitvik pracāra)* has already been obtained otherwise; and therefore, does not need to be expressed again; whereas, the idea of 'red-turban' as the prominent one has not been already expressed otherwise; and therefore, needs to be expressed afresh.

It should be observed here that the expression of the heaven as the most desired *kāraka* item, i.e. as the object (prominent), by the word *'kāmaḥ'* in *'svargakāmaḥ'* is parallel to the expression of the most desired *kāraka* item (i.e. the object) by the accusative case ending. In the accusative statements such as *'svargam yajate'*, the accusative case ending *'am'* expresses the heaven as the most desired item, i.e. the object. Similarly, the word *'kāmaḥ'* in *'svargakāmaḥ'* can express the same heaven as the most desired item. Thus, the word *'svargakāmaḥ'* expresses the most desired (object) status to the heaven in such a statement. Also it should be observed here that the cognition of the person, who desires such a heaven, again is only due to repetition. The idea that the person desires to accomplish an object like heaven has already been obtained through the activity (i.e. activity implies a person who accomplishes an object); and therefore, there is no need that the same idea should be expressed again. Thus, what is intended to be expressed, i.e. enjoined, by the word *'svarga'* in *'svargakāmaḥ'* is really only the heaven as the prominent (i.e. object) as the same heaven alone provides the particular item to be accomplished through the activity.

Now, it may held as follows : The offering of sacrifice, which is expressed by the verbal root *'yaj'* in the scriptural statement *'svargakāmo yajeta'*, is more immediate to the activity, expressed by the conjugational ending *'ta'*, compared to the 'heaven', expressed by the different phrase, i.e. *'svargakāmaḥ'*; and therefore, only former (offering of sacrifice) deserves to be considered as the object with respect to the activity.

However, this position is incorrect. The prescription *'svargakāmo yajeta'* enjoins only the accomplishment of the heaven which is conducive to the achievement of the welfare, i.e. prosperity, of the *yajamāna;* and therefore, the same prescription can not enjoin the accomplishment of the 'offering', i.e. the sacrifice, which is not directly conducive to the achievement of welfare or prosperity. Therefore, the assumption that the 'offering of sacrifice' is the object to be accomplished with respect to the activity is contradictory to the very spirit of the prescription. Moreover, it should be noted that the prescription becomes meaningful only in the theory that the verbal root-meaning, i.e. the offering, is the means, i.e. instrument, to the accomplishment of heaven through the activity; and therefore, the only assumption that the offering is only the means or instrument is not contradictory to the spirit of the prescription.

Further, the semantical competency of the instrumentality of the verbal root-meaning 'offering' for being related to the activity cannot be doubted. The knowledge of such a semantical competency (or lack of it) actually depends on the scriptural science and not on any other means of knowledge. And, since the scriptural science establishes the semantical competency of the instrumentality of the verbal root-meaning 'offering' for being related to the activity, there occurs no untenability of any sort for such a relation. Further, since the root-meaning 'offering' is itself to be accomplished through the agent's activity, the same 'offering' can be considered to be the means with respect to the accomplishment of the heaven due to *adṛṣṭa*. And this phenomenon is established by the fact that all the root-meanings such as cooking etc., which are to be accomplished through the activity of the agent, function as the means of accomplishment of the effect 'rice' etc.

Finally, Siddhāntin answers the Pūrvapakṣin's alternative theory that, since the phrase '*svargakāmaḥ*', expresses the qualifier, namely, the heaven, the same (phrase) cannot express the same (heaven) as the prominent (i.e. as the object). According to the Siddhāntin, an activity requires, i.e. expects, first an object to be accomplished so that it can manifest its accomplishing nature. The activity expects the means of the accomplishment, i.e. the root-meaning 'offering' etc., only indirectly through the object which is to be accomplished as it is of secondary importance. Moreover, the desire, expressed by the word '*kāmaḥ*', in '*svargakāmaḥ*', has only a secondary or alternative reference to the means of the accomplishment etc., since the same is only secondary to the object to be accomplished which is prominent. Thus, it has been establlished that the phrase *'svargakāmaḥ'* expresses the heaven as the prominent, i.e. as the object to be accomplished, with respect to the activity.

Translation (P.192)

Objection of a *Mīmāṁsakaikadeśin* that *'svargakāmaḥ'* expresses the *'niyojyaviśeṣa'*

LVI. 2. The scriptural statements of desire such as *'svargakāmaḥ'* etc., are not intended to convey primarily the knowledge of the object to be accomplished (i.e. are not meant to provide the idea of an object to be accomplished such as heaven). On the contrary, the same statements are intended to express the particular qualified person, who is enjoined or impelled to undertake the performance of the compulsory duty of offering *'niyojya viśeṣa'*. Otherwise, suppose the statements convey only the object to be accomplished, then the relevant contextual information as to 'whom is this instruction valid for', 'who is enjoined or impelled (to undertake the action)', 'who has to undertake this action' etc. would remain unknown. Consequently, since the scriptural statements, i.e. the injunctions (such as *'svargakāmo yajeta'*), would be semantically expecting, or incomplete, the same would become untenable for conveying any meaning.

Note : Some *Mīmāṁsakas*, who hold that the injunctive statements such as *'svargakāmo yajeta'* convey relevant information regarding the person performing the compulsory duty of offering, take objection to the theory that the words such as *'svargakāmaḥ'* in the injunctive statement *'svargakāmo yajeta'*, express the heaven as the prominent, i.e. as the object to be accomplished. According to them, what is important is that the injunctive statements must give all the relevant informations regarding the person who is impelled to undertake an action. It is not important that the injunctive statement should express the object to be accomplished ignoring the relevant information regarding the person enjoined to undertake an activity. Suppose, the injunctive statements do not express the *niyojyaviśeṣa*, then the information as to 'whom is the injunction valid for,' 'what are the qualifications of the person', 'which person should undertake what activity' etc. would remain unsupplied. And consequently, the injunctive statements would become incomplete as far as providing the sufficient information regarding the *niyojyavisśeṣa* is concerned. It is absolutely necessary, therefore, that the phrase *'svargakāmaḥ'* should express only the *niyojyaviśeṣa* and not the heaven as the prominent, i.e. object to be accomplished.

Translation (P.192-3)

Refutation of *Mīmāṁsakaikadeśin's* objection

No, this objection too is not essential (i.e. incorrect). For -

Verse 57

The compulsory undertaking (performance) of the duty of offering by the competent person, desirous of an effect, is understood by implication of competence from the injunctive statement. Otherwise, the cliam or right of the ineligible or incompetent person (to perform the sacrifice with benefit) would become irresistible, i.e. unavoidable.

Translation (P.193-194)

Explanation of verse (57)

LVII. 1. Even he, who considers that the knowledge of (the information regarding) the particular qualified person, impelled to undertake an activity (*niyojyaviśeṣa)* is obtained through the injunctive words, must concede that the implication of the competence (eligibility) is required (expected) in obtaining the knowledge of the competent person enjoined (impelled) to undertake the activity. Otherwise, in the case of the assumption of the power of denotation (in obtaining the *niyojyaviśeṣa)* on account of the words, even the blind and other incompetent persons could claim their right with respect to performing the sacrifice (with benefit) as well, since there are no words barring blind etc. Also, since, in spite of the presence of the denotation of words (expressing the *niyojyaviśeṣa*), the implication of the competence is necessary to be resorted to in understanding the eligibility or competence of the particular qualified person, it would be better that such a competence, i.e. eligibility, is understood with respect to the particular qualified person even without the presence of such (denotation of) words. Thus, it should be realized that 'the qualified person impelled to undertake the performance of sacrifice' (*niyojya*) means the one who is competent to understand the implications of the injunction as well as to practice, i.e. undertake, the activity enjoined by the injunction. Such a '*niyojya*' is, further, qualified as the one who desires to accomplish the effect. This is so because, the '*niyojya*', who is incompetent and non-desiring the effect, cannot be justified, i.e. has no right, in undertaking the sacrificial performance which is either impossible for him to accomplish or which is not desired to be accomplished by him. (Now, since the competence of the '*niyojya*' is to be obtained by implication anyway, the particular qualified person (*niyojyaviśeṣa*) could also be held to have been obtained by implication; and therefore, the phrase '*svargakāmaḥ* can express the heaven as the prominent, i.e. as the object to be accomplished).

Note : Verse 57 refutes the *Mīmāṁsakaikadeśin's* (Prābhakara's) objection. It states that the compulsory undertaking of the performance of the sacrifice by the person, who is competent to undertake an activity, is understood by implication of the competence (eligibility) even without the words expressing such an idea. Otherwise, suppose the competence is not expected to be implied in the person, then even the incompetent persons such as blind, deaf, etc. would become eligible for undertaking the sacrificial offering, and therefore, the barring of such persons from undertaking such activities would become impossible. Therefore, since the competent person, who is impelled to undertake an activity, is to be obtained by the implication of the competence in any case, it would be better to accept that the injunctive statement '*svargakāmaḥ*' expresses only the heaven as the prominent, i.e. as the object to be accomplished. In other words, even those scholars of *Mīmāṁsā*, who regard that the injunctive statement '*svargakāmaḥ*' expresses *niyojyaviśeṣa* (a particular person who is impelled to undertake an activity), must accept that the competence (*sāmarthya*) of such a *niyojyaviśeṣa* is understood only by the implication of the competence. This is necessitated by the fact that otherwise persons who are incompetent such as blind, deaf etc. could not be barred from undertaking the sacrificial performance. Now, since the competence of the *niyojyaviśeṣa* is to be understood anyway by the implication of the competence (despite the expression of the *niyojyaviśeṣa* by the phrase *svargakāmaḥ*), the theory that the *niyojyaviśeṣa* is expressed by the phrase '*svargakāmaḥ*' becomes meaningless. Therefore, it is necessary to accept that the *niyojyaviśeṣa*, who is competent to undertake the sacrificial performance, is implied in the injunctire statement. Thus, the phrase '*svargakāmaḥ*' in the injunctive statement can express the heaven as the prominent, i.e. as the object to be accomplished.

Translation (P.194)

Siddhānta that the effect (object) is not obtained otherwise, and therefore the same should be the expressed meaning of '*svargakāmaḥ*'

Verse 58

In the theory that the phrase '*svargakāmaḥ*', in the injunctive statement '*svargakāmo yajeta*', is intended to express something other than the effect (i.e. the '*niyojya viśeṣa*), the state of heaven being the effect (object) of the (animal ?) cannot be obtained from words. Also, it cannot be held that the notion of the particular effect is obtained due to the untenability of the sacrificial performance otherwise; for, nothing would be untenable without the assumption of the effect, since the undertaking of a sacrificial performance is held, according to the Prābhākaras, as caused due to only the scriptural injunction enjoining a compulsory duty of sacrificial performance.

Translation : (P.194-95)

Explanation of verse (58) that the phrase '*svargakāmaḥ*' is '*phalapara*' and not '*niyojya viśeṣapara*'

LVIII. 1. Suppose the phrase '*svargakāmaḥ*' (one who desires heaven), in the injunctive statement '*svargakāmo yajeta*', is not intended to convey the idea of a distinct (i.e. particular) effect such as heaven, then the state of being the effect of the heaven etc. would not be indicated through the indicative power of words (*svargakāmaḥ*). Also, in that case, the state of being the effect of the heaven etc. could not be implied through the power of implication; for, there occurs nothing that would become untenable without the assumption of an effect such as heaven. Now, without the assumption of an effect such as heaven too, the persons, who are impelled to undertake an activity of performing sacrifice, can be explained as undertaking the performance of the sacrifice due to the sense of the compulsory duty only.

Also, it cannot be held that, in the absence of the reference to the effect by the words, the undertaking of the sacrificial performance would become unjustified. For, the undertaking of the sacrificial performance would not be unjustified as the same is admited as based on the injunction of the compulsory duty only.

Again, it cannot be held that the syntactico-semantical unity (i.e. the singularity) of the sentence *'svargakāmo yajeta'* cannot be explained unless the heaven is understood as the effect. For, no contradiction to the syntactico-semantical unity of the sentence would occur in the absence of understanding of the heaven as the effect. Now it may be held that the contradiction such as one desires something (i.e. heaven), but one undertakes the performance of some thing else (i.e. sacrifice) would become unavoidable due to the fact that one who desires heaven would have to undertake something else, i.e the performance of the sacrifice. However, then, precisely for this reason, we shall insist that let the phrase *'svarga-kāmaḥ'* in the injunctive statement be accepted as intended to express the object (i.e. the effect such as heaven) of the action which is enjoined to be undertaken; and also we shall insist that let the same phrase not be accepted as intended to express the particular person who is enjoined to undertake an action.

Note : The verse 58 explains the *Siddhānta* that the phrase such as *'svargakāmaḥ'* in the statement *'svargakāmo yajeta'* needs to express only the particular effect such as heaven which is not obtained otherwise. According to the Siddhāntin, suppose the phrase *'svargakāmaḥ'* is accepted to express the particular person who is impelled to undertake an action, *(niyojyaviśeṣa)*, then the state of being an effect (i.e. object) of the heaven etc. becomes impossible to perceive as such a sense is not referred to otherwise through any other words. Also, such a state (of the heaven' etc.)

cannot be held as obtained due to the implication of the syntactico-semantical competence (i.e. necessity of such an effect). There is nothing which would become untenable without the assumption of reference to such an effect. For instance, the injunctive statements are found to be impelling the people to undertake certain actions even without the assumption (expectation) of any effect in the case of *nityaniṣedha* and compulsory duty (*adhikāra*); and therefore, the assumption of an effect such as heaven would not be necessary to facilitate the undertaking of the sacrificial offering.

Further, it may be held that although the injunction, impelling the person to undertake the action of offering, does not become untenable without the effect 'heaven', the actual undertaking of the sacrificial performance becomes unjustified so long as there is no effect; and therefore, the assumption of the effect such as heaven becomes necessary through implication. However, this argument is also not correct. For, the Niyogavādin would hold that the undertaking of the sacrificial performance is due to the mere impelling by the injunction; and therefore, such an undertaking does not require any effect as such like in the case of the undertaking of the *nityakarmas* which are without any effects. Also, it should be noted that the syntactico-semantical unity (i.e. the singularity) of the sentence (*ekavākyatā*) of the injunctive statement *'svargakāmo yajeta'* would become utenable unless the phrase *'svargakāmaḥ'* is held to express the effect such as 'heaven'. When the phrase *'svargakāmaḥ'* expresses only a qualified person, enjoined to undertake an activity (and not any effect (heaven) which is to be accomplished), it would mean that the statement *'svargakāmo yajeta'* impels the person to undertake the performance of the activity without any relation to the effect 'heaven' desired by the person. However, since the statement must express an activity, which is conducive to the object of the desire, for obtaining the syntactico-semantical unity (i.e. the singularity of sentence), the statement *'svargakāmo yajeta'* would fail to obtain the syntactico-semantical unity in such a position. On the other hand, when the phrase expresses the effect 'heaven', the syntactico-semantical unity of the statement becomes tenable because the same statement would be taken to enjoin the person's unertaking of an activity, i.e. offering, which has a reference to the effect 'heaven', expressed by the phrase *'svarga-kāmaḥ'* and desired by the person by producing the same. Thus, to facilitate the singularity of the sentence, the phrase *'svargakāmaḥ'* must be held as expressing the effect 'heaven'.

Translation (P.196)

Niyogaprādhānya is untenable

Moreover, it can be stated as follows :

Verse 59

The undertaking of the activity leading to a different thing, i.e. offering, by a person, who desires something quite different, i.e. heaven, and who is controlled by the compulsory duty prescribed by the injunctive statement, is quite contradictory to what he desires. Thus, (due to the contradiction of the prominence of such an undertaking of the activity to the prominence of the desired effect 'heaven'), the prominence of the person's undertaking of the compulsory duty (*niyogaprādhānya*) becomes untenable.

Tranlation (P.197)

Explanation of verse (59) that qualifying nature of the effect does not depend on the *bhāvyatva*

LIX. 1. The Niyogavādin, who states the contradiction in the form such as "one desires something, i.e. heaven, while one undertakes the performance of something else, i.e. offering", forfeits his claim of the prominence of the person's undertaking of the compulsory duty (to the effect 'heaven'). This is so because, the undertaking of the compulsory duty by the person can be caused by only the desire (of the person) to accomplish the effect 'heaven'. Also, persons such as servants, who are controlled by others, i.e. masters, are found to undertake the different activity (i.e. the fighting for masters) on account of the command of the masters (in spite of the fact that they have a desire for something else such as eating etc.); and therefore, the question of contradiction itself can be ruled out as false. Now, the Niyogavādin may hold that the qualifying nature of the heaven with respect to the person impelled to undertake the activity (leading to the offering) is dependent on the fact that such a heaven is to be accomplished (*bhāvya*) by the activity of the same person. However, this argument is also not correct. The same (qualifying nature of the heaven with respect to the person, impelled to undertake an activity) is not related to, i.e. is not dependent on, the eventuality of undertaking the performance of the activity leading to 'offering'. For, the object, which is to be accomplished through the undertaking of some other activity (than the one leading to the offering), could also be considered to be the qualifier with respect to the person impelled to undertake the activity leading to 'offering'. Moreover, the theory that the qualifying nature of the heaven is dependent on the activity because the same is accomplished through the activity leading to 'offering' is not always tenable; for, the motivation to undertake an activity is found even due to the mere existence of a desire to accomplish an effect through the activity (and thus, such an activity may not necessarily be producing such an effect).

Translation (P.198-99)

Refutation of Niyogavādin's counter objection :

LIX. 2. Now, Niyogavādin may counter object that, this way, suppose the heaven (in '*svargakāmo agnihotram juhoti*') is considered to have the state of being what is produced by a particular cause, i.e. offering (*bhāvyatva* or *naimittikatva*), then the state of being the obligatory or necessary rite (*nityatva*) of the Agnihotra offering would be contradicted, since the same (Agnihotra) would be leading to the production of a desired effect, i.e. heaven.

However, this counter objection of Niyogavādin is not tenable. For, we (Siddhāntins) hold that (in our theory that the phrase such as '*svargakāmaḥ*' expresses the effect 'heaven' as prominent) this additional fault (alongwith the fault of considering the heaven as the effect) could be tolerated. Under no circumstance, however, it could be accepted that the knowledge of the effect 'heaven' is caused, i.e. is implied, by the phrase '*svargakāmaḥ*' meant to be expressing the particular person impelled to undertake an activity.

Again, Niyogavādin may counter object that the 'Agnihotra-offering' is perceived as the compulsory duty to be undertaken by the person who desires the heaven as the effect to be accomplished. However, this objection is not tenable. For, how can such an Agnihotra-offering be considered as the compulsory duty to be undertaken by the person when such an offering is not meant to produce such an effect as heaven ? Nevertheless, it may be held as follows : That, like the Kṣāmavatīya-offering, perceived to be the compulsory duty to be undertaken by the person who has kept the *gṛhya* fire, the Agnihotra-offering too could be perceived to be the compulsory duty to be undertaken by the person who has a desire to accomplish the heaven; although no cause and effect relationship between the same offering and the effect heave can be visualised as such.

Further, Niyogavādin may again counter object that suppose the person is motivated to undertake the compulsory duty of performing the Agnihotra-offering, which is not accomplishing the (effect) heaven, then the same person cannot be considered to be the one who desires the heaven (to be accomplished through the offering). However, this objection too is not tenable. For, the state of being the one who desires the heaven (to be accomplished through the offering) is not contradictory to the person who is movivated to undertake the performance of an indifferent action such as twinkling etc. in spite of the fact that the same performance etc. are not conducive to the accomplishment of the desired effect 'heaven'. (Similarly the state of being the one who desires the heaven is not contradictory to the person who is motivated to undertake the performance of offering which is not conducive to the accomplishment of heaven).

Also, Niyogavādin may object that the motivation towards the undertaking of the activity of twinkling etc. is explained due to some other extraneous reason (i.e. avoiding dust etc.). However, this objection too is not tenable, since it can be claimed that here too, the motivation towards the (undertaking of) the activity of Agnitotra-offering is due to the injunction of undertaking the compulsory duty (for the person who desires heaven). Thus, there occurs no fault of contradiction to the state of being the person who desires the heaven to be accomplished.

Note : Verse 59 points out another difficulty in the

Niyogavādin's theory that the phrase *'svargakāmaḥ'* expresses only the person impelled to undertake an activity as the prominent. In the Niyogavādin's theory, the person is controlled by the prescription of the compulsory undertaking of the activity (*niyoga*). And therefore, the Niyogavādin, when holding that the undertaking of a different item (i.e. offering) by a person, who desires something else, i.e. heaven, is contradictory to the desire (*icchā*), concedes the prominence of the desire; and therefore, forfeits the claim for the prominence of the *niyoga*; and further, in its place, establishes the prominence of the effect 'heaven', which is being desired by the person. For, the motivation of the person to undertake an activity is caused by the fact that the same person desires to accomplish the effect through his performance of offering.

Further, Siddhāntin establishes the position that the undertaking of an activity by a person desiring something else (heaven) need not be contradictory. He states that in the case of a master making an injunction (i.e. order) to undertake the activity of fighting, the servants do undertake such an activity despite the servants having a desire to accomplish something else, i.e. eating (*bhojana*). Similarly, there is no contradiction to the person's undertaking some different activity leading to the offering due to the force of *niyoga* (despite the persons having a desire for accomplishing something else, i.e. the effect 'heaven').

Niyogavādin, at this juncture, raises another objection: That effect such as heaven is considered to be the qualifier of the person impelled to undertake an activity (*niyojya*). And, such a nature is tenable only when the same is considered to be accomplished through the activity of the person. Thus, the implying of the effect such as heaven by the phrase *'svargakāmaḥ'*, which is intended to express the *niyojya*, is absolutely necessary. However, Siddhāntin refutes such an objection as follows :

The effect such as heaven has been viewed to be the qualifier of the person impelled to undertake the activity (*niyojya*) only on account of its being the object of desire, and not on account of its being an effect accomplished through the activity enjoined by the injunction (*niyoga*); for, an effect can be viewed to be a qualifier of the person impelled to undertake an activity despite the same effect being not to be accomplished through the activity enjoined by the *niyoga*, provided that the same can be accomplished through some other activity undertaken by the same person. Also, as an alternative, Siddhāntin suggests that it is not necessary to consider that the effect such as heaven is to be accomplished through the activity for facilitating the person's motivation to undertake the activity. For, person's motivation to undertake the activity can be explained due to the person's desire to accomplish the same. Thus, the qualifying nature of the effect can be tenable even without the same being produced by the activity. Thus, there is no need that the phrase *'svargakāmaḥ'* should imply the effect when intended to express *niyojya*.

Niyogavādin objects to the Siddhāntin's theory as follows : Suppose, as explained by Siddhāntin, the effect 'heaven' is established to be something accomplished, then the same heaven would become an effect to be produced from the Agnihotra-offering. Consequently, even the Agnihotra offering becomes the optional rite (*kāmya*) as opposed to the obligatory rite (*nitya);* and hence, the obligatory nature of the same rite becomes contradicted.

However, Siddhāntin, replies as follows :

The eventuality of accepting the Agnihotra-offering as an optional rite meant to produce the effect 'heaven' is a much more preferable alternative compared to the eventuality of accepting the injunctive statement such as *'svargakāmo yajeta'* as expressing only the *niyojya*, i.e. the person impelled to undertake the activity of offering; and therefore, the effect 'heaven' as an implied sense. For, the injunctive statement, expressing the particular *niyojya*, can never be held to imply the sense of the effect 'heaven', since, even without referring to the accomplishment of the effect 'heaven', the injunction prescribing the undertaking of the activity becomes tenable.

Niyogavādin raises now another objection. That the Agnihotra-offering must be held to be conducive to the effect 'heaven' as otherwise the same offering could not be explained as the compulsory duty undertaken by the person desiring the effect, namely, heaven. Thus, it can be accepted that the same phrase *'svargakāmaḥ'* implies the effect. However, Siddhāntin refutes such an objection as well. He states that the Agnihotra-offering could be considered to be the compulsory duty to be undertaken even without producing an effect like heaven as it has been enjoined. And, the undertaking of the compulsory duty, which does not produce any effect, is not contradictory, since it is like the undertaking of the Kṣāmavatīya-offering by the person who keeps *gṛhya* fire even though the same offering does not produce any effect. Also, the undertaking of the Agnihotra–offering, which does not produce any effect, is not contradictory to the person's status as being the one who desires the effect 'heaven' either. For, it is like the undertaking of an indifferent activity like twinkling etc. which do not contradict the person's status as being the one who desires the heaven. Thus, even without the implication of the sense of an effect like heaven, the injunctive statement can be explained as expressing *niyojyaviśeṣa;* and therefore, the Niyogavādin's theory that the phrase, which expresses the *niyojyaviśeṣa,* implies the effect 'heaven' is untenable.

Translation (P.201,202)

Siddhānta that the effect, *'svarga'* cannot be obtained as *niyojya viśeṣaṇa,* and hence, the injunctive statement must express the effect.

LIX. 3. Niyogavādin's objection : This might be so. However, when the (effect) 'heaven' is accomplished, the purpose of undertaking the compulsory duty (*niyoga*) must be held to have been achieved, since the desire (for accomplishing the same heaven) is fulfilled (lit. gone). Otherwise, even the person, who has performed the (Agnihotra) offering, would become necessary to be considered as the one who is yet to carry out his duty of offering prescribed by the injunction; and not as the one who has already carried out the duty by undertaking the performance of the offering. Thus, (the obtainment of the idea of) the accomplishment of the effects such as heaven must be understood as implied from the phrase *'svargakāmaḥ'* due to the inherent ability of the accomplishment of the effect 'heaven' to facilitate the purpose of the undertaking of the compulsory performance of Agnihotra – offering.

Refutation : No, this objection of Niyogavādin is not tenable. The accomplishment (of the purpose) of the undertaking of the compulsory duty of offering can be possible only from the accomplishment of the object of the compulsory duty. And, since the effects such as the heaven, function, according to the Niyogavādin, as only the qualifier of the person enjoined to undertake the performance of the offering (*niyojyaviśeṣa),* the same cannot be considered to be the object of the undertaking of the compulsory duty of offering. Since the accomplishment of the purpose of the undertaking of the compulsory duty is possible only from the accomplishment of the object of the undertaking of the compulsory duty, the idea of the accomplishment of the effect such as heaven is not possible to obtain by implying the same (idea) from the phrase *'svargakāmaḥ'* when held as expressing the person enjoined to undertake the compulsory duty. Otherwise (suppose the accomplishment of the purpose of the undertaking of the compulsory duty is held to be possible from the accomplishment of the fulfilment of the desire, the cause of the undertaking of an activity, then) even the fulfilment of the desire for the even accomplishment of the effect of the *gṛhya* fire would become necessary from the accomplishment of the purpose of the *kṣāmavatīya* offering.

Thus (it is absolutely necessary that) the phrase such as *'svargakāmaḥ'* etc. in the injunctive statements *'svargakāmo yajeta'* etc. are held as intended to express the effects such as the heaven (as the prominent i.e. as the object); and therefore, the theory of the distinction of the accomplishing activity from the action is justified.

Note : The Niyogavādin raises the last of his objections against the necessity of accepting the effect 'heaven' as the expressed meaning of the phrase *'svargakāmaḥ'*. According to him, the undertaking of the compulsory duty of offering is always perceived to be done by only the person impelled. And, the purpose of such an undertaking of the offering, becomes achieved only through the accomplishment of the effects such as heaven, since the attainment of the eligibility of the person is dependent on the fulfilment of the desire for the heaven by the accomplishment of the effect 'heaven'. Otherwise, suppose the purpose of the undertaking is achieved even without the accomplishment of the effect 'heaven' etc., then even the person, who has undertaken the performance of 'offering' (Agnihotra etc.), would become necessary to be considered as the one who has not done his duty. This is so because, the desire for the accomplishment of the effect 'heaven', which functions as the determining cause of the eligibility of the person, remains unfulfilled. Therefore, Niyogavādin argues that it becomes inevitable that the phrase *'svargakāmaḥ'*, in the injunctive statement *'svargakāmo yajeta'*, which expresses the person impelled to undertake the activity leading to Agnihotra – offering (i.e. *niyojya*), be considered as implying the sense of the effect such as heaven as well.

However, Siddhāntin refutes such an argument as untenable. According to him, the theory that, 'when the effect such as heaven is accomplished, the purpose of the undertaking of the compulsory performance of Agnihotra becomes automatically achieved' is not correct. He states that the purpose of the undertaking becomes accomplished only upon the accomplishment of the object of the duty undertaken. And, since only the performance of Agnihotra offering functions as the object of such an undertaking (the effect 'heaven' functions as only the qualifier of the person impelled to undertake the Agnihotra, i.e. *niyojya*, according to the Niyogavādin), the accomplishment of the same effect 'heaven' cannot be considered as automatically facilitating the accomplishment of the purpose of the undertaking. Otherwise, suppose the accomplishment of the purpose of the undertaking is held to be dependent on the desire to accomplish the effect, which functions as the determining cause of the person's eligibility (*adhikāra*), then, on the analogy of such an accomplishment, the accomplishment of the purpose of the undertaking of the Kṣāmavatīya sacrifice could also be insisted to be dependent on the accomplishment of the effect of the *gṛhya* fire; however, since the *gṛhya* fire does not produce any visible effect, the accomplishment of the purpose of Kṣāmavatīya sacrifice would become impossible. Therefore, since the accomplishment of the effect such as heaven cannot automatically facilitate the purpose of the undertaking, the phrase such as *'svargakāmaḥ'* should not be held to express the person, impelled to undertake the performance of Agnihotra – offering, and thereby to imply the sense of the effect 'heaven'. On the other hand, the same phrase must be held as expressing only the effect such as heaven as the prominent, i.e. as the object. And, since the qualifying phrase *'svargakāmaḥ'* in *'svargakāmo yajeta'* expresses the sense of the effect 'heaven', the explanation of the total sentence meaning involving a reference to the distinct accomplishing activity such as 'one should exert in such a way to accomplish the effect 'heaven' by means of offering through the activity' (*yāgena bhāvayet svargam)* becomes tenable. Thus, ends the BHĀVANĀVIVEKA, the composition of Ārya Maṇḍana.

।। श्रीरस्तु ।।

।। भावनाविवेकः ।।

(आचार्यमण्डनमिश्रविरचितः)

संसर्गमोहितधियो विविक्तं धातुगोचरात् ।
भावात्मानं न पश्यन्ति ये तेभ्यस्स विविच्यते ।। १ ।।

I.1 तथाह्याहुः–सामानाधिकरण्यात्तदर्थभेदाभिधानुमा ।
न तादर्थ्यानुमा नाह वृक्षतां शिंशपाश्रुतिः ।। २ ।।

II.1 इह खलु गगनशशविषाणयो रक्रियमाणत्वादभवतोः भवतश्च घटादेस्तत्त्वाद्भवत्यर्थस्य कर्तुः करोतिकर्मता । तथा च भवितुः करोत्यर्थस्य कर्ता प्रयोजक इति भवतेः प्रयोजकव्यापारे णिजुत्पद्यमानः करोत्यर्थमवलम्बते । तेन सा भावना । करोतिसमानाधिकरणाश्च पचत्यादय इति तेषां तादर्थ्यानुमानम् ।

II-2 तदसत्।एकाधिकरणता हि तदर्थभेदाभिधाननिमित्तं नैकार्थ्य मवगमयति । तादृशोस्सहप्रयोगानुपपत्तेः । न खलु वृक्षता शिंशपादिशब्दगोचरः, अपि त्वभिधेयपरिप्रापिततया गम्यमाना तदेवमैकाधिकरण्यं स्फुटं विपर्ययसाधनम् ।

II.3. विशेषाभिधानोन्नयनमेवेत्थमिति चेत् न तस्याः प्रत्ययार्थत्वेनाभ्युपगमात् । प्रत्ययस्य चैकत्वे वाचकभेदादृते वाच्यनानात्वायोगात् ।

II.4. धातवस्तु नानात्मानः करोतिसमानाधिकरणतया तदर्थ विशेषाभिधायिन इति साम्प्रतम् ।

अपि च–

भावाभावे प्रयोगस्य द्विधापि खलु दर्शनात् ।
धात्वर्थवर्तिसामान्यं करोत्यर्थमुपागमत् ।। ३ ।।

III.1. किं करोति घण्टा ? ध्वनतीति न ध्वनिजन्यमन्यत् । सदपि वा

न विवक्षितम्, धात्वर्थमात्रजिज्ञासनात्, तथा च नाभूतप्रादुर्भावनम् । अतो वस्तुतस्तदभावेऽपि प्रयुज्यमानस्य करोतेरिह कुतस्तदर्थः । तथा का क्रिया ? पाकः इति धात्वर्थमात्राभिधानात् ।

भावनाया अपरामर्शान्न भावनाविशेषनिमित्तमैकाधिकरण्यम् ।

III.2. गम्यमानापेक्षमिति चेत् न, तिङन्तेष्वपि प्रसङ्गात् । प्राधान्यात्तिङन्तेष्वभिधेयत्वमिति चेत् न, इहापि तद्विशेषप्रश्नाद्धात्वर्थस्य तल्लक्षणार्थत्वात्प्राधान्यमभिन्नम् ।

III.3. अतः सकलधात्वर्थानुयायिनः करोतेः तत्सामान्यमर्थो नाभूतप्रादुर्भावनमिति शब्दप्रवृत्तिविदः प्रतिपेदिरे । तथा चोचुः– क्रियावचना धातवः। कथं ज्ञायते क्रियावचनाः पचत्यादयः इति ? यदेषां करोतिना सामानाधिकरण्यम् कृभ्वस्तयः क्रियासामान्यवचनाः, क्रियाविशेषवचनाश्च पचत्यादयः ।।

III.4. अथ मतं न भावरहितो धात्वर्थः । सर्वेण तेन किंचिदसदुपजयते इति । तन्न ।

सर्वत्र यदि धात्वर्थे भाव्यं सैवास्तु भावना ।
स्वर्गभूतिसमर्थोऽन्यो व्यापारः कोऽनुपागतः ।। ४ ।।

IV.1. भाव्यभवनसमर्थो हि व्यापारो भावना । धात्वर्थ एव चेत् कस्यचिदात्मलाभानुकूलात्मा, स एव भावना अस्तु न तदतिरिच्यमानशरीरा ।

IV.2. एवं चैतत् न खलु स्वर्गादिफलोदयानुकूलं यागादिधात्वर्थभेदप्रभाव्यं व्यापारान्तरमुपलभामहे यद्भावनाशब्दोऽभिनिविशेत । यागादय एव तु स्वर्गादिफलोदयाय चोदितास्तत्समर्थतया तथाव्यपदेशमर्हन्ति । अव्यापाररूपत्वाद्धात्वर्थस्य नैवम्, इति यदि मन्येत, वक्तव्यो व्यापारः–यदि समीहितकार्यो ऽपजननानुगुणः साध्यस्वभावो धर्मभेदः तदपेक्षया तथा व्यपदेश्यः न धात्वर्थस्तथाविधत्वमतिवर्तते इति । अथ परिस्पन्दः तदा तदात्मनां तावत् धात्वर्थानामविहतं भावनात्वम् ।

अस्पन्दमानकर्तृकेषु आस्ते यजते जानाति इति चात्मकर्तृकेषु तदभावप्रसङ्गः ।

आत्मकर्तृकमेवाह व्यापारं योऽपि भावनाम् ।
कर्त्रन्तरेऽस्य नाख्यातं धीसाम्यान्नोपचारतः ।। ५ ।।

V.1. योऽपि मन्यते सकलपुरुषप्रत्यात्मवेदनीयः चेतनस्यात्मन औदासीन्यप्रच्युत्युपलक्ष्यमाणात्मा प्रयत्नशब्दसंवेदनीयो व्यापारो भावना, कर्त्रन्तरेऽस्य नाख्यातं प्रयुज्येत–कूलं पतति, रथो गच्छति

अग्निर्ज्वलति इति । न च श्रृणोत ग्रावाणः इतिवत्समारोपेण प्रयोगः प्रत्ययस्यावैलक्षण्यात् । नहि रथो गच्छति करी गच्छति इति प्रत्ययो विशिष्यते ।

अपि च-

धातुगोचरनिर्वृत्तिपर्यन्तत्वाच्च कर्मता ।
सर्वत्र तस्य न परः करणाभिमतेऽप्यसौ ।। ६ ।।

VI.1. पुरुषप्रयत्नो हि धात्वर्थनिर्वृत्तिमात्रापवर्गी, सर्वत्र काम्ये नित्ये नैमित्तिके च तत्कर्मताप्रसङ्गः, व्यापारविशेषानुपलम्भात् । नहि काम्येऽपि प्रयोगे करणाभिमतस्य धात्वर्थस्य परस्तात्तत्साध्यस्वर्गादिफलविशेषसाधनः प्रयत्नभेदः समस्ति ।

VI.2. अपूर्वन्नाम न प्रयत्नभेदः न कर्तृव्यापारः करणव्यापारत्वाभ्युपगमात् । अन्यथा व्यापारसङ्करात्कारक-भेदाभावप्रसङ्गादित्यलमनेन ।।

कर्मणो भावभेदं यः फलावधितया वदेत् ।
तस्यादृष्टफलेष्विष्टमनुष्ठानं न युक्तिमत् ।। ७ ।।

VII.1. धातुर्हि कर्म स्वरूपमात्रेणोपादत्ते आख्यातोपसंधानात्तु भावनात्मना अवगम्यते । तथाहि-यावता कर्मक्षणोत्पादनिचयेनेष्टमर्थं साधयति तावत्याख्यातं प्रयुज्यते । अतस्तेन तेन फलेनावच्छिद्यमानः स कर्मक्षणोत्पादनिचयः तेन तेनाख्यातेनाभिधीयते । तदिदं फलावधिकं कर्म भाव्यतया अवसीयते, नाभाव्यमानं फलभावनायालमिति । फलोत्पादिका अवस्था आख्यातार्थः । तथा यतेत यथा यत्किञ्चिद्भवति इति दर्शितम् । एवं अवस्थाभेदेन भावनाकर्मणोर्भेदः । उक्तं च-पूर्वापरीभूतं भावमाख्यातेनाचष्टे व्रजति पचतीत्युपक्रमप्रभृत्यपवर्गपर्यन्तम् इति ।।

VII.2. तत्र प्रतिक्षणमपवर्गवतः कर्मणः कावुपक्रमापवर्गौ ? फलापेक्षया तु कल्प्येते इति यो वदेत् तस्य प्रत्यक्षफलेषु कर्मसु काममारम्भविरामौ कल्प्येते, पुरः परस्ताच्च तत्पर्यन्तकर्मक्षणप्रचयपरि-ज्ञानात् अदृष्टफलेषु त्वनिरूपितफलपर्यन्तपरिमाणभेदेषु कथं प्रवर्तते ? नहि नियुक्तोऽप्यप्रसिद्धविषयविशेषः प्रवर्तितुं प्रभवति । प्रवृत्तौ वा पुरः फलादर्शनात् अकृतशास्त्रार्थमात्मानमवबुध्यमानो न विरन्तुमर्हति । शास्त्रात्फलोत्पत्तिं प्रतिपद्य विरंस्यतीति चेत्-न कृतशास्त्रार्थस्य

फलोत्पत्तेः, फलोत्पत्त्या कृतशास्त्रार्थत्वादितरेतराश्रयप्रसङ्गादित्यलं प्रसङ्गेन ।

प्रकृतमनुसरामः—

धातुप्रत्ययोर्वाच्ये प्रतीयेते नहि क्रिये ।
संबन्धो नावकल्पेत द्वयोः साध्याभिधायिनोः ।। ८ ।।

VIII.1. येषान्तूत्पत्तौ इत्यारव्यातवर्ती धात्वर्थः साध्यः क्रियात्मोपेयते । यदि च प्रत्ययः क्रियान्तरमाचक्षीत क्रियाद्वयं प्रतीयेत– ओदनं पचति, करोति घटमिति यथा । न च तथा प्रतीयते । तस्मान्न धात्वर्थव्यतिरेकिणी आख्यातेषु क्रिया अस्ति ।

साध्यस्य च साध्यान्तरेण समत्वादसंबन्धता । ततश्च तदभिधायिनोः प्रकृतिप्रत्ययोः समभिव्याहारानुपपत्तिः ।

VIII.2. करणत्वाद्धात्वर्थस्यानुपालम्भ इति चेत् न, येषान्तूत्पत्तौ इति विरोधात् न हि तद्भावनाभिप्रायम् । नामपदार्थस्य धात्वर्थसंबन्धे दृष्टार्थता, अपेक्षितसंबन्धप्रतिपादनार्थत्वात् ।

अपि च–

न भावे नापि धात्वर्थे काष्ठैरिति समागमः ।
अक्रियात्वादन्यरोधाच्छाब्दत्वात् करणस्य च ।। ९ ।।

IX.1. न तावद्धात्वर्थसंबन्धिता काष्ठानाम्, करणानां क्रियापेक्षिणां अतदात्मना करणान्तरेण संगमायोगात् । नापि भावनासंबन्धिता, तस्याः करणान्तरोपरुद्धत्वान् नाप्यंशान्तरतया संबन्धः शाब्दत्वात्करणत्वस्य । तदेवं यत्र करणभावः क्रियायां तस्या अवरुद्धत्वात्, धात्वर्थे च अक्रियात्मन्यकरणत्वात् काष्ठैः पचतीति संबन्धाभावः ।

IX.2. अर्थाक्षिप्त–

भावनाद्वारकः संबन्ध इति चेत् –न, अव्यवधानेन संबन्धबोधनात् । नहि मृदा घटम्, काष्ठैः पचतीति समः संबन्धावगमः, एकत्र नैराकाङ्क्ष्यात्, अन्यत्रान्यापेक्षणात् ।।

विक्लिद्यन्ति पचन्तीति न विशेषः प्रकल्प्यते ।
कः प्रत्ययार्थो धातूक्तव्यापारो यदिकर्तृता ।। १० ।।

X.1. अपि च–विक्लिद्यन्ति पचन्ति इत्युभयत्र प्रयोजकव्यापारस्य प्रत्ययेनाभिधानम् धातुभ्यां च विक्लित्तेरिति नार्थभेदः स्यात् ।

X.2. नन्वस्ति तावत्कर्तृभेदेन व्यापारभेदः तदभिधानान्न दोषः । तथाहि–विक्लिद्यन्तीति तण्डुलाः कर्तारः, पचन्तीति देवदत्तादयः । किं पुनर्भवान्कर्तृलक्षणं मत्वैवमाह–यदि साधननियोगादिकम्, कथं तण्डुलानां कर्तृत्वम् ? देवदत्तादय एव कर्तार इत्यविशेषप्रसङ्गः । अथागुणतो धातुना अभिधीयमानव्यापारता, क इदानीं प्रत्ययार्थः कर्तृव्यापारस्य भावनाया धातुनैवाभिधानात् ।

X.3. फलधात्वर्थार्थभावनानात्वाद्धात्वर्थार्थो व्यापारो धातुवाच्यः, फलार्थस्तु धात्वर्थकरणकः प्रत्ययवाच्यः । नैतत्सारम् ।

नहि धात्वर्थकरणफलभेदप्रभावनः ।
धात्वर्थं फलभेदं च व्यापारो दृश्यतेऽन्तरा ।। ११ ।।

XI.1. योऽपि व्यवहितफलेषु दृश्यते, धात्वर्थान्तरात्मकः प्रयत्नान्तरजन्मा, न प्राचीनधातुगोचरप्रभावनीय इति ।

कर्मणा च करोत्यर्थो व्याप्तोऽतस्तदयोगतः ।
तदभावः प्रत्ययार्थसाधनेऽपि विभक्तयः ।। १२ ।।

XII.1. करोतेः सदा सकर्मकत्वात्तद्योगविरहेण करोत्यर्थाभावं प्रतीमः ज्वलनविरहेणेव धूमाभावम् । तथाहि–न जातु यजेत स्वर्गम्, शयीत स्वास्थ्यम् आसीत सुखम् इति दृष्टचरः संसर्गः ।

XII.2. यदि मन्वीत सङ्गतिसमर्थविभक्तिभेदाभावादेवम् ।

तथाहि–धात्वर्थसाधनावगाहिन्यः सुब् विभक्तयः प्रत्ययार्थकर्मणि नियोज्ये स्वर्गकामादौ तददर्शनात् ।

तच्च वार्तम्, एवं सति शेषसंबन्धहेतोः षष्ठ्या अव्याहतप्रसरत्वात् । अपि च प्रत्ययार्थभावनाकरणधात्वर्थनामधेयेभ्यो विश्वजिदादिभ्यः करणविभक्तिमीक्षमाणो नेदमध्यवसातुमर्हति ।

XII.3. अस्त्येव कर्मसंबन्धो यजेत स्वर्गकामः इति चेत्–न, पुरुषविशेषणत्वेन (त्वात्) साक्षादसंबन्धात् । स्वर्गाय यजेत इति साक्षात्सङ्गतिरिति चेत्–न अकर्मरूपत्वात् कर्मरूपसंबन्धाभावस्य च भावनाभिधानाभावहेतुत्वात् । अकर्मता च चतुर्थीनिर्देशात् । स्वर्गाय यागः इति च धात्वर्थेनापि संबन्धात् ।

तुल्यार्थत्वं भावयति भवतीति प्रसज्यते ।
कः प्रत्ययार्थो धातूक्तव्यापारे खलु कर्तरि ।। १३ ।।

XIII.1. भावयति घटं कुम्भकारः, भवति घटम् इत्यपि प्रसज्येत,

तुल्यार्थत्वात् । तथाहि-एकस्य (त्र) कर्तुः कुम्भकारस्य व्यापारं णिजाचष्टे, अन्यत्राख्यातप्रत्यय इति न भिद्यतेऽर्थः ।

XIII.2. प्रयोजकव्यापारो णिजर्थः, कर्तृव्यापार आख्यातार्थ इति नानार्थत्वं यो मन्यते, वक्तव्यस्तेनेह कर्तृप्रयोजकभेदः । यदि साधनानां प्रवर्तयिता निवर्तयिता च कर्ता, स चैकः कुम्भकार एवेति तद्व्यापाराभिधानात्तुल्यार्थत्वम् ।

XIII.3. घटः कर्ता, प्रयोजकः कुम्भकारः इति चेत् कथमनीशितुः साधनप्रवृत्तिनिवृत्त्योर्घटस्य कर्तृत्वं तादृशं कुलालमतिक्रम्य । अथागुणतो धातुना अभिधीयमान व्यापारत्वम्कस्तर्हि-इदानीमाख्यातार्थः । धातुना अभिहितत्वात्तद्व्यापारस्य । नच व्यापारभेददर्शनम् येन धातुप्रत्यययोर्विषयविभागः स्यात् ।

XIII.4. करणत्वं च शब्दतोऽन्यतो वा धात्वर्थस्योभयत्राप्यविशिष्टमिति दुर्वारं तुल्यार्थत्वम् । अतो न प्रत्ययो भावनावचन इति सूक्तम्-ण्यन्तस्य भवतेरर्थः केनांशेनाभिधीयते इति ।।

किञ्च-

कर्तृव्यापार इष्टश्चेत् पच्यादावपि भावना ।
धात्वर्थान्तररूपः स्यात्सोऽप्यधिश्रयणादिकः ।। १४ ।।

XIV.1. यदि च कर्तृव्यापारो भावना, स च पच्यादिष्वधिश्रयणादिकः तं पचिरेवोपादत्ते, अन्यथा सिध्यतिविक्लिद्यतिभ्यामविशेषःस्यात् ।

अथापि नोपाददीत, तथाप्याधिश्रयत्यादिधात्वन्तरार्थ इति नान्यो धात्वर्थाद्भावनापदार्थः ।

XIV.2. अथ मतं-करोतीत्यन्विताभासप्रत्ययविषयतया अनुवृत्तात्मा व्यावृत्तावग्रहग्रहणगोचरेभ्यो धात्वर्थेभ्योऽन्यो भावनापदार्थ इति-तदसत् । एवं हि सामान्यलक्षणानुपातितया धात्वर्थसामान्यमेव स्यात् न पदार्थान्तरं भावनापदार्थः ।

XIV.3. अथ मतं-सत्यं साध्यतया सामान्यम्, न गोत्वादिवत्तद्रू-पतया । तस्याः प्रतिपुरुषं शीघ्रं करोति, मन्दं करोतीति स्वसामान्यविशेषाभ्यां योगात् । धात्वर्थवर्ति तु करणरूपं सामान्यम-न्यदेव ।

उक्तं हि–

अन्यदेव हि धात्वर्थसामान्यं करणात्मकम् ।
अन्यच्च भावना नाम साध्यत्वेन व्यवस्थितम् ।। इति ।।

तदेतदपेशलम् । तथा हि–

न क्रियाकरणाकारे द्वे ज्ञाने अनुयायिनी ।
यतः प्रतीमः सामान्ये द्वे साध्यसमवायिनी ।। १५ ।।

XV.1. नहि करणं करणमिति क्रियाकारकव्यतिरिक्तेऽर्थे पच्यादिषु प्रत्ययः, यतः क्रियारूपव्यतिरिक्तं करणात्मकं धात्वर्थसामान्यं कल्प्येत । शीघ्रमन्दादिषु तु धात्वर्थसामान्यस्यैव करोतिवाच्यस्यावान्तर सामान्यभेदः शोणकर्कादिरिवाश्वत्वस्य ।

उक्तं च–

न हि धात्वर्थकरणः फलभेदप्रभावनः ।
धात्वर्थं फलभेदं च व्यापारो दृश्यतेऽन्तरा ।। (इति) ।।
वाच्यो लक्षणभेदश्च ननु धात्वर्थभावयोः ।
भावः परिस्पन्द इति यजत्यादावसम्भवः ।। १६ ।।

XVI.1. अवश्यं च भावधात्वर्थभेदवादिना तयोः स्पष्टो रूपभेदो दर्शयितव्यः । अस्पन्दात्मा धात्वर्थः, स्पन्दात्मको भाव इति चेत् अस्पन्दमानकर्तृकेषु यजते जानति इत्याख्यातार्थेषु तदभावप्रसङ्गः । गच्छत्यादौ च धात्वर्थस्य भावनात्वप्रसङ्गः । चेतनव्यापारस्तु पुरस्तात्प्रत्युक्तः ।

XVI.2. कश्चैष परिस्पन्दः ? न खल्वयमाश्रयाभिमताद्भेदेन गम्यते । कथं न गम्यते ? यदा सत्यप्याश्रये प्रत्यक्षे कदाचिच्चलतीति प्रत्ययप्रादुर्भावः, (अतः) तदतिरिक्तार्थालम्बनः ।

नैतत्सारम्–

कार्यं विभागसंयोगलक्षणं चलतीति धीः ।
आलम्बतां ततो नान्यो विशेषो गम्यते स्थितात् ।। १७ ।।

XVII.1. स खलु परिस्पन्दो ऽक्षगोचरः पूर्वोत्तरदेश विभागसंयोगफलोऽभ्युपगम्यते । तथा च तावेव गोचरयत्वेष प्रत्ययः । न खलु पूर्वोत्तरदेशहानोपादाने अप्रतिपद्यमानश्चलतीति बुध्यते । न च स्थितान्निपुणतोऽपि निरूपयद्भिरन्यो विशेषः चलतीति लक्ष्यते ।

XVII.2. ननु चलित्वा स्थितोऽपि संयोगविभागवानेव न चलतीति गम्यते । अन्यतरकर्मजन्मनोश्च

संयोगविभागयोर्द्विष्ठत्वेनोभयत्रक्रियाप्रत्ययप्रसङ्गः । स्थाणुश्येनयोर्विभागमात्रम्, एकत्र समुदितयोस्तद्धेतुत्वमिति चेत् अन्यतरकर्मजन्मनोरुभयोरपिः प्रसङ्गः यदा स्थाणुरेकेन श्येनेन संयुज्यतेऽन्यतश्च वियुज्यते । न च क्रमविशेषवन्तौ तदालम्बनम् पुरःसंयुक्तश्येनान्तरविभागपुरस्सरेऽपि श्येनान्तरसंयोगेऽभावात् ।

उच्यते-

अच्छिन्नोत्पत्तयो देशविशेषत्यागसङ्गमाः ।
तद्गोचराः पदार्थानामाकाशो देश इष्यते ।। १८ ।।

XVIII.1. न खलु संयोगविभागमात्रे चलतीति प्रत्ययः । अपित्वविच्छिन्नोत्पादसंयोगविभागप्रबन्धे । स्थिते च तदभावः । नच स्थाणौ देशविशेषविषयौ संयोगविभागौ, संयोगिमात्रस्यादेशत्वात् न हि श्येनौ स्थाणोर्देशाविति प्रतियन्ति लौकिकाः । आकाश एव तु सकलदेशिपदार्थानां देश इति प्रतीमः । अतस्तत्प्रदेशसंयगोगविभागावेव तदालम्बनमिति स्थाणौ न प्रसङ्गः ।।

XVIII.2. ननु व्योम्नोऽप्रत्यक्षत्वाद्वायुवनस्पतिसंयोगविभागवत्तत्संयोगविभागानां प्रत्यक्षावृत्तित्वेनानैन्द्रियकत्वादिन्द्रियजन्मनः प्रत्यक्षस्य विषयता न युक्ता ।

न न युक्ता । अन्यथा-

कथं गम्येत वयसो नियताधारदेशता ।
चलतोऽक्षातिवृत्ताश्चेद्विहायोदेशसङ्गमाः ।। १९ ।।

XIX.1. अप्रत्यक्षत्वे हि नभोविभागसंयोगादीनां कथं पतति पतत्रिणि देशभेदाधिकरणज्ञानम् ? क्रियया कारणेन कार्यानुमानादिति चेत्-न, नियतदेशाधिकरणप्रतीतेः । इह प्राप्तः नेह इति नियतप्रत्ययो न देशविशेषसंयोगाप्रत्यक्षतायमवकल्पते ।

XIX.2. वियद्विततालोक निवहभेदादुपपन्न इति चेत्-स एव तर्ह्याकाशदेश इति तद्वर्तिसंयोगविविभागौ प्रत्यक्षौ ।

अपि च-प्रत्यक्षाप्रत्यक्षवृत्त्योरपि संयोगविभागयोः सिद्धयोः प्रत्यक्षत्वकल्पना युक्ता, न त्वसिद्धस्य कर्मणः ।

XIX.3. ताभ्यामेव तर्हि

संयोगविभागाभ्यां क्रियामनुमिमीमहे, कादाचित्कयोरहेतुत्वानुपपत्तेः । कादाचित्कत्वादेव चाश्रयमात्रहेतुत्वायोगात् हेत्वन्तरापेक्षणात् ।

नैतत्सारम् यतः-

नित्यत्वे सर्वदा जन्म स्यात्संयोगविभागयोः ।
अनित्यत्वेऽस्य यो हेतुस्तयोरेवास्तु तेन किम् ।। २० ।।

XX.1. तद्धि कर्म संयोगविभागाभ्यां नित्यमनित्यं वा अनुमीयते । नित्यत्वे हेतुसन्निधानाद्धेत्वन्तरानपेक्षत्वाच्च सदा संयोगविभागोत्पादप्रसङ्गः । अनित्यत्वे तु तस्यापि हेतुमत्वात्तद्धेत्वभिमतादेव तत्सिद्धिरिति किमन्तर्गडुना कर्मणा ।

XX.2. यस्तु मन्यते-नित्यत्वादन्तरङ्गत्वाच्च कर्मैव कारणं संयोगविभागयोः, न प्रयत्नादि, बहिर ङ्गत्वात् व्यभिचारित्वाच्च । तथा हि-कर्मैकार्थसमवायिनः संयोगविभागसंस्काराः । कर्मणि च सति नियोगतस्तत्सद्भावः, कार्यानुमितस्य हेतोस्तदभावे सत्ताप्रमाणाभावात् । प्रयत्नस्त्वात्मस्थः । सत्यपि च प्रयत्ने बहुषु संयुक्तेषु कश्चिदेव प्रयत्नाद्देशान्तरं प्राप्नोति ।

स वक्तव्यः-

प्रसिद्धस्यान्तरङ्गत्वान्नित्यत्वाद्धेतुता भवेत् ।
अकारणत्वमन्यस्य यदि कर्म ततः कथम् ।। २१ ।।

XXI.1. बहुसमवधाने हि नित्यत्वान्तरङ्गत्वाभ्यां प्रसिद्ध सद्भावं वस्तु हेतुरिति व्यवस्थाप्यते, नत्वप्रसिद्धसद्भावस्य कल्पना । तद्विपरीतस्य हेतुत्वमनुपपन्नमिति, तादृशमप्रसिद्धसद्भावमपि परिकल्प्यत इति यदि मतम्, हन्त तर्हि कर्मणोऽपि तदकारणमापतति ।

XXI.2. अथ मतं व्यधिकरणमपि सम्बन्धात् कुतश्चिच्च प्रतिबन्धाद् दृष्टव्ययभिचारमपि तत्कर्मणः कारणम् संयोगविभागाभ्यां किमपराद्धम् ? येन दृष्टं कारणं परित्यज्यादृष्टं मृग्यते । प्रायेण च कर्महेतवः संयोगविभागैकाधिकरणा इति यत्किञ्चिदेतत् ।

हेतुसत्ता च कार्येण ततः प्रागनुमीयते ।
वर्तमानावभासः स्यान्न क्रियाधिगमस्ततः ।। २२ ।।

XXII.1. कार्योपजननं प्रत्यनन्तर कालीनं हेतसत्त्वं तदुपयोगि, न कार्यकालम्, तस्य तदा सिद्धत्वात् । अतः कार्येण कारणमनुमिमानः

तत्प्राक्कालमेवानुमिमीते, न वर्तमानकालम्। तथा च फललिङ्गात्मजन्मा ततः प्राक्कलक्रियागोचरः प्रत्ययो न वर्तमानावग्रहः स्यात्।

अपि च–

संयोगान्तं वर्तमानं तत उन्नीयते कथम्।
विभागतो मीयमानं स्थाणावप्येतदापतेत्॥ २३॥

XXIII.1. संयोगान्तं कर्म संयोगोत्पादज्ञानक्षणोत्तरकालमनुमीयमानं न वर्तमानम्। संयोगविभागौ तु वर्तमानौ। ज्ञानानुरूपश्च विषयो न तद्विपरीतः। तस्मात्तयोरेव चलतीतिप्रत्ययविषयता, न तु कर्मणः।

XXIII.2. अथ विभागानुमेयत्वात्तमुपजनय्य आसंयोगोत्पादं व्यवस्थानाद्वर्तमानमनुमीयत इति। तदसत्। स्थाणावपि प्रसङ्गात्, विभागस्य तुल्यत्वात्।

XXIII.3. तत् गुणविशेष एव धातूपादानः किया, न तु तदतिरिच्यमानात्मा क्रियापदार्थः, यः प्रत्ययस्य धातोर्वाअभिधेयः स्यात्।

XXIII.4. यदप्यनुमानम्–यत्सर्वेषु साधनेषुसन्निहितेषु सत्सु कदाचित्पचतीति प्रत्ययो भवतीति तन्न–

सिद्धेर्गुणविशेषेण पचतीत्यपि संविदः।
क्रियापदार्थस्यान्यस्य नानुमानं प्रकल्पते॥ २४॥

XXIV.1. यः खलु तण्डुलावयवेषु विभागलक्षणः प्रशिथिलसंयोगलक्षणो वा गुणभेदस्तस्य सन्निहितेष्वपि साधनेषु कदाचिद्भावात्तन्निबन्धनः पचतीति प्रत्यय इति न तत्र क्रियापदार्थानुमानं युक्तम्।

XXIV.2. तत एव तर्हि गुणविशेषात्कादाचित्कात्तदस्तु। अन्यथा साधनसन्निधिमात्र एवैष स्यात्। न, कर्मण्यपि तथा प्रसङ्गात् कर्मान्तरानुमाने चानवस्थाप्रसङ्गात्, अग्निसंयोगस्य च क्रमेण भावात् प्रकृष्यमाणत्वाच्च तद्धेतोर्न तस्य साधनसन्निधिमात्र एव भावः। तस्यैव तर्हि संयोगस्य कारणं कर्मेति चेत्, न, प्रयत्नादेरेव कर्महेतोस्तद्धेतुत्वात्।

तदित्थं यागादिव्यतिरिक्तभावनाभावात्–

यागेन भावयेत्स्वर्गमित्यर्थः परिकल्पितः ।
स्वर्गकामस्य यागे तु नियोगः सम्प्रतीयते ।। २५ ।।

XXV.1. सत्यां हि भावनायां यागस्य करणत्वम्, कर्मापेक्षित्वाच्च तस्यापेक्षायां पुरुषविशेषणस्यापि इष्टेः सामर्थ्यात्कर्मत्वमवधार्यते । तदभावे तु मन्दान्विप्रलब्धुमेष परिकल्पननिमित्तो वाक्यार्थो–यागेन भावयेत्स्वर्गमिति । पुरुषविशेषस्य तु नियोगो यागेऽवगम्यते ।

XXV.2. तस्मिंस्त्वनुष्ठिते स्वर्गादिफलं स्वतोऽन्यतो वा कुतश्चिद्भविष्यति, नैव वा, नत्वयमर्थः शक्योऽभ्युपगन्तुम् ।

XXV.3. ननु पुरुषविशेषणमप्येतन्न संभवति अयोगान्ययोगात्यन्तायोगानामन्यतमस्यापि व्यवच्छेदासंभवात् । जात्या च तस्याभावात् ।

XXV.4. साध्यत्वमपि तर्ह्यनुपपन्नम्, स्वर्गस्य तथा अनिर्देशात्, विशेषणस्यैव चार्थाद्भावनासम्बन्धाभ्युपगमात् वर्तमानेच्छा विशेषणत्वमितरस्याप्यविरुद्धम् ।

XXV.5. न, फलनिमित्तयोरन्यतरापत्तेः । निमित्तत्वे च यावज्जीव श्रुत्युपसंहारे तदानर्थक्यम्, अनुपसंहारे त्वेतस्याः ।

XXV.6. स्यात्तावदेष नित्येषु परिहारो नानित्येषु । अपि चानर्थक्यं स्यादित्यनर्थो नावगन्तुं शक्यत इत्युक्तम् । पुनरुदेशाद्वा स्वर्गकामः पुनः प्रयोक्ष्यत इति नानर्थक्यम् ।

बुद्ध्वैतदेवं भगवान्ददर्श खलु बादरिः ।
न द्रव्यगुणसंस्कारव्यतिरिक्तेऽस्ति शेषता ।। २६ ।।

XXVI.1. द्रव्यगुणयोः खलु योग्यता । अतः कारकविभक्तितो वा क्रियायां शेषभावोऽवगम्यते । संस्कारोऽपि सम्मार्गादिः शब्दतो वस्तुतो वा कर्मसम्बन्धी, तत्र आपन्नशेषत्वः तन्मुखेन क्रियायां शेषभावं यायात् ।

XXVI.2. यागस्तु प्रकृत्या अकर्मको देवताकर्मको वा कथं स्वर्गेण सम्बध्येत ? भावनाकर्मणा तेन तव्द्यवहितः संबध्येत । सा च नास्तीति मन्यमानो भगवान्बादरिर्द्रव्यगुणसंस्कारेष्वेव शेषभाव इति मेने–इति पूर्वः पक्षः ।।

अत्रोच्यते-

अनेकार्थत्वमन्याय्यं तेनैकाधिकरण्यतः ।
करोतिना तिङन्तेषु भावभेदोऽनुमीयते ।। २७ ।।

XXVII.1. घटं करोतीत्यत्र तावज्जननोत्पादनादिश्रुतिविषयां भावनां करोतिराचष्टे । स च पचत्यादिसमानाधिरकरणोऽपि नान्यत्र वर्तितुमर्हति । अनेकार्थत्वेऽप्यनैकान्तिकत्वात् ततोऽभिधेयनिश्चयायोगादप्यव्यवहारापत्तेः । परिगतसामर्थ्यानुसारेण च प्रयोगोपपत्तौ सामर्थ्यान्तरपरिकल्पनायोगात्, प्रतीतबाधादप्रतीतकल्पनाच्च, प्रयोगान्तरेऽपि प्रयोगान्तरनिर्ज्ञातस्यैव प्रत्ययात् ।

XXVII.2. किं करोतीति चोत्पादनाया एवाधिगमात् । एवं भावनाभिधानेन करोतिना समानाधिकरणतया आख्यातपदानां तद्विशेषाभिधायित्वमनुमीयते ।

XXVII.3. यद्यपि प्रत्यययोऽभेदान्न विशेषावगमायालम्, पदन्तु प्रकृतिभेदभिन्नं प्रकृत्यर्थानुरक्तप्रत्ययार्थप्रधानम् । प्रत्ययोऽपि पौर्वापर्यनियमात् पदवन्न स्वतन्त्रः सामान्यमात्रे धियमादधाति, अपि तु प्रकृत्यपेक्षया आचक्षाणः स्वार्थमेव समर्पयति । सर्वथा तावत्पदं विशेषे वर्तते । तेन तावत्स्वतो भेदवत्या अपि धात्वर्थोपधानव्यज्यमानस्फुटविशेषायास्तत्र विशेषाभिधानमविरुद्धम् ।

XXVII.4. ननु प्रत्ययस्य सामान्यमभिधेयमिष्टम् तत्कथमुभयोस्सामान्याभिधायिनोरैकाधिकरण्यम् ?

उच्यते-

भेदोपहितसामान्यवचनेऽप्यपृथक्श्रुतिः ।
को राजा याति ? पाञ्चालराज इत्यभिवीक्ष्यते ।। २८ ।।

XXVIII.1. प्रश्नवर्तिना हि सामान्यशब्देन व्यवच्छिन्नसामान्यविषयाः श्रुतयः परिदृष्टसमानाधिकरणप्रयोगाः, को राजा याति ? पाञ्चालराज इति यथा ।

XXVIII.2. युक्त एवोत्तरे सामान्यनिर्देशः, अन्यथा प्रश्नगतं तदपेक्षणीयं स्यात्, विशेषतस्तु भावनाया असंविज्ञानपदभेदत्वात्परोपधानव्यज्यमानस्फुटविशेषायाः । तस्मान्न सिद्धसाधनम्, न विपर्ययसाधनम्, न दृष्टान्ताभावः ।

भावाभावे प्रयोगस्तु द्विधापि न निरीक्ष्यते ।
अन्ततस्सोऽस्ति धात्वर्थगोचरो लक्ष्यते तथा ।। २९ ।।

XXIX.1. घण्टा ध्वनतीति भाव्याभावेन भावनाया अभाव उच्यते । सर्वश्च धात्वर्थः किञ्चिदसदुत्पादयति । ध्वननमपि सुखं दुःखं ज्ञानं वा । अन्ततो धात्वर्थ एव भाव्यः ।

XXIX.2. नहि सर्वत्र धात्वर्थस्य करणतैव, कर्मतापि तु क्वचित्तन्मात्रनिर्वृत्तिविवक्षायाम् ।

XXIX.3. का क्रिया ? पाकः इति च, द्विविधत्वाच्छब्दार्थस्य श्रौतलक्ष्यमाणभेदेन । अतो नाभावो भावनायाः शब्दतः, तद्विशेषलक्षणार्थत्वात्पाकशब्दस्य ।

तिङन्तेऽपि तर्हि लक्ष्यमाण एव भावोऽस्तु नैतत्सारम् । यतः–

कः पाकः पचतीत्यत्र बुद्धिभेदमपह्नुते ।
न भावनापरामर्शमन्तरेण च भाव्यता ।। ३० ।।

XXX.1. इदं भवान् पृष्टो व्याचष्टाम्–पाकः पचतीत्यनयोर्धात्वर्थोभिद्यते, न वा भिद्यते, इति । को हि स्फुटं प्रत्ययभेदमवजानीते । तथाहि–तिङन्ते भाव्यः स गम्यते न तथाभूतो (रूपो) घञन्ते, भावे तद्विधानात्, शुद्धस्य च धात्वर्थस्य तत्त्वव्याख्यानात्–धात्वर्थः केवलः शुद्धो भाव इत्यभिधीयते इति ।।

XXX.2. तत्तर्हि भाव्यत्वं भावनासंस्पर्शकृतमिति तिङन्तानां सा अर्थः । गम्यमानत्वे हि तिङन्तघञन्तयोः नैव धीर्भिद्येत, अविशेषात् ।

XXX.3. नच साधनसम्बन्धाद्भेदः, गम्यते स्थीयते इति प्रसङ्गात् ।

किञ्च–

पाकं करोति पचतीत्याख्यातार्थो निदर्श्यते ।
भेदेन शब्दवृत्तिज्ञैः पाकादौ नत्वयं क्रमः ।। ३१ ।।

XXXI.1. पचति, पाकं करोतीति तिङन्तपदार्थं भेदेन निदर्शयति नाप्रतिपद्य भेदम्, पाकादिषु तु न तथा भेदप्रतिपत्तेरभावादिति गम्यते ।

XXXI.2. परिकल्प्य भेदं तथोपदर्शनम्, पाकस्याभिनिर्वर्तनं करोतीति यथेति चेत्–न, पाकादावनिदर्शनात् । शब्दोपकल्पितस्तिङन्तेष्वपि भेद इति चेत् अस्तु तावच्छब्दार्थभेदः, वस्तुन्युप

पादयिष्यते ।

XXXI.3. नन्वेवं भावनाया अपि साध्यरूपायाः प्रतीतेर्भावनान्तरापातः, तदपि तथैवेत्यनवस्था । यदपि मतं व्यापारो हि सा, रूपमेव तस्याः तादृशमपराधीनोपजननम्, अतो रूपात्तथात्वसिद्धिः नान्यसंस्पर्शव्यपेक्षितेति ।

XXXI.4. धात्वर्थोऽपि तर्हि तथा अस्तु । तथा हि-सोऽपि वस्तुतस्तथाभवन् न वा आपादिततथाभावः स्वशब्दैः व्यापारात्मोपादीयते, घञादिष्वपि कारकसम्बन्धोपपत्तेः, अन्यथा अव्यापारे कारकसम्बन्धायोगात्, अव्यापारसम्बन्धिनः कारकत्वानुपपत्तेः, क्रियासम्बन्धप्रभावितत्वात्कारकभावस्य । बुद्धिभेदस्तु पाकादिषु प्रत्ययोपात्तेन सिद्धभावेनाभिभवात्, अनभिभवाच्च पचत्यादौ । तच्चानभिभूतं रूपमन्यथाशक्यनिदर्शनं व्यापारान्तरसंस्पर्शेनैव निदर्शयन्ति भावनाया इव । नच सिद्धसाध्यतयोरैकशब्द्यं विरुद्धम् भेदाभेदयोरिव गोत्वादिषु, भिन्नप्रकृतिप्रत्ययोपादानत्वात् भाव्यरूपप्रतीतिनिदर्शनाभ्याञ्च धात्वर्थस्य तिङन्तेषु भावनामिच्छतो धात्वर्थस्य कर्मत्वप्रसङ्गः, करणत्वं न स्यात् । तस्माद्धात्वर्थ एव व्यापारात्मा स्वशब्दोपादानः फलभवनसमर्थो भावना क्रिया चेति साम्प्रतम् ॥

तदेतदसमञ्जसम्-

दृश्यमाने वस्तुभेदे नेष्टा शब्दार्थमात्रता ।
प्रत्ययार्थेनाभिभवः सिद्धे तद्भावनिश्चये ॥ ३२ ॥

XXXII.1. दर्शयिष्यते ह्यव्यापारात्मनो धात्वर्थाद्भेदवती क्रिया । न अतो शब्दसामर्थ्यविलसितमेवैतदिति युक्तम् । असति वस्तुनि तथा नाम भवेत् । सम्बन्धग्रहणापेक्षत्वाच्च शब्दस्य न वस्तुस्वरूपक्लृप्त्यै विभवः । निश्चिते च धातुभिःभाव्यताया इहोपादाने अभिभवाभिधानं युक्तम् । न च तथा, प्रमाणाभावात्, साधनसम्बधस्य गम्यमानभावनाविषयत्वात्, तथापि निदर्शनात् शङ्कुलया खण्डः इति ।

विक्लिद्यन्ति पचन्तीति न विशेषः प्रकल्पते ।
ऋते व्यापारनानात्वात्कर्तृभेदोऽपि वै कुतः ॥ ३३ ॥

XXXIII.1. न तावत्तिङन्तेषु धात्वर्था एव व्यापारात्मोपादीयते,

विक्लिद्यन्ति पचन्तीति धात्वर्थाभेदात्प्रत्ययाभेदप्रसङ्गात् । कर्तृभेदान्नैवमिति चेत्-न, व्यापारभेदमन्तरेण तदनुपपत्तेः । यथा साधनानां नियोक्तृत्वे कर्तृलक्षणे यज्ञदत्तादय एव कर्तारो न तण्डुलाः, अभिधीयमानव्यापारत्वे तु तण्डुला एव । अनेन भिनत्ति, दलति, छिनत्ति, द्विधाभवतीत्यादयो व्याख्याताः । तस्माद्धात्वर्थातिरिक्तो व्यापार उपेयः यत्कृतोऽर्थभेदः कर्तृभेदश्च ।।

XXXIII.2. अपरः कल्पः-स्यान्मतं कर्मसमवायिक्रियेष्वेव धात्वर्थातिरिक्तो व्यापारो गम्यते । कर्तृस्थक्रियेषु कथम् ? उच्यते-

ऋते व्यापारनानात्वात्कर्तृभेदोऽपि वै कुतः ?

ऋत्विजो यजन्ति, यजते यजमानः इत्यगुणतो धातुना अभिधीयमानव्यापारस्य कर्तृत्वात् सङ्कल्पविशेषस्य च यज्यभिधेयस्य यजमानव्यापारत्वात् यजन्ति याजकाः इत्यनुपपत्तिः । धात्वर्थातिरिक्तव्यापारप्राधान्यविवक्षायां तूपपद्यते ।

XXXIII.3. नन्वनभि-

धानेऽपि व्यापारभेदस्य द्रव्यपरित्यागसङ्कल्पमात्रस्याभिधानेऽपि यजतिना स्वातन्त्र्यविवक्षाभेदात् कर्तृभेदः करणभेद इवातिशयविवक्षाभेदादुपपद्यते । किमिदं स्वातन्त्र्यम् ? साधनानां नियोक्तृत्वम् । काष्ठादीनि पचन्तीति कथम् ? नियोज्यान्तराभावात् नियोगविवक्षया प्रयोगो न स्यात् । तस्मात्प्राधान्येन प्रतिपाद्यमानव्यापारता स्वातन्त्र्यमित्यास्थेयम् । तथा चोक्तम्-स्थालीस्थे यत्ने कथ्यमाने स्थाली स्वतन्त्रा इति ।।

XXXIII.4. भवतु व्यापारभेदः, (स च) धातूपादान एवास्तु । तथा च पचिना देवदत्तादिव्यापारोपादानात् विक्लिदिना चानुपादानात् विक्लिद्यन्ति पचन्ति इत्यर्थभेदकर्तृभेदौ । यजिना च ऋत्विजां व्यापारस्य तादर्थ्यादभिधानादृत्विजां कर्तृत्वोपपत्तिः । यथोक्तम्-तदभिसन्धिपूर्वकं प्रेषणमध्येषणं वा युक्तं तत्सर्वं पच्यर्थ इति ।।

नैतत्सारम्-

विक्लित्तिमात्रसङ्कल्पविशेषैकावलम्बनौ ।
ज्ञायमानतदर्थत्वान्नेष्टावन्याभिधायिनौ ।। ३४ ।।

XXXIV.1. पाकः यागः इति विक्लित्तिमात्रं सङ्कल्पमात्रं चाचक्षते पचियजी, न तदतिरिक्तं कर्तृव्यापारम्, पाकस्य क्रियेत्यनिदर्शनात् ।

XXXIV.2. तथा पच्यन्ते तण्डुलाः स्वयमेव यजते यजमानः इति, तन्मात्रस्यैव तद्व्यापारत्वाभ्युपगमात् । तथा च पचति देवदत्तः यजन्ति याजकाः इति प्रज्ञायमानतदर्थस्य नार्थान्तरविषयत्वं युक्तम् ।

XXXIV.3. अव्यभिचाराद्धि तावन्मात्रमर्थः, नाधिकम्, व्यभिचारात्, शब्दान्तरनिबन्धनत्वाच्च, प्रत्ययागमे हि प्रतीयमानः तदर्थ एव कर्तृव्यापारः । प्रधानानाञ्च प्रायेण प्रत्ययार्थत्वात्प्राधान्यादपि प्रत्ययार्थत्वम् ।

XXXIV.4. अस्त्यादिषु व्यभिचार इति चेत्-न, वस्तुतोऽभावेऽपि शब्दात्प्रतीतेः । अन्यथा अस्ति भावः सत्तेत्यभेदात् ।

XXXIV.5. सत्ताया एव साध्यरूपेण धातुनोपादानात् साध्यताप्रतीतिः, न पुनः प्रत्ययेन भावनाया अभिधानात् । सत्ता भाव इति सत्ताया धातुनैव सिद्धरूपेण उपादानात् सिद्धरूपप्रतीतिः, न पुनः प्रत्ययेन भावनाया अनभिधानात् व्यापारसंस्पर्शकृतस्य साध्यत्वस्य पच्यादौ निश्चयात्

XXXIV.6. इहैव तर्हि व्यभिचारः यजते यजमानः पच्यन्ते स्वयमेव तण्डुलाः इति । व्यापारान्तरोपगमे वा धातोरव्यभिचारः । न, अभ्युपगमात् लेनाभिधानस्य, तन्निबन्धनत्वात्तस्यान्यथा(पि)सिद्धेः पाकादिषु व्यभिचारात्, भेदेनानिदर्शनादप्रतीतेः, इतरत्र तैर्निष्कर्षणात्, अतुल्यार्थत्वात्तन्निष्कर्षः सामान्यविशेषयोः साध्यसाधनभावायोगात्, सामान्यस्यासाध्यत्वात्, अनभिधेयाख्यानापत्तेः ।

किञ्च-

तदेव तस्य करणं न वै कर्म च कल्पते ।
भावनां सङ्गिरन्तेऽतो धात्वर्थव्यातिरेकिणीम् ॥ ३५ ॥

XXXV.1. यजेताश्वमेधेन, ईजे बहुभिर्यज्ञैः, स्वं यज्ञं यजति इत्येकत्वे क्रियाकारकभावानुपपत्तिः । सामान्यविशेषभेदोऽपि न क्रियाकारकसम्बन्धमुपपादयितुं क्षमः सामान्यस्यासाध्यत्वे-नाक्रियात्वात्, विशेषणविशेष्यसम्बन्धे तु कारकविभक्तिविरोधः ।

XXXV.2. नाप्येकदेशयोः क्रियाकारकभावः, उभयत्रापि समुदायस्य शब्दोपादानत्वात् । नापि धातूपादानायामप्यन्त-र्भूतसामान्यकर्मकरणिकायां विशेषकर्मकरणसम्बन्धः-यथा मुण्डयति माणवकम् मालिन्योपश्लोकयति इति, स्वं यज्ञम्, बहुभिर्यज्ञैः इत्यपि

धातुना भावनोपादानात् विशेषभावनाभ्युपगमात् विशेषणविशेष्य-सम्बन्धप्रसङ्गात् ।

XXXV.3. अनुपादाने च सिद्धव्यभिचारोऽसौ न तिङन्तेऽपि तामुपादातुमर्हति । एतेन ओदनपाकं पचति इत्यादयो व्याख्याताः । तस्माद्यत्रैष कारकभावो नामपदोपादानधात्वर्थस्य विभक्तिभिर्व्यज्यते, स तदतिरेकी तिङन्तेषु प्रत्ययोपादानः करोत्यर्थः प्रतिज्ञायते वृद्धैः । इष्टवान्यज्ञैः इत्यपि द्रव्यप्रधानभावनाधिगमान्निष्ठादिषु तथा प्रतीतेरविरोधः ।।

यत्तूक्तं भावनाविषयत्वप्रतीतेः करणत्वहानिः, तदनिरूपितकरण (त) त्वस्य ।

तथा हि-

करणं खलु सर्वत्र कर्तृव्यापारगोचरः ।
तिरोदधाति कर्तारं प्रधानं तन्निबन्धनम् ।। ३६ ।।

XXXVI.1. न खलु कर्तृव्यापारलक्षणभावानाप्त्या धात्वर्थस्य कर्मत्वप्रसङ्गः करणत्वबाधो वा, परश्वादिषु तथा प्रसङ्गात् । न छिदादिषु साक्षाद्व्याप्रियते कर्ता, किन्तु परश्वादिकरणे । तव्द्यापारःतदुद्यमननिपातनादिलक्षणः परशुगोचर एव । अतः तस्याव्यवहितव्यापारतया क्रियासिद्धेः साधकतमत्वम् । तव्द्यपाद्दवारायत्तप्रवृत्तितया च करणस्य कर्तुः स्वातन्त्र्यमारादुपकारिणोऽपि, अन्यथा करणतैव न स्यात् ।

अपि च-

साधनानामभावस्स्यात्कर्तृकर्मातिरेकिणाम् ।
साधनानां नियोगो हि कर्तृव्यापार इष्यते ।। ३७ ।।

XXXVII.1. प्रलीनेदानीं कर्तृकर्मातिरिक्तसाधनान्तरसङ्कथा साधननियोगः कर्तृव्यापार इति तन्नियोगविषयतापत्त्या सर्वत्र कर्मत्वापातात् ।

XXXVII.2. कस्तर्हि कर्मेतरविभागः ? कथञ्च करणपरिक्षयिणि कर्तृव्यापारे तदाप्तिविरहिणः कर्मता । उच्यते-

अन्यार्थाप्तिविवक्षायामकर्मातिशयाद्विना ।
उद्देशादन्यवृत्त्यापि फलमेवेष्यतेतराम् ।। ३८ ।।

यत्खलूद्दिष्टवस्त्वन्तराया नान्तरीयकत्वेन विषयतामुपयदभिसंहितं

तदकर्म अतिशयाभावात् । उद्देश्यं तत्कर्मान्यगोचरयापि क्रियया तस्यैवाप्तुमिष्यमाणत्वात् तदभिसन्धिप्रवर्तिताया इतरसंबन्धस्य नान्तरीयकत्वात् । अतः करणस्यापि धात्वर्थस्य साध्यत्वप्रतीतिनिदर्शने अविरुद्धे ।

यथा परशुना छिनत्तीति परशोरुद्यमननिपात्यमानत्वप्रतीतिः परशुमुद्यच्छति निपातयति द्विधाभवनायेति निदर्शनं प्रयुङ्क्ते चेति ।

यत्तु कर्तृव्यापारोऽधिश्रयणादिः धात्वर्थान्तरात्मक इति, अत्राहुः-

कथ्यमानाद्रूपभेदाद् द्विधा धात्वर्थसङ्गतिः ।
अन्योत्पादानुकूलात्मा भावना किं प्रदुष्यति ।। ३९ ।।

XXXIX.1. सर्वथा पचति यजतीति प्राक्प्रयुज्यमानगोचरो न भवतीति प्रतिपादितम्, धात्वन्तरैस्त्वभिधानं करोतिभावयतिभ्यामिव न पक्षक्षतिमावहति ।

धातूनामभिधानीयान्कर्तृकर्मसमाश्रयान् ।
लब्धात्मनोऽक्रियारूपान्विशेषान्प्रतिजानते ।। ४० ।।

XL.1. यथा श्रयतेश्चुल्लीस्थालीसंयोगविशेषः आसिञ्चतेरासिच्यमानाधारसंयोगविशेषः । एवं सर्वत्र यावत्पचेस्तण्डुलावयवानां विभागाः प्रशिथिलावयव संयोगविभागाः ।

उदासीनत्वविच्छेदलक्ष्यं धात्वर्थकारणम् ।
स्पन्दव्यापारपर्यायं करोत्यर्थं प्रचक्षते ।। ४१ ।।

XLI.1. तथाहि-अधिश्रयति उदकमासिञ्चति पचति पठतीति वा अधिश्रयणादिसंयोगभेदेभ्यो व्यापारात्मको भेदेन करोति स्पन्दते चेष्टते व्याप्रियते इति व्यापाररूपमध्यक्ष्यते । न चैष तज्जन्यत्वाभिमतविशेषालम्बनः प्रत्ययः, यतः-

व्यापारबुद्ध्युपजनो न संयोगविभागयोः ।
सतोरपि हि चेष्टित्वा विरामं समुपागते ।। ४२ ।।

XLII.1. न चलित्वा स्थिते क्रियाप्रभवपूर्वोत्तरदेशविभाग संयोगाभावः, तदालम्बनो व्यापारप्रत्ययो न जातु विरमेत् ।

विभागेन समुच्छेदात्संयोगप्रचयः कुतः ।
भविष्यद् वृत्तिसंयोगविभागाध्यक्षता कथम् ।। ४३ ।।

XLIII.1. यदप्यविच्छिन्नोत्पाददेशसंयोगविभागप्रचयालम्बन इति ।

तदपि न सम्यक् । नह्युत्तरसंयोगः पूर्वविभागादृते । न विभागः संयोगेन सहैकत्र । तद्विभागोच्छेदात्कुतस्तत्प्रचयः ?

अच्छिन्नोत्पादश्च नियोगभाव्युत्तरसमवेतता वर्तमानानां । तेषु वर्तमानानागतेषु तदविषयं कथमिन्द्रयं धियं जनयेत् ?

मनोऽपि चागणितकुशलस्य नैवमर्थम् । अपि च स्थाणौ पूर्वोत्तरश्येनाभ्यां संयोगविभागाभ्यां व्यापारधीः स्यात् ।

आधारदेशसंयोगविभागाभ्यां सेति च न युक्तम् । तथाहि-

जलावयवसंयोगविभागौ स्थिरमूर्तिषु ।
जलाधारेषु मत्स्येषु व्यापारप्रत्ययाद्विना ।। ४४ ।।

XLIV.1. प्रतीतं हि जलं देशो मत्स्यानाम्, न स्थाणोरिव श्येनो न देशः । तदवयवसंयोगविभागसद्भावेऽपि तेषु महत्त्वादकम्पनीयेषु बलवद्विधारकप्रयत्नविधृतात्मसु न क्रियावत्त्वाभ्युपगमः । तरमान्न तन्निबन्धनः ।

नभसस्त्वप्रत्यक्षत्वात् तद्भन्यत्त्योः संयोगविभागयोर्दुर्लभा प्रत्यक्षता ।

न च वियद्वितितालोकनिबन्धनः, सन्तमसे झटिति विद्युति क्रियाप्रत्ययात् ।

तस्मादस्ति धातूपादानतदाहितविशेषातिरिक्तात्मा क्रियापदार्थो भावनापर्यायः ।

XLIV.2. नन्वेवं भावनातो धात्वर्थनिष्पत्तिः, ततः फलस्येति कथं तन्निष्पाद्यो धात्वर्थः तस्याः करणं ? स्वर्गादि वातत्साध्यं कर्म ?

तस्मात् स एव धात्वर्थस्तथा भावना अस्तु, स्वर्गं धात्वर्थञ्चान्तरा व्यापारान्तरानुलब्धेरित्युक्तम् ।

उक्तोत्तरमेतत् । तथाहि-

फले न साक्षात् करणे कर्तुश्चेष्टा फलार्थिनः
करणत्वं प्रधानांशे ताद्रूप्यं वा यतस्ततः ।। ४५ ।।

XLV.1. नेमे अन्यकर्मकरणत्वविलक्षणे फलधात्वर्थ-कर्मकरणत्वे । दर्शितं परशुना छिनत्तीत्यपि न द्विधाभवने कर्तृव्यापृतिः, अपितु करणे साधननियोगादिलक्षणत्वात्कर्तुः तत्रैव चैष व्यापारः तदभिसन्धानात् अनन्यप्रकारत्वात् ।

इयांस्तु विशेषः-धात्वर्थस्योत्पादेन विनियोगः परश्वादेस्तु

सिद्धस्योद्यमननिपातनादिना । वृक्षादेस्तु कर्मत्वं द्विधाभवने कर्तृत्वात्तदर्थं परशुनिपातनोद्यमनलक्षणम् ।

द्विधाभवनं प्रति करणत्वं च परशोः छिनत्तौ प्रधानापेक्षम्, ताद्रूप्यस्य वा तदधीनत्वात् ।

नह्युद्यमननिपातनमात्रमसंभवद् द्विधाभवनं छिनत्तीति निरूप्यते ।

तस्मादिहापि धात्वर्थस्योत्पादकोऽनुग्राहको वा कर्तृव्यापारः समुद्दिष्टफलभवनतया प्रतिलब्धभावनाव्यपदेशो धात्वर्थोपनिबद्धप्रधानांश ताद्रूप्यफलकर्मको धात्वर्थकरणकश्चेति न दोषः ।

XLV.2. न हि द्विधाभवति (भावयति) परशुनेति परशुं द्विधाभवनं चान्तरेण कर्तृव्यापार एकोऽपरसाध्योऽपरसाधन उपलभ्यते । न च करणत्वं विरुद्धम्, प्रधानांशनिष्पत्तेस्तदधीनत्वात् । तथेहापि

फलभूतक्रियांशापेक्षत्वात्कारकविभक्तिविभागव्यवस्थायाः ।

तथाहि–

प्रधानांशमुपादाय साधनान्येकवाक्यताम् ।
व्रजन्ति नान्यव्यापारो रूपतो ह्यन्यसाधनः ।। ४६ ।।

XLVI.1. तस्मादनुपालम्भोऽयं व्यापारानुपलम्भ इति यत्त्वात्मकर्तृकेषु यजत्यादिष्वसंभव इति, तत्र केचित्–

भाष्ये यततेति गिरा प्रयत्नं प्रतिपेदिरे ।
अचेतने प्रयोगस्य प्राचुर्यान्नोपचारधीः ।। ४७ ।।

XLVII.1. तथा यतेत यथा यत्किञ्चिद्भवतीति फलभा (भ)वनानुकूलः प्रयत्न एवाख्यातार्थो दर्शितः । अचेतने त्वाख्यातप्रयोग उपचारात् । प्रयोगप्राचुर्यान्नौपचारिकः (कप्र) प्रत्ययः ।

XLVII.2. इदन्तु समाधानं सिद्धे तद्भावे स्यात् । न च प्रत्यये समाने हेत्वन्तरे चासति तत्प्रसिद्धिरस्ति, विपर्ययावगमस्याशक्यवारणत्वात् ।

उदासीनत्वविच्छेदसामान्यात्मा ततो मतः ।
करोत्यर्थो द्वयोश्चेह तद्रूपप्रत्ययोद्भवः ।। ४८ ।।

XLVIII.1. उदासीनत्वविच्छेदो हि करोत्यर्थः, उदासीने क्रियाज्ञानाभावात् ।

उदासीनताप्रच्युतिधियश्च द्वैधम्, आत्मनि प्रयत्नात् अन्यत्र परिस्पन्दात् । तथाहि–

प्रयत्नवन्तमात्मानमनुदासीनं कुर्वाणं व्यापारवन्तमवैति, परिस्पन्दमानं चान्यत् । अतः प्रयत्नपरिस्पन्दयोरौदसीन्यविच्छेदसामान्ययोस्तदाभासधीविषयत्वेन क्रियापदार्थत्वान्नात्मकर्तृकेषु तदभाव इति ।

तदुक्तम्-न परिस्पद एवैकः क्रिया नः कणभोजिवत् इति । अथापि परिस्पन्देन प्रयोजनम्, असौ-

मनोभूतपरिस्पन्दः आत्मनस्तत्प्रयत्नजः ।
विक्लित्त्यादिर्यथा तस्मिन्साधनोपनिपाततः ।। ४९ ।।

LIX.1. आत्ममनस्संयोगविशेषाद्विज्ञानसङ्कल्पाद्युत्पत्तिः तन्निबन्धनमात्मसमवेतादृष्टप्रयत्नहेतु मनसि कर्म परिस्पन्दरूपमुपेयते । आत्मप्रयत्नापेक्षश्च भूतेषु द्रव्योपादानादिलक्षणः परिस्पन्दः । उभयोऽप्ययमात्मनस्तदधीनत्वात्, विक्लित्त्यादिवत् विक्लित्तिच्छिदाभिदास्तण्डुलादिसमवायिन्योऽसमवेता अपि देवदत्ते तत्क्रियाः, तासु तस्य कर्तृत्वात्, प्रधानक्रियायां सर्वकारकोपनिपातात्, एकवाक्यत्वात् । न हि स्वव्यापारविषयः करणादिभावः कारकाणाम्, तेषां भेदादेकवाक्यत्वानुपपत्तेः ।

एवञ्च कर्तृविनियोज्यतया सर्वसाधनानां तद् व्यापारः कर्तुरिति तेषां भावनान्तर्गतिः तन्मुखेन साधनताप्युपपन्ना ।।

परोपाधिक्रियारूपो ज्ञायते न क्रियान्तरम् ।
सम्बन्धादेव साध्यत्वमतः करणसङ्गतिः ।। ५० ।।

L.1. धात्वर्थस्य भावनामनुरञ्जयतः तद्विषयताप्रतीत्या तत्परामर्शकृतं तदन्तर्गतस्य क्रियात्वमिति कुतः क्रियाद्वयप्रत्ययः ? नहि जातिगुणोपरक्तेषु द्रव्येषु तद्रूपभेदः ।

भावनासम्बन्धितयैव तस्य साध्यता न तत्सम्बन्धं विहन्ति, तदभावे तस्याप्यभावप्रसङ्गात् । अतश्च करणसम्बन्धोऽप्युपपन्नः, भावनाविषयत्वमनुपयतः करणतायोगात् साध्यताप्रतीतेः क्रियारूपापत्तेः ।

प्रधानव्यापृतिर्यस्य धात्वर्थं प्रत्यपीष्यते ।
स कर्तातः पचन्तीति विक्लिद्यन्तीति भिद्यते ।। ५१ ।।

LI.1. न वै खल्वगुणतः धातुना अभिधीयमानव्यापारः कर्ता, येन प्रत्ययार्थः पर्यनुयुज्येत, अपि तु धात्वर्थं प्रत्यभिसंहितप्रधानव्यापारः, सर्वत्र धात्वर्थस्य कर्तृव्यापारं लक्ष्यमभिधेयं वा प्रति विशेषणत्वात् । तेन विक्लिद्यन्तीति तण्डुलव्यापारस्य

ज्वलनावयवाभिघातजन्मनोऽवयवाश्रितस्य स्थाल्युदकाद्यनुसरणात्मकस्य धात्वर्थं प्रति प्रधानस्याभिधानम्, पचतीत्यत्र तु देवदत्तव्यापारस्याधिश्रयणादेः प्रत्ययेनाभिधानादर्थभेदः कर्तृभेदश्च सिद्ध्यतीति न प्रत्ययार्थपर्यनुयोगावकाशः । कथं पनस्तुल्यार्थत्वात्पचिना विक्लिदेः परेण प्रत्ययेन तण्डुलव्यापार एव प्रयोक्तृभिः विवक्ष्यते, न देवदत्तव्यापारोऽपि पचेः परेणै(णे)व ? प्रकृतीनां रूपभेदात्तुल्यार्थत्वेऽपि स्वार्थे प्रत्ययस्य शक्तिभेदात् ।

भार्या दारा जलान्याप एकार्थत्वेऽपि दृश्यते ।
प्रकृते रूपभेदेन प्रत्ययार्थो विशेषवान् ।। ५२ ।।

LII.1. जलानीति प्रकृत्यर्थसमवायि तदेकार्थसमवायि वा बहुत्वं बहुवचनार्थः, तथा भार्या इति । आपो दारा इति तु प्रकृत्यर्थावयवसमवायि तदाश्रयैकार्थसमवायि (वा), प्रकृतिरूपभेदात्तदपेक्षत्वात्प्रत्ययस्याभिधानशक्तेः ।

तथेहापि पचिपरो धात्वर्थैकार्थसमवायिनं व्यापारं कर्मकर्तृविषयः प्रत्यय आह, भिन्नाश्रयं वा अन्यत्र । विक्लिदिपरस्तु प्रकृत्यै (त्यर्थै) कार्थसमवायिनमित्यनवद्यम् ।

अग्निं चिनुत इत्यत्र स्वं यज्ञं यजतीति च ।
दर्शनात्कर्मयोगस्य नाभावस्तदभावतः ।। ५३ ।।

LIII.1. धात्वर्थस्य हि चयनस्येष्टकाः स्थलं वा अव्यवधानात्कर्म, न व्यापारान्तरव्यवधीयमानो व्यभिचार्यग्निः । स तु भावनाकर्म । अग्निशब्दश्च न स्थलवचनः अपि तु ज्वलनवचनः । एवं ह्युक्तम्-अत्र ह्येषप्रसिद्धः इति । स्वं यज्ञं यजति इति तु न भावनातोऽन्यत्र कर्मत्वमिति वर्णितम् ।

तथा महाभाष्ये कर्मद्वयसम्बन्धो विक्लित्तेर्भावनाभेदेनैव दर्शितः-इह तावत्तण्डुलानेदनं पचतीति, व्द्यर्थः पचिः, तण्डुलान्विक्लेदयन् ओदनं निर्वर्तयति इति ।

प्रयोजकक्रियामाहुः कर्तृव्यापारगोचराम् ।
कर्तृव्यापारविषयो धातोरर्थो विवक्ष्यते ।। ५४ ।।

LIV.1. स्वव्यापारे सर्वस्य (कर्तृत्वात् अन्यथा कारकत्वायोगात्) नियोगात्कर्तृव्यापारविषयः प्रेरणादिः प्रयोजककर्तृव्यापारो णिजर्थः, धात्वर्थविषयः कर्तृव्यापारस्तिङर्थ इति न

भवति भावयत्योस्तुल्यार्थतेति ।

> तदेवं भावनार्थत्वादाख्यातप्रत्ययस्य हि ।
> यागेन भावयेत्स्वर्गमित्यर्थः शब्दनिर्मितः ।। ५५ ।।

LV.1. तत्कथम् ?

> अपेक्षितत्वाद्भाव्यस्य कामशब्दा हि तत्पराः ।
> विशेषणप्रधानत्वं दण्डीत्यादिषु दर्शितम् ।। ५६ ।।

LVI.1. यद्यपि स्वर्गादयः पुरुषविशेषणत्वेन श्रूयन्ते, तथापि कामश्रुतयः तत्प्रधानाः, दण्डीप्रैषानन्वाह, लोहितोष्णीषा ऋत्विजः प्रचरन्ति इति दर्शनात् । कुतः ? भावना (न) या भाव्यस्यापेक्षितत्वात् स्वर्गादीनां च काम्य (मान) तया भाव्यत्वप्रतीतेः द्वितीयान्तप्रयोग इव तयापि इष्टत्वप्रतिपादनात् । तेन पुरुषप्रतीतिः स्वर्गकामपदेऽनुवादः । स्वर्गमित्येतावद्विधित्सितम्,

भाव्यविशेषपरत्वात्, धात्वर्थस्य श्रौतस्यापि विधिज्ञानविरोधादकर्मत्वात् । करणत्वेऽपि श्रुत्यनुग्रहादविरोधात्, शास्त्राधीनत्वाद्योग्यायोग्यत्वयोरज्ञानात्, (योग्यत्वस्य अयोग्यत्वाज्ञानात्) सर्वफलभावनानां च धात्वर्थविशेषसाधनत्वात् ।

स्यान्मतम्–स्वर्गादिविशेषणपरत्वेऽपि गुणभावः स्वर्गादेः स्यात् । न, भाव्यस्य प्रथममपेक्षणात्, साधनेषु चोपचारादिच्छायाः ।

LVI.2. ननु न भाव्यप्रतिपत्तिप्रधानाः कामश्रुतयः, अपितु नियोज्यविशेषप्रतिपादनपराः । अन्यथा कस्यायमुपदेशः, को नियुज्यते, कस्येदं कर्तव्यम्, इत्यज्ञानात्सापेक्षमसमाप्तमप्रतिपत्तिकरमेव शास्त्रं स्यात् ।

नैतत्सारम्, यतः–

> प्रतीयते नियोगोऽर्थात्समर्थस्य फलार्थिनः ।
> अन्यथा ह्यसमर्थानां दुर्वाराधिकृतिर्भवेत् ।। ५७ ।।

LVII.1. योऽपि हि शब्दान्नियोज्यविशेषावसायं मन्यते सोऽपि नियोज्यविशेषप्रतिपत्तौ सामर्थ्यमुपैति । अन्यथा शब्दवशेन शक्तिकल्पनायामन्धादीनामप्यत्रार्थेऽधिकारः स्यात् । सत्यपि चेच्छब्दे सामर्थ्यमुपाश्रीयते नियोज्यावगमे तदसत्येवास्तु । तस्माद्यो नियोगार्थं प्रतिपत्तुं तद्विषयं चानुष्ठातुं समर्थः फलार्थी स च नियोज्यः असमर्थस्यानर्थिनोऽशक्येऽनभिलषिते (वा) यागे प्रवर्तनायोगात् ।

किञ्च–

अतत्परत्वे फलता (स्वर्गादेः) पश्वादेर्नास्ति शब्दतः ।
न सामर्थ्यादनुष्ठानं नियोगैकनिबन्धनम् ॥ ५८ ॥

LVIII.1. यदि स्वर्गकामादिश्रुतयो न फलभेदाधिगमनपराः न शब्दवती फलता स्वर्गादीनाम्, नापि सामर्थ्यतः, अनुपपद्यमानाभावात् ।

अन्यथा (पि) नियुज्यमाना (न) भावात् । अनुष्ठानमयुक्तमिति चेत्–न, तस्य नियोगमात्रायत्तत्वाभ्युपगमात् । एकवाक्यत्वमिति चेत्–

को विरोधः ? अन्यदिच्छति अन्यत्करोतीति स्वर्गकामो यागं कुर्यादित्ययमेव विरोधः (इति चेत्) अत एव तर्हि न पुरुविशेषपराः स्वर्गाकामादिश्रुतयः, फलपरास्सन्तु ।

अपि च–

नियोगपरतन्त्रस्य पुरुषस्यान्यदिच्छतः ।
क्रियान्यस्य विरुद्धेति न नियोगप्रधानता ॥ ५९ ॥

LIX.1. अन्यदिच्छति अन्यत्करोति इति विरोधं वदतो नियोगप्राधान्यं हीयते, फलार्थिताहेतुत्वान्नियोगस्य । दृश्यते च नियोगसामर्थ्यादन्यदपीच्छतामन्यक्रिया परतन्त्राणाम् । भाव्यस्यैव सतो विशेषणत्वमिति चेत्–

न, नियोगविषयासंबन्धात्, ततः क्रियान्तरभाव्यस्यपि विशेषणत्वात् इच्छामात्रप्रवृत्तिदर्शनाच्चायुक्तमैवैतत् ।

LIX.2. नन्वेवं नैमित्तिकत्वे चाग्निहोत्रादीनां नित्यत्वव्याघातः । अयमप्यपरो दोषोऽस्तु, न तु नियोज्यविशेषपरात्फलप्रतिपत्तिः । ननु स्वर्गकामस्य यागः कर्तव्योऽवगम्यते । कथं च स तस्य कर्तव्यः यदि तं न निष्पादयति ?

न, गृहदाहवत इवेच्छावतः किञ्चिदसम्पादयतोऽपि कर्तव्यता स्यात् । यदि तर्ह्यसम्पादयति स्वर्गं यागे पुरुषः प्रवर्तते न तर्हि स्वर्गकामः । न, निमेषादिष्वतथाभूतेष्वपि प्रवर्तमानस्य स्वर्गकामत्वाविघातात् । हेत्वन्तरात्तत्र प्रवृत्तिरिति चेत्इहापि नियोगादिति न दोषः ।

LIX.3. स्यादेतत्–स्वर्गसिद्धाविच्छापगमे नियोगनिष्पत्तिः । ञन्यथा कृतयागोऽपि नियोज्य एव स्यात्, न कृतनियोगः अतो

नियोगार्थनिष्पत्तिसामर्थ्यात्स्वर्गादिसिद्धिः (निष्पत्तिः) । न, विषयसिद्ध्या नियोगनिष्पत्तेः, स्वर्गादेश्च नियोज्यविशेषणत्वेनाविषयत्वात् । अन्यथा गृहदाहादेरप्यपगमप्रसङ्गः ।

तस्मात्फलपराः स्वर्गकामादिश्रुतय इति मनोहरम् ।

इत्यार्यमण्डनस्य कृतिर्भावनाविवेकोऽवसितः ।।

BIBLIOGRAPHY

Bhatta, V.P. Epistemology, Logic and Grammar, Published by Eastern Book Linkers, 5825, New Chandrawal, Jawahar Nagar, Delhi. 2 Vols. 1991, 1992.

Burrow, T. Indian Theories of the Nature of Meaning, T.P.S. 1936.

Caland, W and Henry V.L' Agniṣṭoma, 2 Vols. Paris, 1906-7.

Chakravarti, P.C. The linguistic speculations of the Hindus, University of Calcutta, 1933.

Datta, D.M. The six ways of knowing, George Alean and Unwin, London, 1932.

Franklin Edgerton, Mīmāṁsanyāya Prakāśa or Āpadeâi, Translated intc English. New Haven, Yele University Press, 1929.

Gánganatha Jha. Translation of Mīmāṁsā Nyāya Sūtras, Sacred Books of the Hindus, Vol. X Part 1;

The Prābhākara School of the Pūrvamīmāṁsā, Allahabad, 1911; Pūrvamīmāṁsā in its sources, Benares Hindu University, 1942.

Ingalls, D.H.H. Materials for the Study of Navyanyāya Logic, Harvard Oriental Series, 40 Cambridge, Mass. Harvard University Press, 1951.

Jaimini. The Aphorisms of Mīmāṁsā, Edited by Pandit Maheśachandra Nyāyaratna, Bibliotheca Indica, 2 Vols. 1973-1889.

Kane, P.V. A brief sketch of the Pūrva-Mīmāṁsā System, Poona, 1924.

Kauṇḍabhaṭṭa. Vaiyākaraṇabhūṣaṇasāra, Edited by S. Sastri, Anandasrama Sanskrit Series, 135, Poona, Anandasrama Press, 1957.

Keith, A.B. The Religion and Philosophy of the Vedas and Upaniṣads, Harvard Oriental Series, 31 Cambridge, Mass. Harvard University Press, 1925;

The Karma Mīmāṁsā, Association Press, Calcutta, 1921.

Kumarila Bhaṭṭa.Mīmāṁsā Ślokavārtika, Edited by Rama Sastri Tailangava, C.S.S. Vol. 3. Benares, 1898-1899; Translation by Ganganatha Jha, Bibliotheca Indica, 1900-1908.

The Tantravārtika, Edited by Gangadhara Sastri, Benares Sanskrit Sereis, 1903; Translation by Ganganatha Jha. Bibliotheca Indica, 1903, 1924.

Kunjunni Raja, K.Indian Theories of Meaning, Adyar Library Series. 91, Madras, Adyar Library, 1963.

Mādhavācārya.Jaiminīya Nyāyaratnamālā, Edited by Śivadatta Paṇḍita, Ānandasrama Sanskrit Series 24, Poona, 1982.

Maṇḍana Miśra.Vidhiviveka, Published in the Pandit, N.S. Vols. 25-28, Benares 1903-1906.

Matilal, B.K.The Navya nyāya Doctrine of Negation, Harvard Oriental Series, 46. Cambridge Mass. Harvard University Press, 1968; The Word and the World, Delhi, Oxford University Press, Oxford, New York, 1990.

Bhimacarya Jhalakikar, Nyāyakośa, Bombay Sanskrit Series 49. Bombay 1893.

Pāṇini. Aṣṭādhyāyī, Edited by Otto Böhtlingk, Georg Olms verlagsbuch handlung Hildesheim, 1964.

Patañjali. Vyākaraṇa Mahābhāṣya, Edited by F. Keilhorn, Bombay Sanskrit Series, 18-20. Bombay 1892.

Pārthasārathi Miśra. Nyāyaratnākara, A Commentary on Ślokavārtika, Chowkhamba Sanskrit Series, II Benares, 1988. Śāstradīpikā, Edited by Dharmadatta Suri, Bombay, Nirnaysagar Press: 1915.

Tantraratnam, Edited by Genganatha Jha, Vidyavilas Press, Bombay, 1930.

Prabhākara Miśra. Bṛhatī, Edited by S.K.R. Sastri, Madras University Sanskrit Series, 3, Madras 1934.

Raja, C. Kunhan and Sastri. S.S. Mānameyodaya, Theosophical Publishing House, Madras, 1933.

Ramanujācārya.Tantrarahasya, Edited by R. Sharma and Sastri, and introduction by K.S. Ramaswami Sastri,

Oriental Institute, Baroda, 1956.

Śabara. Śābarabhāṣya, Bibliotheca Indica, 45. Calcutta, Asiatic Society of Bengal, 1889.

Śālikanātha. Prakaraṇa Pañcikā, Edited by Mukunda Sastri and Laxman Sastri Dravida, Chowkhamba Sanskrit Series, 17, Benares 1904.

Vidyabhusana, S.C. Nyāyasūtras of Gautama, Text and translation, Sacred Books of the Hindus, Vol.8 Allahabad, Pāṇini Office, 1913.

SELECT GLOSSARIAL INDEX